14

||||| ||| || |||| ||||| || |||| ||
D1460693

John R. Young,
Glasgow, 1997

SCOTTISH SPORT IN THE MAKING OF THE NATION

Sports, Politics and Culture
A series of books from Leicester University Press

Series editors: **Stephen Wagg**
Department of Sociology, University of Leicester
John Williams
Sir Norman Chester Centre for Football Research,
University of Leicester

Published:

Rogan Taylor	*Football and its Fans*
John Sugden & Alan Bairner	*Sport, Sectarianism and Society in a Divided Ireland*
Neil Blain, Raymond Boyle & Hugh O'Donnell	*Sport and National Identity in the European Media*

Forthcoming titles:

John Bale	*The Landscape of Modern Sport*
Stephen Wagg	*Football and Society in Different Continents*

SCOTTISH SPORT IN THE MAKING OF THE NATION
NINETY MINUTE PATRIOTS?

EDITED BY
GRANT JARVIE
AND
GRAHAM WALKER

LEICESTER UNIVERSITY PRESS
LEICESTER, LONDON AND NEW YORK

DISTRIBUTED IN THE UNITED STATES AND CANADA BY ST. MARTIN'S PRESS

Leicester University Press
(a division of Pinter Publishers Ltd)
25 Floral Street, London WC2E 9DS

First published in Great Britain 1994

© The editors and contributors 1994

Distributed exclusively in the USA and Canada by St. Martin's Press, Inc., Room 400, 175 Fifth Avenue, New York, NY 10010, USA

British Library Cataloguing in Publication Data
A CIP catalogue record for this book is available from the British Library.

ISBN 0 7185 1454 8

Library of Congress Cataloging-in-Publication Data
A CIP catalog for this title is available from the Library of Congress

Typeset by Florencetype Ltd., Kewstoke, Avon
Printed and Bound in Great Britain by Biddles Ltd of Guildford and King's Lynn

CONTENTS

THE CONTRIBUTORS

Alan Bairner teaches at the University of Ulster at Jordanstown. He is co-author (with John Sugden) of *Sport, Sectarianism and Society in a Divided Ireland* (Leicester University Press, 1993).

Neil Blain teaches at Glasgow Caledonian University. He is co-author (with Raymond Boyle and Hugh O'Donnell) of *Sport and National Identity in the European Media* (Leicester University Press, 1993).

Raymond Boyle teaches at the University of Stirling. He is co-author (with Neil Blain and Hugh O'Donnell) of *Sport and National Identity in the European Media* (Leicester University Press, 1993).

Gerry Finn teaches at the University of Strathclyde. He has written extensively on racism, religion and social prejudice in Scottish football and society.

Chris Harvie is Professor of British and Irish Studies at the University of Tubingen. He is author of numerous books and articles including *Cultural Weapons* (Polygon, 1991) and *The Rise of European Regionalism* (Edinburgh University Press, 1993).

Richard Holt teaches at the University of Stirling and the University of Leuven. He is author of *Sport and the British* (Oxford University Press, 1989) and editor of *Sport and the Working Class* (Manchester University Press, 1990).

Grant Jarvie teaches at the University of Warwick. He is author of *Highland Games: The Making of the Myth* (Edinburgh University Press, 1991) and co-author of *Sport and Leisure in Social Thought* (Routledge, 1994).

John Lowerson teaches at the University of Sussex. He is author of *Sport and the English Middle Classes* (Manchester University Press, 1994).

Bert Moorhouse teaches at the University of Glasgow. He has written extensively on various aspects of Scottish football and is author of *Driving Ambition, an Analysis of American Hot Rod Enthusiasm* (Manchester University Press, 1992).

Hamish Telfer teaches at the University of Lancaster. He has written a number of articles on sport and recreation in Argyllshire.

Neil Tranter teaches at the University of Stirling. His historical research has contributed greatly to our understanding of sport in nineteenth and early twentieth century Scotland.

Graham Walker teaches at Queen's University of Belfast. He is author of *Tom Johnston* (Manchester University Press, 1988) and co-editor of the book (with Tom Gallagher) *Sermons and Battlehymns, Protestant Popular Culture in Modern Scotland* (Edinburgh University Press, 1991).

ACKNOWLEDGEMENTS

We would like to thank our contributors both for their enthusiasm for the project and the relatively painless task they gave us as editors. The manuscript was prepared with the help of a small research grant from the University of Warwick's research and innovation fund. The book would not have been possible without the support, skill and patience of Carolyn Ison who produced the final manuscript. While the editors may not share all the views expressed in the text nonetheless they recognise the complexity of sport in the making of the nation. We are indebted to Bob Crampsey for his helpful and informative comments.

1

NINETY MINUTE PATRIOTS?
SCOTTISH SPORT IN THE MAKING OF THE NATION

Grant Jarvie and Graham Walker

The great problem is that Scotland has too many ninety minute patriots whose nationalist outpourings are expressed only at major sporting events.
Jim Sillars ex-MP, Scottish National Party,
The Herald, 24 April 1992, p.1.

Everybody who saw him has his own memories, mine is Wembley 1967, and Scotland with their provincialism, fed by the grandeur of England's World Champion status, were putting it on. McCreadie went down the left . . . and Baxter, in midfield, called for the ball, in some infection of Baxteritis, McCreadie not normally given to flights of megalomania as a player, stopped the ball about fifteen yards from the half-way line, turned round and walked away from it. Baxter strolled across, can you see the slightly hen-toed saunter, the socks crumpled, the gallus expression? and as he prompted his team mates into more advantageous positions, he played keepie uppie. (Cited in Jenkins, 1983, p.iii)

The above extracts encapsulate some of the intensity of feeling about sport in Scotland and the elevated place that the subject holds for many Scots. The infamous 'ninety minute patriot' phrase made by Jim Sillars, shortly after the 1992 General Election results, is in many ways similar to Ralph Miliband's statement of the early 1960s that sport itself is not conducive to any form of consciousness – a theme which is also borne out in the work of his fellow Marxist, Eric Hobsbawm. Yet as this text clearly illustrates sport in Scotland has not only continually contributed to ideas about Scotland but in all its different forms sport has helped to define different aspects of class, gender and community in Scotland (see Alan Bairner's discussion on Football and the Idea of Scotland, Chapter 2, and Graham Walker's explanation of some of the social and political circumstances that influenced Motherwell's international swimming fame in the 1940s, Chapter 10).

Sillars' comment is a classic expression of the view that sport has functioned as a substitute for political nationalism in modern Scotland. This is a widely held view among Scots; there are many who share Sillars' exasperation and even more who regard the matter in a resigned way as proof that Scotland lacks the will to control its own destiny. The concept of sport as a 'substitute' in this sense has not been subjected to much critical interrogation; indeed, it has virtually attained the status of another national myth.

A fixation with this concept has hitherto impeded critical examination of sport's role in Scottish life. The 'substitute thesis' is at once too static and too one-dimensional to help us explain the way sport has reflected Scottish life in its different political, social, and cultural manifestations. It is a thesis which implies that the passion aroused by sport is in a sense misleading; that it does not reflect a people with enough pride in their nation or confidence in themselves to press for independence. This, we would argue, is too simplistic: it elides the different kinds of Scottish nationalist and patriotic feeling and overlooks changing expressions of nationalist sporting fervour. It is just as valid to argue that sporting passions can reflect prevailing political moods and sociological images. Thus one of the most obvious examples of mass patriotic fervour in the recent past – the Hampden and Wembley football internationals against England – could be said to have reflected quite accurately the centrality of the mainly west of Scotland working class to Scotland's social profile and the Labourist character of their political views with their tongue-in-cheek regard for displays of 'tartanry'. On the other hand, the more contemporary example of the crowd's part in Scotland's rugby triumph over England in 1990 reflected something different: a more socially-mixed, more 'establishment'-oriented crowd giving vent in a more self-consciously political way to the impact of the 'New Nationalism' of the 1980s.

Certain chapters in this volume further illustrate the ways sport can be said to have reflected political and social moods, rather than in some way concealing or distorting them. Graham Walker's chapter on Nancy Riach is concerned with a kind of nationalist feeling which desired to emphasise Scotland's contribution to wider British and Imperial/Commonwealth causes, and to show that Scottish pride and self-respect was still very much intact within the wider British structures. Richard Holt demonstrates that the popular view of Denis Law in Scotland in the 1960s was related to the emergence of a new style of nationalist politics and a 'changing national atmosphere'. Alan Bairner's contribution on Scottish football fans indicates that the divergence in the Scots' behaviour from that of their English counterparts in the 1980s is related to a changed perception of the Scottish-English rivalry: a perception now based on a more confident, if gratuitously self-congratulatory, sense of an independent and outward-looking Scottish identity, and on a corresponding perception of the English as stuck in a jingoistic time-warp. Bairner's points about the respective attitudes to the national team of some Rangers and Celtic supporters also can be said to reflect significant changes of a political and cultural kind.

The second piece of prose is from Alan Sharp's essay 'The Dream of Perfection' and perhaps is indicative of the fact that as an aspect of Scottish popular culture, football in particular may be enjoyed, worked at, discussed or disliked, but rarely ignored. In Scottish football folklore there are many different versions of how Baxter taunted the English in that memorable international back in 1967. Other novelists such as Robin Jenkins, whose work covers the whole spectrum of social life in contemporary Scotland, could not avoid commenting upon the meaning and significance of football within Scotland's industrial mining communities. Born in Lanarkshire, into the depression of the 1920s, the 1926 General Strike confirmed, for Jenkins, the injustice of a social system which forced ordinary workers to do without during hard times. Although the General Strike of 1926 is rarely mentioned in his novels its influence is evident in many of his writings. The significance of football, community, working-class politics and industrial action are some of the many factors which form the backcloth to *Thistle and the Grail* (1954). The efforts of Drumsagart Thistle Junior Football Club clearly illustrate that football in Scotland is much more than just an expression of region or class or even escapes into fantasy. Drumsagart's vain search for the Holy Grail (the Junior Cup) clearly reinforced a collective commitment to community.

In some cases it is easier to accept the idea that sport or sporting relations help to reproduce, solidify, transform or even construct different forms of community without accepting the idea that any ideal imagined or homogenous community exists. In many ways the notion of community is akin to that of nation and yet when one talks of Scottish sport in the making of the nation it is important to recognise the similarities and differences between the different people, communities, and images which have been active not only in the making of Scottish sport but also the making of the Scottish Nation. While many of the people mentioned in this book, such as Nancy Riach, Liz McColgan, Denis Law, Jim Watt, Lachie Stewart, Jim Baxter, John Jeffries, and Belle Robertson, might all share the similar experience of representing Scotland in sport they are divided by a number of factors, the principal of which are gender, class, locality, and in some cases the historical period through which they experienced a sense of Scotland (see in Chapter 8, Hamish Telfer's account of sport and recreation in Argyllshire during the late nineteenth and early twentieth centuries and Neil Tranter's observations on women in sport in nineteenth century Scotland in Chapter 3). In short while Scottish sport has both contributed to a sense of nation, class and even community it is important to ask the question whose nation? whose community? and during what time period?

The importance of Scottish sport is also reflected in the effect that it has on other aspects of Scottish culture such as the composition of the newspapers and the time devoted to sport on television (see Neil Blain and Raymond Boyle's coverage of sports journalism in Scotland, Chapter 9 and Richard Holt's account of the way in which the Scottish Press presented Denis Law as a national sports idol in the 1960s, Chapter 5). Like the Scottish press, aspects of Scottish sport are strongly nationalist in outlook. The fact that certain sports are organised along national and not British lines has often been used by political scientists to reinforce the idea that sport in Scotland, like the Royal Burghs, education, the Church of Scotland and certain legal practices, has a strongly national character. For instance, the crystallisation of distinct Scottish and English football structures along national lines dates back to an incident in the late 1880s. On 30 October, 1886, during a third round Football Association cup match between Preston North End and Queen's Park, Jimmy Ross, a Scots player with Preston North End, fouled Harrower, the Queen's Park centre forward, before a crowd of 15,000. The pitch was invaded by

Queen's Park supporters and Ross had to be smuggled out of the ground. The incident brought to a head the differences between the Football Association and the Scottish Football Association (SFA), as a result of which the SFA announced on 10 May 1887 that clubs belonging to the Association shall not be members of any other National Association and, consequently ordered Scottish teams to withdraw from the FA cup competition.

The Royal Family have played a key role in regulating a particular definition of Britishness, a process which has involved the emergence of certain social codes, social calendars and social closure among not just the hereditary privileged but also those who aspire to belong to the upper circles of both British and Scottish society. In Scotland events such as the Braemar Royal Highland Society Gathering, the grouse and deer shooting season and the Argyllshire Gathering and Oban Ball contribute not only to a Scottish sporting social calendar but also a British sporting calendar which includes such events as the Epsom Derby, Ascot flat racing week, which includes the Gold Cup, various polo matches, Henley Regatta, Cheltenham National Hunt racing week and the Grand National at Aintree. Sport and leisure seem to occupy an important symbolic and social space within the social structure of both Britain and Scotland: a social space which requires the sponsorship of various intersecting upper circles of power. Introduction to the monarchy used to be the ultimate sign of acceptance for some. Playing the royal game in this sense involved being the referee over certain social codes, prescriptions and prohibitions concerning not only social class and gender but also the reproduction of a distinct form of anglo-British nationalism (see Grant Jarvie's discussion on sport, monarchy and the politics of the environment, Chapter 11).

Leading up to the 1992 General Election it was not football nor Hampden Park, the national football stadium, which seemed to reflect the feelings of the Scottish electorate but rugby union and in particular the events during and leading up to the clash between Scotland and England at Murrayfield, the national rugby union stadium. Those on the terraces were caught up in a particular expression of nationalism, different in some respects from that experienced at Hampden, especially in the late 1970s. Sport, it might be argued was reacting to a new social movement, a distinct and specific set of tensions at a particular point in time. Murrayfield itself was packed with a capacity crowd of 59,000 whose loyalties had been emotionally charged by a complex number of factors, the prospect of a Scottish victory over the 'auld enemy', memory of England's grand slam victory of 1991, the Scottish flanker John Jeffries leading out the Scottish team in his last home international before retirement, the contrast of styles between England's dour pack and Scotland's fleet-footed backs, and the strains of the respective national anthems, the English 'God Save the Queen' and the Scottish 'Flower of Scotland'. It should be noted that for some Scots 'Flower of Scotland' has not yet reached the status of a national anthem. However the adoption by such a conservative Scottish institution as the Scottish Rugby Union of the populist national anthem 'Flower of Scotland' at one level might seem insignificant and yet at another level it was a profound gesture of sentimentality which in part encapsulated for a brief instant the mood of many Scots. When the song was first written it was much less popular because it was associated with the Scottish Nationalist Party.

Perhaps idealistically some political commentators at the time were suggesting that the game itself had taken on a much greater importance. In the words of one correspondent (*The Guardian*, 28 October 1991, p.24):

> The message of Murrayfield this weekend was bigger than scrummaging techniques and line-out skills. It seemed etched in emotion on the faces of the players as they sang Flower of Scotland. It boiled constantly around the arena. Sometimes events happening send a clearer signal than a thousand pieces of newspaper. Murrayfield was a message of Scottish identity and nationhood.

It goes without saying that sport does not provide the healthiest foundation upon which to mobilise a campaign for national or regional separatism and yet it is equally idealistic to suggest that sport and sporting relations are not affected by post-modernist or post-nationalist conditions. Sport itself in all its different forms reacted to the complexity of Scottish feelings and emotions about the 1992 General Election. During October 1991 the aforementioned emotions at Murrayfield were seen by some as an indicator of the apparently widening fissure within the fabric of the original 1707 Act of Union of the parliaments. By March 1992 both the chairman and club manager of Glasgow Rangers Football Club, David Murray and Walter Smith, had both publicly declared their support for the Unionist option. One correspondent quoted Murray as saying 'I believe very strongly that the Union has served us well' (*The Herald*, 27 March 1992, p.8). As alluded to earlier, after the election Jim Sillars, a former deputy leader of the Scottish National Party (SNP), insisted that 'the great problem we have is that we sing Flower of Scotland at Hampden or Murrayfield and that we have too many ninety minute patriots in this country' (*The Herald*, 24 April 1992, p.1).

There are many more convincing explanations of the SNP performance at the General Election than to suggest, as the former deputy leader clearly does, that those on the terraces exhibited a degree of false consciousness when it came to voting for the nationalist cause. It might be said, in any case, that the mood of Murrayfield 1991 was reflected in April 1992 in an increased SNP vote and in the overall vote for parties which stood for constitutional change. While it is crucial not to overstate the contribution which sport has made to either cultural or political forms of nationalism or Scottish civil society, it is equally important not to dismiss the sporting contribution. Cricket in the Caribbean during the late 1950s and early 1960s became a powerful expression of Caribbean progress and nationhood. C.L.R. James' text *Beyond a Boundary* (1963) remains a classic statement of the link between cricket, black nationalism, Caribbean identity and anti-colonial struggle. Since 1948 both the African National Congress and the Nationalist Party in South Africa have regarded sport as an area of popular nationalist struggle in the Republic of South Africa. Slightly nearer home the Gaelic Athletic Association (GAA) played a prominent role in Irish Nationalist politics during the late nineteenth century and the first quarter of the twentieth century. Formed in Dublin, in 1884, the GAA acted as a bulwark against

6 *Scottish Sport in the Making of the Nation*

what is described as those English imperial games of cricket, rugby and soccer.

Indeed given that Scotland and Ireland have much in common it is perhaps surprising that, especially in the Highlands, no equivalent organisation to that of the GAA emerged in Scotland (for a discussion on this theme see Chris Harvie's analysis in Chapter 4). Paradoxically Michael Davitt, founding member of the Irish Land League, strong supporter of the GAA, was also a staunch supporter of Glasgow Celtic Football Club (see Gerry Finn's discussion on politics, religion and ethnicity in Scottish Football in Chapter 7). As patron of the club, Davitt laid the first patch of soil, specially transported from Donegal, at Celtic Park in 1892. Perhaps Davitt's association with Celtic Football Club, despite his GAA connections, was an indication that the Irish in Scotland were about to go their own way, that is to commit themselves to a different union and thus to weaken the original ties with Ireland. This is not an assertion that Irish-Scots did not identify with Irish causes, but that they became more involved with socialist concerns and the labour movement in Scotland which, while recognising the important cultural and political links with Ireland, in the last instance was pro-unionist in its orientation. Despite the relationship between revolutionary socialism, Irish Nationalism, and land agitation in the Highlands, Scotland at this point in its political history did not want to break out of the Act of Union and in this fact alone, lies one of the many reasons why a similar organisation to the Gaelic Athletic Association did not develop in Scotland.

Furthermore it has to be said that while periods of Scottish social development have witnessed attempts to establish separate kingdoms and local fiefdoms, such as the Lordship of the Isles during the fifteenth century, in general nationalists whether they be Gaelic, Irish, or Scottish have tended to support moves for home rule in Scotland and Ireland but not home rule for the Highlands or the Gaidhealtachd. In a simple sense while the Gaelic Athletic Association could readily identify with a form of Irish nationality, in the early twentieth century, in either modern or post-modern times no nation existed for gaelic culture in the Highlands to identify with other than Scotland. Indeed many celtic historians have suggested that the divisions within the Gaidhealtachd are as great as the integrating factors and while one might talk of a Scottish consciousness or even Celtic spirituality, it is perhaps spurious to talk of a unified celtic consciousness in the Highlands of Scotland. There was certainly no specific modern political organisation that was marching for home rule or devolution for the Highlands and as such no political party for any potential nationalist sporting organisation to attach itself to.

A great deal of sympathy existed between the Irish Land League, formed in 1879, and the Highland Land League, formed in 1883. Unlike the GAA, the Camanachd Association and other sporting associations in the Highlands failed to consolidate any strong political links with either the Highland Land League (HLLRA) or the Scottish Home Rule Association (SHRA) which itself was founded in 1886. Yet it would be misleading and indeed incorrect to suggest that key personnel within either the HLLRA or the SHRA failed to see the political significance of sport or leisure. Like Davitt, John Murdoch openly attacked not only the landlord system, but also the systematic development of the Highlands as a leisure playground for the southern aristocracy. The formation of the HLLRA was in no small part due to the tireless campaigning of John Murdoch through *The Highlander*, the paper which he launched in Inverness in 1873. This paper regularly reported on Irish Nationalist politics, anti-landlord agitation in the Highlands and developments within the game of shinty.

Like Murdoch, John Stuart Blackie from the Chair of Greek at Edinburgh University supported Highland land reform, gaelic revivalism, Irish home rule and Scottish devolution. Blackie prompted the campaign for the establishment of the Chair in Celtic studies at Edinburgh, became Vice-President of the HLLRA, was regularly quoted and supported by Charles Stewart Parnell and was first Chairman of the SHRA. Blackie's interest in Gaelic politics and culture included sport and he became the first president of Edinburgh University Shinty Club, formed in 1891. Shinty, or Camanachd as it is traditionally known, was viewed not only as the embodiment of Scottish Gaelic culture and identity, but also as a link with the past. At one level the relationship between people, politics and various cultural forms, including sporting forms, may seem insignificant and yet a shared interest in all things Celtic was the product of a radical, nationalist and, for some, a socialist internationalism brought about by the mistaken belief that Scotland and Ireland stood in a similar relationship to England's imperial power.

As to the role of sport in the making of nations or communities at a general level, a number of common arguments have, in the past, been put forward:

(i)   that sport itself is inherently conservative and that it helps to consolidate official or centre nationalism, patriotism and racism;

(ii) that sport has some inherent property that makes it an instrument of national unity and integration, for example, in peripheral or emerging nations;

(iii) that sport helps to reinforce national consciousness and cultural nationalism;

(iv) that sport provides a safety valve or outlet of emotional energy for frustrated peoples or nations;

(v)   that sport has at times contributed to unique political struggles some of which have been closely connected to nationalist politics and popular nationalist struggles; and

(vi) that sport, whether it be through nostalgia, mythology, invented or selected traditions, contributes to a quest for identity be it local, regional, cultural or global (for discussion of some of the popular myths which have mediated discussions about such sports as golf and football in Scotland see the contributions by John Lowerson, Chapter 6, and Bert Moorhouse, Chapter 12).

Some or all of these might be helpful in understanding certain aspects of Scottish sport at particular points in Scotland's social development. Like sporting experiences and memories of sporting action all forms of nationalism and expressions of nationhood are timebound, selective, particular and expressive. It might be that sport in Scotland has not been centrally concerned with self-determination or political devolution but rather has been an assertion of Scottishness on the part of a diverse group of interests and people whose identities and ways of life have been part of the process of Scottish development. Sport itself in all its different forms certainly contributes to and is constitutive of Scottish history, politics and social development. It can also contribute to our understanding of Scotland in a pre- and post-nationalist era.

The unity of this book derives from the simple postulate that something that absorbs so much of the nation's physical and emotional energy needs to be confronted and explained. In general it is hoped that this book will indicate that different and competing identities, all claiming the term national and all laying claim to forms of patriotism of one kind or another, have expressed themselves through Scottish sport, and that analysis of them has to transcend the myths which have been constructed out of sport's power to grip emotions. The contributions to this book convey not only the complexity of Scottish sporting experiences but also the complexity of Scotland. Sport in all its different forms continues to contribute to the process of Scotland. Sport may at times contribute to a notion of Scottishness and yet within each of the amorphous identities and expressions of nationhood which make up Scotland it is almost impossible to distinguish what exact identity is being reflected, symbolised, reproduced or even imagined. It is certainly far too simplistic to claim that sport is simply reactive to political culture, or that sport contributes to a sense of false consciousness about community and nation. Yet when everything has been subject to critique and counter-critique there is still something down there, something deep rooted about sport that needs to be explained. It is hoped that collectively, *Scottish Sport in the Making of the Nation Ninety Minute Patriots?:* not only makes a small contribution to our understanding of Scotland but also illustrates that no dialogue on Scotland or Scottish civil society is complete without acknowledging the social space occupied by sport.

BIBLIOGRAPHY

Harvie, C., 1977, *Scotland and nationalism: Scottish society and politics 1707–1977*, George Allen & Unwin, London

James, C. L. R., 1963, *Beyond a boundary*, Stanley Paul, London

Jarvie, G., 1991, *Highland games: the making of the myth*, Edinburgh University Press, Edinburgh

Jenkins, R., 1983, *The thistle and the grail*, Macdonald and Co, Glasgow

Kellas, J., 1989, *The Scottish political system*, Cambridge University Press, Cambridge

Lynch, M., 1991, *Scotland a new history*, Century, London

Linklater, M. and Denniston, R., 1992, *Anatomy of Scotland: how Scotland works*, Chambers, Edinburgh

McCrone, D., 1992, *Understanding Scotland: the sociology of a stateless nation*, Routledge, London

Walker, G. and Gallagher, T., 1990, *Sermons and battle hymns: protestant popular culture in modern Scotland*, Edinburgh University Press, Edinburgh

2

FOOTBALL AND THE IDEA OF SCOTLAND

Alan Bairner

It is undeniable that there exists a Scottish national identity which differs markedly both from the national identity of Britain as a whole and from the identities of the other component parts of the United Kingdom. Robert McCreadie refers to 'the existence among Scots of all classes, and particularly the educated classes, of a quite *conscious* awareness of Scotland's status as a nation – in other words, the existence of a specifically Scottish consciousness' (McCreadie, 1991, p.39). But how cohesive is this consciousness? To what extent does it form the basis of a coherent and unifying world view?

This chapter addresses these issues by examining the role which football plays not only in forging a sense of what it means to be Scottish but also in promoting the kind of divisions which militate against the development of a uniform sense of national identity.

One need not subscribe to the late Bill Shankly's somewhat fatuous view that football is more important than life and death to recognise the significance of the game for Shankly's fellow Scots. As Don Lindsay comments, 'football plays a disproportionate and some would say overtly intrusive part in Scottish culture' (*The Independent*, 19 March 1991). Ample proof of the Scottish passion for football is found in the response of Archie McGregor, editor of Scotland's leading general football fanzine, *The Absolute Game*, to the question – could Scotland survive without football? 'People would get fairly desperate – it would be like having no sex. It's been important for Scotland culturally for the past one hundred years, particularly for the working class and a lot of us like to claim Scotland as the cradle of football' (*Scotland on Sunday*, 5 April 1992).

As well as adopting football as their national game, Scots have made an important contribution to the development of the game's popularity worldwide. According to Richard Holt, 'considering its population size and resources, no other country has sustained the scale and quality of professional football attained in Scotland' (Holt, 1989, p.256). For many Scots, however, football represents more than simply a popular game which their ancestors helped to introduce to the farthest corners of the globe. It is also a symbol of Scottish nationality.

Scotland's status within the United Kingdom after the Act of Union of 1707 was and remains a peculiar one. The Scots were left with a number of institutions of civil society which have ensured the existence of a separate identity despite the absence of political channels through which this can be more formally articulated. Indeed, even after the Union, it was open to Scots to develop their own forms of association separately from their English neighbours and other members of the United Kingdom.

The Scottish Football Association (SFA) was formed in 1873, ten years after the Football Association (FA). At first, Scottish clubs continued to play in the FA Cup competition but in 1887 the differences between the two associations became irreconcilable and the SFA ordered its members to withdraw from the English competition. From that time onwards, in the words of Christopher Harvie, 'the new proletarian, professional game was organised on national, not on British lines' (Harvie, 1977, p.38). As a result, Scottish football took its place alongside the Church of Scotland, Scottish regiments, the educational and legal systems and a distinctive form of local government as the newest, and perhaps the most emotionally charged, symbol of the Scottish nation.

Scotland is of course by no means unique in having assigned a quasi-political role to sport. As H.F. Moorhouse observes, 'Scotland is characteristic of "submerged nations" in that sport, and soccer in particular, has an overdetermined significance' (Moorhouse, 1991, p.201). An obvious comparison can be made with Catalonia where football, according to Jay Rayner, 'has been appropriated, over the years, as something of a metaphor for the whole Catalan tradition' (*The Independent on Sunday*, 28 June 1992). So important is football in this respect to many Scots that the performance of the national team can have a direct impact on the fluctuating fortunes of nationalist feeling. For example, political commentators have expressed the opinion that a significant factor in the outcome of the 1979 referendum on the issue of devolved government was the lamentable performance of the Scottish team at the 1978 World Cup Finals (Kellas, 1980, p.148). According to Tom Gallagher, 'Scotland's ignominious exit from the World Cup in June 1978 may also have been a final blow to faith in Scottish capabilities, given the crucial importance of football for sustaining a sense of patriotism within the Scottish working class' (Gallagher, 1991, p.106).

In this regard, 1992 may come to be regarded as a year in which football actually came to the rescue of Scottish national sentiment. The result of the April General Election was a bitter blow to the aspirations of the majority of Scottish voters. For the fourth consecutive time, they were faced with government by a Conservative Party which they had rejected. Furthermore, despite the fact that almost three quarters of the Scottish electorate had voted for candidates who supported constitutional change, the newly elected government's majority was such that it would be under no pressure during its term in office to consider Scotland's constitutional position.

In terms of football, however, 1992 was to be a good year for the Scots. A hopeful sign was the achievement of the national under-21 squad which reached the semi-final of the European Championships having beaten Germany in the previous round. Nevertheless, most of Scotland held its collective breath when the full national squad set off in June to compete for the first time in the European Championships final stage. Memories were of past failures in World Cup Finals. But the pessimism proved to be unfounded. The Scottish team played with a combination of passion and skill which led to narrow defeats at the hands of Holland and Germany, two of the pre-tournament favourites, and a 3–0 victory over the Commonwealth of Independent States (CIS). National coach, Andy Roxburgh, dealt with the media with courtesy and good humour in some contrast with his English counterpart, Graham Taylor. Last but not least, Scotland's travelling support – the Tartan Army – proved to be first-class ambassadors whose behaviour charmed their Swedish hosts and contrasted markedly with that of some of the followers of Holland, Germany, Sweden and, most significantly, England. The election result was all but forgotten. It was good to be Scottish and, at least as importantly, to be recognised as such.

It is symptomatic of the complex character of Scottish identity that many foreigners are unable to differentiate the Scots from the English or Britain from England. This misunderstanding is related to the confusion which many Scots have about their national identity. As Bernard Crick observes, 'many Scots, like many Welsh, have a vivid sense of dual nationality, and for most purposes live with it comfortably . . . and find an enhanced quality of life in being able to live in two worlds, enjoying two cultures and their hybrids' (Crick, 1991, p.18). Thus, they think of themselves as Scottish *and* British through a process described by Tom Nairn as 'the internalisation of duality' (Nairn, 1991, p.6). This condition of dual nationality presents few practical problems since there are only limited opportunities in a modern, developed society to openly declare one's national allegiance. Wars are few and far between and there is nothing noble or exhilarating about signing a hotel register. It is at major sporting events, therefore, that modern men (and, to a lesser extent, modern women) proclaim their loyalties. At that level, dual nationality still creates few problems for Scots. Although Scots participate in British teams in a number of sports, more often, as in the case of football, they represent Scotland. The performances of Scottish teams and players can be viewed, therefore, from the relatively unobstructed perspective of a single national identity. However, as far as football's popularity is concerned, Scottish national identity possesses its own dual character.

David Daiches argues that there are two ways in which a people, placed in the situation experienced by Scots since 1707, can respond in cultural terms to the loss of political independence. On one hand, 'it can attempt to rediscover its own national traditions and by reviving and developing them find a satisfaction that will compensate for its political impotence'. Alternatively, by 'accepting the dominance of the culture of the country which has achieved political ascendancy over it, it can endeavour to beat that country at its own game and achieve distinction by any standard the dominant culture may evolve' (Daiches, 1952, p.8). The manner in which Scots have chosen football as their national team sport indicates that these rival responses may become interwoven in practice.

By adopting football, together with rugby union and, to a lesser degree, hockey and cricket as national team sports, Scots chose the second of the two options outlined by Daiches and responded in sporting terms to English domination according to a pattern followed in the British-controlled regions of southern Asia, the Caribbean and in south and east Africa as well as in New Zealand. Distinction in sport was to be attained by beating the English at their own games. Despite the existence of a native sport in the form of shinty, the vast majority of Scots chose not to take the route followed by north Americans, some Australians and, above all, the Irish nationalists who established the Gaelic Athletic Association and construct a sporting nationalism centred around distinctively national traditions.

However, the precise character of Scotland's adoption of football suggests that the former of the options presented by Daiches was not entirely eschewed. This is manifested in at least two ways. First, there is widespread acceptance of the idea that Scots have imparted to the game of football their own innate qualities to the extent that there exists a particular Scottish style of play. Scottish players are identified with aggression, passion and, in particular, skill. The English, by comparison, are thought of as strong, well organised but essentially lacking in flair – hence the historic reliance of major English clubs on talented Scots in key positions. Like all attempts to create national stereotypes, the grain of truth which these conceptions contain is no match for objective reality. However, the image is what matters for many Scots and the image suggests that Scottish football differs from English football and, by implication, that the Scots are qualitatively different from the English.

The second indication that native traditions were not entirely forgotten when football became the national game comes from the public image of the Scottish football fan. His tartan is a tribute to a bygone Scotland, fondly but inaccurately remembered. His songs are of hills and glens despite the fact that he is likely to live in a housing scheme in an industrial city or town. His tunes of glory recall victories on foreign battlefields. The message is clear. Beating the English at their own game is important but it is given greater poignancy if carried out to an accompaniment which is unmistakably Scottish. Thus, the Scottish approach to football combines both of the responses to lost nationhood outlined by Daiches. A universally popular vehicle is selected to convey national aspirations but it is bedecked in the regalia of an antiquated and even mythical Scotland.

This dualism cannot be disassociated from the relationship between the Highlands and Lowlands of Scotland which is the first of the divisions affecting national identity which are revealed in an examination of Scottish football and which this chapter will now describe. The Tartan Army is a typical representation of the attempt by lowland Scotland to assimilate a certain conception of the Highlands in the construction of Scottish identity. The phenomenon is especially ironic given the marginalisation of the Highlands in the development of Scottish football.

The distinctiveness of the Highlands, well established by historical, linguistic and religious differences, is further secured by a separate sporting tradition which embraces not only shinty but also the Highland Games (Jarvie, 1991).

Despite the potential for the construction of an exclusive brand of sporting nationalism, however, football has been taken up throughout the region with considerable enthusiasm, a fact which remains largely unacknowledged in the structure of the game in Scotland. The Highland League operates separately from the Scottish League and there is no mechanism for automatic access from the former to the latter. Highland League clubs have repeatedly and, so far, unsuccessfully sought entry to the Scottish League when the claims for re-election of existing members have been considered. Particular pressure has come from Inverness, home to three Highland League clubs and the major Highland urban centre. In 1974, however, when the Scottish League authorities were most recently given the opportunity to choose a new club to augment their numbers, they turned to Ferranti Thistle FC (now Meadowbank Thistle FC), an East of Scotland League member based in Edinburgh which was already home to two Scottish League teams. Currently, therefore, the only access which Highland League clubs have to national competition is by way of qualification for entry to the Scottish cup. The exclusion of the Highlands from senior football is not, however, the only example of the way that regional variations have an impact on Scottish football. Significant differences also exist between the Borders of Scotland and the central belt and between the cities (particularly Glasgow) and small-town Scotland.

Like the north west, a substantial area of southern Scotland possesses its own sporting tradition, with rugby union replacing shinty as the most popular team game in many towns and villages. In spite of rugby's strength, however, football is played extensively throughout the Borders. But as in the Highlands, most senior clubs are organised in separate leagues and may only compete with Scottish League teams by qualifying for the Scottish Cup competition. Scottish League membership extends to the region's extremities to include Stranraer FC and Queen of the South FC (based in Dumfries), both of which are in the south west and Berwick Rangers FC situated ironically in north east England.

All of this suggests that the term *Scottish* League is something of a mis-nomer. With the exception of Berwick Rangers, the remaining thirty-seven member clubs are located between two roughly drawn lines stretching from Dumbarton in the west to Aberdeen in the north east and from Dumfries in the south west to Edinburgh in the east. Compare this with the situation in England where Football League clubs are spread throughout the country and all other professional and semi-professional clubs can gain admission because of a system of promotion and relegation involving a network of subsidiary leagues.

A different type of geographical division, containing an added economic dimension, exists between the cities (and their clubs) and the provincial towns (and their clubs) and between Glasgow and the rest of urban Scotland. Scottish football competitions have been dominated traditionally by clubs from the cities of Glasgow, Edinburgh, Aberdeen and Dundee. Between them they have won the Scottish League championship on 93 occasions, the Scottish Cup 86 times and the Scottish League Cup in 42 out of 46 contests. In addition, 80 per cent of all Scottish League support gathers at the grounds of city-based clubs. Together these factors have created a climate of suspicion and dislike. The leading clubs are unhappy about the influence which small town clubs exert in the world of Scottish football. For their part, the small provincial sides and their supporters resent the arrogance of the city-based clubs who purport to speak on behalf of the national game and whose affairs dominate the sports pages of the Scottish press. The proposal made in June 1992 by five city clubs (Rangers FC, Celtic FC, Heart of Midlothian FC, Aberdeen FC and Dundee United FC) to resign from the Scottish League and set up a Super League from the 1994–95 season will do nothing to heal these wounds (*Scotland on Sunday*, 28 June 1992). Jack Steedman, a former Scottish League President, expressed the views of many officials and supporters of small-town Scottish clubs.

> It's high time the view of the majority of clubs was made known. I've never known so much anger in all my years in football. And that's only a few hours after the group made their plans known. Quite frankly, their arrogance is breathtaking. In fact, if they pursue their ideals it could blow Scottish football apart. (*Sunday Mail*, 28 June 1992)

Nevertheless, whether the Super League comes about or not, it is inevitable that the Scottish League will experience some structural reform which will widen further the gap between the Big Five and the rest. The idea of a Big Five, however, is itself misleading. The history of Scottish football has been dominated by only two of the elite group, namely the Old Firm of Celtic and Rangers. This is one of the key elements in the division caused by the city of Glasgow's hegemonic position in Scottish football.

Only Celtic and Rangers are big clubs in international terms. The Old Firm fixture enjoys a worldwide reputation. It continues to attract the biggest attendances in British league football. Despite the clubs' apparent symbiotic relationship, however, since the 1980s it has seemed that one of them, Rangers, is on the brink of setting out on its own to create a Scottish elite with a single member, its sights firmly set on success in a British or perhaps a European arena. Despite the resentment felt about the successes of Celtic and Rangers, smaller clubs have benefited from their status, not least in financial terms. Moorhouse argues that, under the chairmanship of David Murray and since the managerial period of Graeme Souness, 'Rangers activities have pulled others along in their wake and many a club now boasts some foreign international players, an Englishman, a few ground improvements, giving the whole of the Scottish game a much more cosmopolitan and confident veneer than it has ever had' (Moorhouse, 1991, pp.207–8). Far from attracting gratitude, however, Rangers current role has merely increased their unpopularity outside the ranks of their own supporters. This point was not lost on Souness who 'acidly – and accurately – observed that nobody in Scotland outside the club's own following ever wanted Rangers to win anything' (*The Independent*, 13 May 1991). Part of the explanation for this is to be found in the club's sectarian image which will be discussed later in this chapter. It can also be traced, however, to the traditional values of Scottish political culture.

The idea of an inherent Scottish predilection for socialism and democracy is another of these stereotypes which are all too easily contradicted by fact. Nevertheless, whatever its ideological implications, a strong feeling of distaste for those who 'get above themselves' exists among Scots. In the recent past Celtic have enjoyed success comparable with that of Rangers but in spirit they remain closer to the small clubs. As Moorhouse puts it, Celtic 'cling to a conventional view of what football "is about" in Scotland, a posture which seems to block any initiative and to stultify any sensible response to the big changes which European developments seem likely to forge' (Moorhouse, 1991, p.209). Research has also indicated that Celtic's support remains more solidly working class than that of Rangers and thus more closely linked to the historic roots of Scottish football (*Scotland on Sunday*, 1 September 1991). This contrast together with the charitable purposes for which the Celtic club was founded help to explain the description by Rangers supporters of their rivals as 'The Beggars'.

For these reasons, and others which relate to the problem of sectarianism, Celtic tend not to provoke the same hostile feelings as Rangers. Indeed, in recent years, an Edinburgh club, Heart of Midlothian, have become closest to Rangers in terms of popular demonology as their high profile, business-oriented chairman, Wallace Mercer, has eagerly sought to follow the modernising example set by Rangers. Nevertheless, Hearts are still regarded as a small club by Old Firm standards and Celtic remain tainted by the impression that Glasgow exercises a hegemonic position in Scottish football of which their success and that of Rangers are only examples.

In addition, the main governing bodies of Scottish football, the SFA and the Scottish League, are based in Glasgow as is the *Daily Record*, the most influential Scottish newspaper in terms of football coverage. In a symbolic sense, however, the clearest indicator of Glaswegian hegemony is the fact the city plays host to the overwhelming majority of major fixtures, including nearly all of Scotland's senior international matches. This has caused rancour in the past when one or both Scottish cup semi-finalists have considered the choice of a Glasgow venue to be unfair and inappropriate. The problem has intensified, however, because the deteriorating condition of the national stadium, Hampden Park, has prompted a search for alternative venues. One suggestion was to play international games at Scottish rugby's headquarters, Murrayfield in Edinburgh. The response of SFA chief executive, Jim Farry, however, was that there was not a 'snowball's chance in hell of the SFA agreeing to such a scheme' (*Daily Record*, 8 July 1991). His explanation was of particular interest to those who view Glasgow's dominance with suspicion.

> Glasgow and west central Scotland is the hub of football in the country, Edinburgh and the east more the rugby playing region. Murrayfield is also needed on Saturdays, which limits its use to us. It is not far away from Tynecastle. Hearts would need to play on Wednesday nights and so would we. (*Daily Record*, 8 July 1991)

Mr Farry's statement revealed a remarkable degree of ignorance of Scottish geography, sporting traditions and, most surprisingly, of the arrangements made for major football fixtures. First, situated in the west end of Edinburgh, the Murrayfield ground is only an hour's drive from Glasgow and within easy reach from the rest of the central belt. Second, although rugby is undeniably a popular sport in Edinburgh, as indeed it is in Glasgow, the pre-eminent game in the capital city in terms of participation and spectator interest is football. The city is home to three senior clubs: Hearts, Hibernian FC and Meadowbank Thistle, chosen for admission to the Scottish League despite the rival claims from clubs in both the Highlands and the Borders. Furthermore, a short distance from Edinburgh are such traditional hotbeds of football as West Lothian and West Fife. Finally, Mr Farry claimed that there would be problems with fixture clashes involving both the Scottish Rugby Union and Hearts whose Tynecastle ground is also in Edinburgh's west end. The fact is that nowadays Scotland seldom plays international football games on Saturdays and never at times when Murrayfield would be needed for rugby. As for the problem of Tynecastle's proximity, it is inconceivable that Hearts, or virtually any other football club in Scotland, would arrange a match in direct opposition to an international fixture. If a problem did exist, it would presumably also apply to Glasgow clubs with grounds close to Hampden.

Few followers of Scottish football were convinced by Mr Farry's arguments. One correspondent to *The Absolute Game* asked, 'are not the arguments being put up against the use of Murrayfield typical examples of the parochial, introspective thinking of the West Coast Mafia that runs and reports on football in Scotland?' (*The Absolute Game*, 27, 1992). A less emotional response was offered by Robert McElroy, secretary of the Scottish Programme Club and himself a Glasgow resident.

> Full use could be made of both Ibrox Stadium (the home of Rangers) and Murrayfield for Cup Finals and Major internationals, with Aberdeen and Perth included on the rota for certain fixtures, and obviously the new Stadiums planned by clubs such as Celtic and Hearts coming into the equation as and when ready.

Public sentiment notwithstanding, it seems unlikely that while the future of Hampden is being decided, major international games will be moved any further than Ibrox in Glasgow. Thus, Scottish football will miss the opportunity to follow the example set by other European countries which use two or more stadia, in different cities, for games featuring their national sides.

In terms of football's role in the creation of national identity, the most unfortunate product of Glasgow's virtual monopoly of international fixtures is that many Scots find it difficult, if not impossible, to see the national team play. Whereas the Tartan Army abroad represents every corner of Scotland, the crowds at international matches at Hampden Park with 8.00pm kick-offs are dominated by supporters from west central Scotland and, thus, primarily by followers of Rangers and Celtic. Graham Spiers described how this manifested itself during Scotland's 2–1 victory over Switzerland in a European Championship qualifying game in October 1990. 'For sure, the singing and clapping was hearty, but this was an almost exclusive Rangers-Celtic preserve. One tribe chanted one song, the other answered back' (*Scotland on Sunday*, 21 October 1990).

While this describes a significant by-product of the regional divisions which affect Scottish football, Spiers' observation alerts us to the problem of sectarianism which arguably does more than anything else to undermine Scottish football's capacity to forge a unified national consciousness. Not only regional differences, but a number of other factors, of which sectarianism is the most pronounced, weaken the claim for football as a cornerstone of national unity. These will now be discussed.

Even at international matches, when one might expect the national cause to be of paramount importance, the Protestant followers of Rangers and the Catholic supporters of Celtic have traditionally taken their places at their respective 'ends' of Hampden and proclaimed their sectarian allegiances. Behind the scenes, a debate rages concerning the degree of loyalty to the national interest which each club and its supporters exhibit.

According to Graham Walker, between the wars and in the immediate post-World War Two era, Rangers were a part of 'a celebration of Scottishness which was underpinned by a strong unionism or loyalism' (Walker, 1990, p.146). This is understandable particularly given the origins of their leading rivals, Celtic, a club founded by Irishmen with the expressed purpose of helping Glasgow's Catholic poor, many of whom were Irish or of Irish extraction. However, as Brian Wilson points out, the name 'Celtic', rather than 'Hibernian', 'Harp' or 'Shamrocks', was chosen by the club's founders precisely because it has Scottish as well as Irish connotations (Wilson, 1988, p.14). Moreover, whereas Rangers have traditionally employed only Protestant players, Celtic have consistently signed both Catholics and Protestants. In a predominantly Protestant country, there might be an element of utilitarian good sense in this approach. The end result, however, has been that Celtic, rather than Rangers, have shown a willingness to employ any Scot, regardless of religion. According to Wilson, by appointing a Protestant, Jock Stein, as club manager in 1965, 'Celtic had confirmed the message that had been repeated throughout the decades – that, while proud of its origins and distinctive identity – the club had always eschewed sectarianism in its employment policies' (Wilson, 1988, p.128). Such remarks, containing as they do an implicit criticism of Rangers, are regarded by Walker as the product of 'a tendency to "ideologise" the Old Firm rivalry, with Celtic cast in the role of progressives on account of their roots, and Rangers in the role of the reactionaries or oppressors' (Walker, 1990, p.150). By an ironic twist of fate, however, although recent developments at Ibrox have included the signing of a leading Catholic player, Maurice Johnston, and a move away from earlier employment practices, they have tended to confirm the popular image of Rangers as the wealthy overlords of Scottish football.

It is possible that the differences between the two clubs are lessening or at least being transformed from matters of sectarian allegiance to considerations of finance, ambition and the capacity to adapt to a changed economic and cultural environment. Moorhouse, for example, suggests that some commentators overemphasise the role of sectarianism in contemporary Scotland and Scottish football.

Of course, 'identities' are situationally relevant, and people can move through levels speedily in certain eventualities, but talking of Glasgow as 'a divided city' with 'simmering hostilities' and so on has been pretty dubious for at least twenty years and now Rangers have suddenly exploded a lot of the old verities about this matter in relation to Scottish football. (Moorhouse, 1991, p.205).

Bob Purdie is less sanguine about the influence of sectarianism. 'Sectarianism is a more powerful force than it appears on the surface; for generations it has been part of the culture of some of the most heavily industrialised and densely populated areas of Scotland' (Purdie, 1991, p.78). (Also, see chapters by Finn and Moorhouse in this volume.)

Certainly sectarianism continues to influence football support in Scotland. Supporters do not leave the small towns, far less the cities, to watch the Old Firm simply because they wish to associate themselves with success, although that is a partial explanation. The choice of club is what really matters. That choice is directly related to the histories of Celtic and Rangers and to the persistence of religious division in Scotland of which those histories are part. Furthermore, there are doubts as to whether Celtic and Rangers supporters are equally devoted to the national cause or, indeed, whether either group identifies with the national team to the same extent as the followers of other teams.

Doubts about the Scottish loyalty of Rangers centre around the club's traditional commitment to the Union. The team's red, white and blue strips mirror the Union flags waved by their followers. This, together with the signing of many English players during the Souness era, has prompted supporters of other clubs to serenade Rangers with 'Flower of Scotland', the people's national anthem, once monotonously reserved, in domestic football circles, for Berwick Rangers. In defence of Rangers Scottishness, however, and in opposition to the unionism of club chairman, David Murray, some Rangers fans have spoken out. For example,

> He [David Murray] is entitled to his views and opinions, just as long as these are not seen as portraying the will or opinion of the majority of Rangers fans. If a poll was conducted among Rangers fans on the issue of which flag they would want between the Union Jack and the Saltire, I firmly believe the Saltire would win and, contrary to a lot of folk's beliefs, most of the fans are either Labour or SNP supporters. (*Scotland on Sunday*, 16 February 1992)

A very different picture is painted, however, by a correspondent to the Rangers fanzine, *Follow, Follow*. Signing himself 'Tartan Tory', he writes

> Real Scots are proud to be British. Bogus nationalists hate post-reformation Scotland and its symbols of union (the Crown, the Kirk and the Scottish Regiments). What has all this got to do with Rangers? Everything. Because our club is a popular symbol of explicit unionism.
>
> . . . . . .
>
> The English are not the enemy, they are friendly rivals in sport. Ulstermen are not the enemy, they are Scots by descent and loyal by instinct. No, the enemy is republicanism, be it the terrorism of the Provos or the scum in the media. (*Follow, Follow*, 24, 1992)

Although extreme in its tone, this statement is accurate in its depiction of some Rangers followers as less antagonistic towards England than are the vast majority of Scottish football fans. This was most evident when England captain, Terry Butcher, was a Rangers player. In general, however, most Rangers supporters share the anti-English sentiment and are fully behind the efforts of the national team. Doubts persist, however, about the club's commitment to the national effort.

It has sometimes been felt that Rangers have been reluctant to release players for international duty. This impression was particularly strong during the Souness era. Relations between current Rangers captain, Richard Gough, and Andy Roxburgh appeared strained, for example, until the recent European Championship Finals, in the light of numerous call-offs by Gough from international duties in the past.

It is also suggested that Rangers play little part in the development of football talent. The policy instead has been to buy non-Scottish players or Scots whose careers began with other clubs. Significantly, Rangers players contributed little to the successful 1991–92 campaign of the Scottish under 21 squad. Aberdeen and Dundee United, on the other hand, provided several players each as did Celtic whose managers over the years have made a point of showing their eagerness to support the national teams' efforts. Set against this, however, are serious doubts about the commitment of their club's followers to the national cause.

The nationalism of many Celtic supporters remains directed towards Ireland rather than Scotland (Boyle, 1991). This tendency has arguably grown with the improved fortunes in recent years of the Republic of Ireland team. On the eve of the 1990 World Cup finals for which Scotland and Ireland both qualified, one Celtic supporter expressed his views to *Que Sera Sera*, a fanzine devoted to the exploits of the Scottish national team.

> As World Cup fever sweeps the land I would like to take this opportunity to explain to you why I, and many other Celtic fans like myself, just could not give a damn about how Scotland perform in Italy. I would like to explain why we hold this attitude towards the country of our birth. (*Que Sera Sera*, 2, 1990)

The writer went on to list a number of factors ranging from the presence in the Scottish squad of Maurice Johnston, a former Celtic player and the only Catholic internationalist to have been signed by Rangers, to the bias shown by the SFA, Scotland fans and managers towards Celtic fans and players. 'For the above reasons', he concluded, 'you will find me supporting the Republic of Ireland this summer'. Again the argument is extreme but the general position was corroborated to some extent in a recent interview given by Celtic player, Charlie Nicholas, himself a former Scottish internationalist.

> I have not been picked for ages, and I don't expect to be picked. I am quite happy with that position. I would play for Scotland if I was asked, as I'm sure any player would. We shouldn't kid each other on, there are not a great deal of Celtic supporters who follow Scotland. I think the burden always falls on ex-Celtic players who never won enough caps, and I will probably be tagged along with Bobby Lennox, Jimmy Johnstone, some of the great Celtic players of the past. (*Once a Tim, Always a Tim*, 10, 1992)

Astonishingly a player such as Jimmy McGrory who scored 550 goals was capped only seven times for Scotland and never played at Wembley. To some extent the patriotism of Celts like Stein and another former manager, Billy McNeill, must have helped to counteract the disaffection of Celtic fans with the national team. Arguably, however, the problem was exacerbated by the fact that in 1991 Celtic appointed former Irish internationalist, Liam Brady, as manager. The club is certainly conscious of the problem as is testified to by the publication in the official programme of an article arguing that Celtic supporters should follow Scotland rather than Ireland (Boyle, 1991). Its author acknowledges that 'in the past it has neither been fashionable, nor frankly very common, to be passionately interested in both the fortunes of Celtic and our national team, Scotland' (Celtic versus Dunfermline Athletic Official programme, 30 November 1991). 'Call it the siege mentality if you like', he goes on, 'but the grievance amongst many Celtic supporters down the years has been that neither their players nor their presence at matches appeared to be WANTED by those who ran and those who followed the Scottish team'. However, 'that should no longer be seen as the case though and the time has come for Celtic supporters to get right behind their country, especially with Scotland having done so wonderfully well to get to the finals of the European Championships in Sweden'. 'It was a little sad', he concludes, 'that some Celtic supporters, Scots born and bred, seemed completely non-plussed by Scotland's achievement and that a number of these same people would have been happier to see the Republic of Ireland reach Sweden'.

It is unlikely that the presence of a substantial Rangers contingent in the Scottish team which played in Sweden will have done anything to diminish anti-Scottish feelings amongst a section of Celtic followers. However, they are not alone in being excluded or excluding themselves from identification with the national football team and sectarianism is by no means the only social division which weakens the link between football and national identity in Scotland. Three are particularly worthy of comment.

First, although class is an increasingly slippery concept, it is employed in virtually every assessment of Scottish football. Football is the working class sport; rugby union, on the other hand, is presented as the team game of the Scottish middle class. The only exception to the latter rule which is usually made is the Borders where rugby is deemed to transcend class divisions. In fact both general propositions are misleading. To begin with, football is played and watched by many middle-class Scots. In addition, it is too simplistic to suggest that in the Borders rugby is the people's game whereas else-where in the country it belongs to an occupational and economic elite. It is safer to say that throughout Scotland rugby enjoys a large middle-class following, guaranteed by the sporting preferences of the country's fee-paying schools, but that it also benefits from the contribution of working-class Scots. For all of these people, the fortunes of the Scottish football team, whilst by no means unimportant, are secondary to those of the national rugby side. It is also worth noting that the Scottish Rugby Union chose to adopt the people's favourite. 'Flower of Scotland', as the anthem to precede international matches. For many years, on the other hand, the SFA had insisted on retaining the British anthem, 'God Save the Queen', regardless of the fact that it had long since ceased to be audible due to the torrent of abuse from the Tartan Army. As a compromise they have since adopted 'Scotland the Brave' which is played at the Commonwealth Games for Scottish gold medal winners. In terms of appealing to the current sense of national identity, however, the SRU's choice puts it well out in front.

A second and very large group of people who are resistant to the lure of the Scottish national game are women. As psychologist, Nanette Mutrie observes, 'football is very important for male culture, it gives a focus they can share, something to talk about and they can identify with a successful and striving team which lends a certain status' (*Scotland on Sunday*, 5 April 1992). There are, of course, many Scottish women who watch and, indeed, play football. Their number is small, however, in comparison with other European countries and Scottish men tend to exhibit towards women's football the amused and patronising attitudes which have long since disappeared in countries like Norway and Sweden. As a result, for many Scottish women the main significance of the final results each Saturday is to be able to gauge the mood of a returning husband, boyfriend or son. Of course, most of these women are happy when the Scottish national team does well but that is a long way from confusing football with matters of life and death.

Thirdly, Scotland has substantial Italian and Jewish communities, each estimated to consist of between 25,000 and 30,000 people. An additional 50,000 are of other ethnic origin, about 65 per cent being Asian and fifteen per cent Chinese (*The Guardian*, 11 March 1992). Of these various groupings, only the Italians, with well-known players such as Lou Macari and Peter Marinello, have made a significant contribution to Scottish football. One obvious explanation of this is that of Scotland's largest immigrant groups only the Italians (and, of course, the Irish) belong to a football culture. However, one cannot help but wonder to what extent young Asians are dissuaded from involving themselves in football by the racism which infects Scottish League grounds. Both Paul Elliot of Celtic and Mark Walters of Rangers were subjected to extensive racial abuse during their brief periods in Scottish football. In part, of course, this was a manifestation of the hostility which the Old Firm clubs provoke from rival supporters. But that is a partial explanation and not an excuse. Scots have long prided themselves on having a more tolerant attitude towards ethnic minorities than is shown by the English. The treatment afforded to Elliot, Walters and others suggests that some of this pride is misplaced.

All of the above divisions must be taken into account before one begins to examine the consciousness of the Scottish football fan as that of the typical Scot. Nevertheless, the Tartan Army, although predominantly composed of white, Protestant, working-class men from the central belt, transcends the divisions in Scottish society to a limited degree and for every Scot who makes the journey to the major championships like those in Sweden, thousands more back home identify not only with the Scottish team's performances but with the activities of their travelling representatives. To what extent, then, can the Tartan Army be regarded as the vanguard expression of a shared national identity (Giulianotti, 1992)? And, what do its image and behaviour tell us about that identity?

Research by Giulianotti has already partially explained the activities of Scotland's tartan army of fans during the 1990 World Cup in Italy (Giulianotti, 1992). In comparing the behaviour of Scottish football fans before and after 1980 Giulianotti illustrates how the symbolism attached to Scottish fans has in fact changed over time. Giulianotti succinctly points out that the significance of the 'Tartan Army' is in part explained by considering the social interaction between a myriad of audiences and groups, not least of which included local people in Italy, Swedish and Brazilian supporters, the Scottish football authorities, and the English media and supporters.

In the not too distant past, the arrival of Scottish football supporters on foreign soil was greeted with considerable trepidation due essentially to the activities of fans who visited England, in particular for the biennial meetings of England and Scotland at Wembley Stadium. The 1977 international match, for example, culminated in a pitch invasion with Scottish followers breaking the goalposts and removing large sections of the playing surface. Scots were also associated in those days with widespread anti-social behaviour in the vicinity of the stadium and this factor was cited amongst others by the FA when it decided to abandon annual games between the two countries since 1989.

In 1992, however, 5,000 Scottish fans travelled to the European Championships and behaved so well that an SFA member was presented with a special award on their behalf immediately before the final at the Ullevi Stadium in Gothenburg. Indeed, the admirable conduct of the Tartan Army in Gothenburg itself and in Norrkoping prompted one Swedish newspaper, *Folkbladet*, to carry the headline, 'Thank you, Scotland' (*Daily Record*, 20 June 1992). Lennart Johansson, president of European football's ruling body, UEFA, and himself a Swede, commented: 'Scotland and their supporters have treated the Championship as a festival and that's how it should be' (*The Independent*, 19 June 1992). So what explains the apparent transformation of the Scottish football fan?

First, supporters' behaviour abroad often mirrors their conduct at home and there is no doubt that the general atmosphere at Scottish grounds has improved immeasurably since the 1970s. This is partially true of England and yet English supporters abroad still have a bad reputation, enhanced by their activities during the 1992 European Championships. Credit for the improved behaviour of Scotland's travelling support, therefore, must also go to the SFA's Travel Club which keeps in close touch with Scottish fans and to the presence of many more women and family groups than would be found in the ranks of the English following (*Scotland on Sunday*, 28 June 1992). More controversially, it is probable that Scots generally exhibit a different attitude towards foreigners and foreign places than the type of young Englishmen who follow their national team (Giulianotti, 1992). This has less to do with innate internationalism than with the fact that Scotland's small nation status fails to generate the xenophobic and chauvinistic outlook which affects some English people and a disproportionately large percentage of those who travel abroad to support the English football team. Nevertheless, it is a factor.

That said, it would be dangerous to arrive at a totally benign view of the Tartan Army. Indeed, it is a sad comment on the contemporary world that so much newsprint was devoted to the fact that 5,000 people could travel to another country for a sporting event and enjoy themselves while acting within the law. Nor is the Scottish reputation for international fraternity entirely warranted. During the European Championship game with Germany in Norrkoping, Scotland supporters chanted 'One Bomber Harris, there's only one Bomber Harris', revealing the extent to which old enemies continue to be viewed with suspicion and even dislike. This brings us conveniently to the perverse role played by England and the English in the transformation of the Scottish football supporters' behaviour.

One of the most pertinent observations during the European Championships of 1992 came from Gosta Welander, deputy commissioner of the Stockholm police. Responding to the bad behaviour of England supporters, he commented, 'I can't understand what makes these people act like this. The Scottish people behaved extremely well and are very happy. We are happy to have them too. It's strange that on an island two groups of people can behave so differently' (*The Guardian*, 19 June 1992).

For many Scots, that was the most satisfying aspect of the whole European Championships campaign because at the heart of Scottish national identity, in football as in much else, is the attitude towards the more powerful southern neighbour. This can be understood partly within a footballing context. As Moorhouse observes, English football conditions are themselves 'essential elements in Scottish football and these feed themes which turn, not on class and class resistance, but on other kinds of social identities, on a very particular kind of nationalism, on what it means to be Scottish' (Moorhouse, 1986, p.53). According to Holt, 'the economic domination of English football aggravated a broad, if politically unfocussed, resentment against the English' (Holt, 1989, p.257). Consequently, the sort of animosity felt by many supporters in Scotland towards the Old Firm is transferred to the English game and English football becomes a metaphor for a more generalised economic domination. Thus, beating the English in every conceivable way assumes deep significance.

Shortly before the European Championships began, Andy Roxburgh conveyed a good luck message to his English opposite number (ITN Sport, 9 June 1992). He was no doubt aware that on this occasion at least he was not speaking for his fellow countrymen. An irate correspondent to the *Sunday Mail* said as much. 'Why on earth did Andy Roxburgh wish the England team all the best in the European Championships? Surely, every real, true Scot wants to see England defeated in every sport and [on] every occasion' (*Sunday Mail*, 21 June 1992).

So accurate is the viewpoint expressed here that one can safely say that for a majority of Scots, the most popular result in the entire championships was not Scotland's 3–0 victory over the CIS but Sweden's 2–1 win the previous night which eliminated England from the competition. The good behaviour of the Tartan Army must also be understood in the light of anti-English sentiment. English fans have a reputation for misconduct. Their behaviour in Sweden was predictable. For their part, Scottish supporters engaged in what Graham Spiers describes as 'moral brinksmanship: the showing up of the violent, ugly, bastard English' (*Scotland on Sunday*, 28 June 1992).

In important ways, therefore, the identity of the Tartan Army and those whom it represents is essentially negative. Antagonisms which might otherwise divide its membership are transcended by a shared consciousness which owes little to an idea of Scotland and much to fanatical anti-English feeling. But what of the positive, Scottish elements that characterise the Tartan Army and Scottish football support in general?

The Scotland of the Tartan Army is essentially the mythical land of Brigadoon. The men who wander the streets of foreign cities in full Highland regalia would be unlikely to do so in their home towns and villages. Their colourful presence, however, confirms the well-established but largely artificial image of Scotland and the Scots. The Scottish football supporter represents one side of the dualism which is the essence of Scottish national identity. For the most part, the countries visited by the Tartan Army witness only one aspect of the national character. Their people are understandably relieved and amused. But they are also amused by the visit of a circus. This does not imply an endorsement of the circus way of life. One suspects, indeed, that there is some relief when the circus and the Tartan Army leaves town. The pity (but it is also a blessing) is that they have not seen the Scots in all their moods. They remain unaware of the deep divisions in Scottish society, to which football contributes, and they see instead the representatives of what Lindsay Paterson memorably described as 'a community of pawky inadequates' (Paterson, 1981, p.70).

However, if Scotland is ever to enjoy a degree of political independence, instructed by a realistic sense of what it is to be Scottish, then real Scots, with all their differences, must act. It is dangerous to take the Tartan Army's latest successful public relations exercise as evidence of national well-being. As Purdie correctly points out, 'only by recognising that unity within Scotland is produced by the present relationship with England, and that it cannot be assumed that it will survive a changed set of relationships, can the necessary negotiation and agreement be carried through, so as to maintain unity' (Purdie, 1991, p.75). In an independent Scotland, the differences between Highlands and Lowlands, the central belt and the rest, the cities and the small towns, Catholics and Protestants, men and women, working class and middle class and black Scots and white, all of which impinge on the day-to-day life of football, would become political issues of pressing importance. It is possible, however, that Scottish football support indicates that independence is a long way off.

Naturally the exploits of the national team and its followers in 1992 heartened most Scots. That for many it made up for the General Election result, however, is illuminating, notwithstanding the sour comments of Jim Sillars about Scottish voters being 'ninety-minute patriots' (*Daily Record*, 24 April 1992). The Scots wear their nationalism more comfortably and more flamboyantly when they watch sport than when they act politically. The result is the persistence of a form of nationalism once described by N.T. Phillipson as 'noisy inaction' (Phillipson, 1969, p.186). Given that our examination of Scottish football reveals that only resentment of the English provides the basis of a unified national consciousness, perhaps that is what Scottish nationalism should remain, at least until the nation's divisions have been healed. Other forces, however, may yet serve to quicken the pace of a football-inspired political nationalism.

In 1984, the FA and the SFA agreed to bring to an end the British Home International Championship which had been in existence since 1883. Since 1989, in addition, there has been no senior international match between England and Scotland. In purely football terms, therefore, it might seem that the break-up of Britain is in process. Paradoxically, however, it is more likely that conflicting, unifying forces may have the more decisive impact on the growth of political nationalism in Scotland. The five Scottish League clubs which plan to create a Super League have raised the spectre, so often raised before, of a British (or at least Anglo-Scottish) competition. Already Third World countries, and others, are demanding that the United Kingdom should be represented at international level by only one side as befits a single nation-state. A British competition would enhance their case. It is undeniable that because of its role as a symbol of the Scottish nation, any threat to the separate existence of the national team would be a potent force. Then, and perhaps only then, would the Scottish people join with the Tartan Army to offer more than 'noisy inaction'.

ACKNOWLEDGEMENTS

I would like to thank Archie McGregor of *The Absolute Game* and Kevin McCarra of *Scotland on Sunday* for sharing with me their thoughts on the Old Firm and Scotland support and my father for first taking me to East End Park.

BIBLIOGRAPHY

The absolute game, 27, 1992

Boyle, R., 1991, *Faithful through and through: a survey of Celtic Football Club's committed supporters*, National Identity Research Unit, Glasgow Caledonian University, Glasgow

Celtic match programme, 30 November 1991

Crick, B., 1991, A tale of four nations, *Chapman*, 67, pp.17–21

Daiches, D., 1952, *Robert Burns*, G. Bell and Sons, London

Daily Record, (Glasgow), various dates

Follow, Follow, 24, 1992

Gallagher, T., 1991, The SNP and the Scottish working class, in T. Gallagher (ed.), *Nationalism in the nineties*, Polygon, Edinburgh, pp.102–25

Giulianotti, R., 1992, Scotland's tartan army in Italy: the case for the carnivalesque, *Sociological Review*, 39(3), pp.503–27

Harvie, C., 1977, *Scotland and nationalism. Scottish society and politics, 1707–1977*, George Allen and Unwin, London

Holt, R., 1989, *Sport and the British*, Clarendon Press, Oxford

The Independent, (London), various dates

The Independent on Sunday, (London), various dates

ITN Sport, 9 June 1992

Jarvie, G., 1991, *Highland games. The making of the myth*, Edinburgh University Press, Edinburgh

Kellas, J., 1980, *Modern Scotland*, 2nd edition, George Allen and Unwin, London

McCreadie, R., 1991, Scottish identity and the constitution, in B. Crick (ed.),

National identities. The constitution of the United Kingdom, Blackwell, Oxford, pp.38–56

Moorhouse, H. F., 1986, Repressed nationalism and professional football: Scotland versus England, in J. A. Mangan and R. B. Small (eds), *Sport, culture, society. International historical and sociological perspectives*, E. and F. N. Spon, London, pp.52–59

Moorhouse, H. F., 1991, On the periphery: Scotland, Scottish football and the new Europe, in J. Williams and S. Wagg (eds), *British football and social change*, Leicester University Press, Leicester, pp.201–19

Nairn, T., 1991, Scottish identity: a cause unwon, *Chapman*, 67, pp.2–12

Once a Tim, always a Tim, 10, 1992

Paterson, L., 1981, Scotch myths – 2, *The bulletin of Scottish politics*, 2, pp.67–71

Phillipson, N. T., 1969, Nationalism and ideology, in J. N. Wolfe (ed.), *Government and nationalism in Scotland*, Edinburgh University Press, Edinburgh, pp.167–88

Purdie, B., 1991, The lessons of Ireland for the SNP, in T. Gallagher (ed.), *Nationalism in the nineties*, Polygon, Edinburgh, pp.66–83

Que sera sera, 2, 1990

Radio Sweden ('Sixty Degrees North'), 3 July 1992

Scotland on Sunday, (Edinburgh), various dates

The Scottish programme club bulletin, May 1992

Sunday Mail, (Glasgow), various dates

Walker, G., 1990, 'There's not a team like the Glasgow Rangers': football and religious identity in Scotland, in G. Walker and T. Gallagher (eds), *Sermons and battle hymns. Protestant popular culture in modern Scotland*, Edinburgh University Press, Edinburgh, pp.137–59

Wilson, B., 1988, *Celtic. A century with honour*, Collins Willow Books, London

3

WOMEN AND SPORT IN NINETEENTH CENTURY SCOTLAND

Neil Tranter

Between the middle years of the nineteenth century and the outbreak of the First World War there occurred what many historians have described as a 'revolution' in British popular sport. Levels of player and spectator participation in sport increased dramatically. The social composition of participants widened and deepened. Rules of play became more formalised, standardised and generalised. Clubs and other forms of institutional structure proliferated, and the practice of sport became increasingly competitive, organised and commercialised (Bailey, 1978, pp.35–146; Tranter, 1990; Vamplew, 1988; Walvin, 1978, pp.83–96).

By far the main beneficiaries of this revolution in sporting activity were males. Men dominated the lists of sport club directors, shareholders, office bearers and patrons and comprised the overwhelming majority of those who played and watched sport. Women, by contrast, were grossly under-represented, both in comparison with the number of men involved and with the total size of the adult female population. This was particularly the case for working class women. In the early years of the twentieth century, as in the early years of the nineteenth, for the vast bulk of English working class females opportunities for participating in sport and physical recreation were negligible, largely restricted to the passive role of spectating at pedestrian events, horse race meetings and cricket matches (Guttmann, 1986, pp.63–64, 66–67, 78–79; Hill, 1986, p.109). By comparison, the numbers of English working class women who participated in sport as players were small and, so far as we can tell from the limited amount of evidence available, in the course of the period may even have declined as an earlier, more extensive involvement in footraces and other types of pedestrian contest, rowing, prizefighting and cricket decreased (Brailsford, 1991, pp.8, 78–89, 133–35). Lacking an established tradition of team games at school and hampered by a combination of low income, the demands of employment and domestic duties and opposition from both working class men and middle class women, the English Victorian and Edwardian working class female was effectively excluded from an active participation in the new sporting culture. The handful who did participate in sports like cricket, hockey, pedestrianism and soccer or who had the good fortune to work for the occasional, enlightened, sport-conscious employer like Cadbury or Rowntree were infrequent and distinct exceptions to the rule (McCrone, 1991; Williams and Woodhouse, 1991, p.89).

For the working class women of nineteenth and early twentieth century Scotland the situation was no different. To judge from newspaper comments on the substantial representation of women among the large crowds attracted to Highland Games gatherings like that at the Port of Menteith in 1895 and from the frequency with which those at places like Alexandria in 1867, Blackford, Inverkeithing and Strathblane in 1870, Crieff in 1881 and Denny in 1896 were associated with the declaration of local holidays to allow workers to attend (*Stirling Journal*, 1867, 13 September; 1870, 5 and 19 August, 30 September; 1881, 26 August; 1895, 21 June; 1896, 7 August), Highland Games events almost certainly drew large numbers of working class female as well as male spectators. Significantly, as at the St Fillans Games of 1828 and 1831 and the Gartmore, Port of Menteith and Buchlyvie Games of 1880, whenever harvesting was in progress attendances fell noticeably below expectations (*Stirling Journal*, 1828, 4 September; 1831, 8 September; 1880, 10 September). Among the 'thousands' of women who attended the Hawick tradesmen's horse race meeting, too, there must have been numerous working class females just as there must have been among the vast crowds attracted to horse race meetings elsewhere in Scotland (Scott, 1984, p.13). The size of the attendances at these and other popular sporting spectacles like regattas and pedestrian events would simply not have been possible without a considerable working class male and female presence.

In Scotland as in England, however, the extent to which working class women played rather than merely watched sport was minimal. Trawls through the literature reveal only the most peripheral active involvement. In the late eighteenth or early nineteenth centuries the fisherwomen of Musselburgh are reported to have played golf and the fisherwomen of Musselburgh and Inveresk football (Browning, 1955, p.121; Fittis, 1891, p.155 and 164). At the Stirling Chapmen sports of 1842 the 'most novel of all the races was by the women for 1lb of best tea'. A similar race was included on the programme at the same event three years later and at the Old Handsel Monday Games at Arnprior in 1853 and 1854 and Kippen in 1856 (*Stirling Journal*, 1842, 26 August; 1853, 28 January, 1854, 27 January; 1856, 25 November; *Stirling Observer*, 1845, 25 September). One of the six races at the inaugural Alloa Regatta in 1853 was for two-oared boats pulled by women, a race that offered three cash prizes of £1. 10s, £1 and 10s and caused 'much amusement to the spectators, the distance being short and the competitors well-matched' (*Stirling Journal*, 1853, 12 August). In an attempt to stimulate public interest, rowing matches between Newhaven fishwives were included in the programme of events at the yachting regattas organised by the Duke of Buccleuch and Lord John Scott on the Forth in the mid 1820s (*Stirling Journal*, 1865, 26 May). A rowing match involving fisher girls from Broughty Ferry was one of ten races at the Perth Regatta of 1872 (*Stirling Journal*, 1872, 13 September). In 1867 a curling match, described as 'rather novel', was recorded between six males and six females employed by the

Duke of Buccleuch while at Stirling in 1896 'even shopgirls' were reported to have taken up cycling (*Bridge of Allan Reporter*, 1867, 9 February; *Stirling Journal* 1896, 9 May). Overall, however, such examples of active female working class participation in sport are few.

Among women of the upper and middle classes, levels of participation in organised sport were greater and, recent work has shown, at least by the later decades of the nineteenth century more extensive than it was once customary to suppose (Mangan and Park, 1987, pp.3–4; McCrone 1987, pp.97–129; Parrat, 1989). In Scotland upper and middle class females figured prominently in the crowds at many of the major spectator sports: at the Christmas shinty matches at Rothiemurchus in the early nineteenth century (Tod, 1988, p.267–68): at curling bonspiels (Murray, 1981, p.98): above all, at cricket and rugby matches, boatraces, highland games gatherings and horse race meetings. In July 1834 a 'great concourse of ladies and gentlemen' attended a cricket match between the Grange and Brunswick clubs in Edinburgh. In September 1834 a cricket match between the officers and men of the Glasgow Garrison and a combined team from the Glasgow University and Lanarkshire clubs on Glasgow Green was watched by 'numerous spectators, among whom were many ladies'. In May 1837 the Stirling Kings Park 'was graced with an assemblage of rank and beauty seldom surpassed' for a match between the Stirling Cricket Club and a team drawn from the 76th Regiment. At games between the Westerton and Caledonian and Westerton and Perth clubs at Bridge of Allan in 1850 'the ground was enlivened by many of the fair sex'. The fact that 'fewer ladies than usual graced the field' for a match between the Stirling and Clydesdale clubs in the Kings Park in 1854 clearly implies that their presence in substantial numbers was normal. In June 1867 the 'promenade' at Livilands for a game between the Stirling Garrison and the 6th Royal Warwicks was 'crowded with ladies and gentlemen the whole day'. A 'large number of ladies' attended a match between Stirling County and officers of the 42nd Regiment at Livilands in May 1868: a 'fair sprinkling' of ladies that between Stirling County and the Garrison and Reserve Forces at the same venue in May 1871. With the temporary decline of cricket as a major spectator sport in central Scotland during the late 1880s and early 1890s female as well as male spectators largely disappeared. Even so, at a game between Stirling County and Perthshire in 1894, the one occasion in the later years of the century when 'for Stirling a good turnout of spectators' was reported, 'many ladies' were in attendance (*Stirling Journal*, 1834, 4 July, 5 September; 1837, 2 June; 1850, 12 July; 1854, 26 May; 1867, 28 June; 1868, 29 May, 24 July; 1871, 12 May; 1894, 3 August).

For as long as it remained a significant spectator sport rugby, too, attracted considerable numbers of middle class female onlookers. In a crowd of 'over three hundred' at a game between the Stirling and Dollar clubs in February 1874 were 'a large number of ladies'. A 'sprinkling of ladies' attended a Stirling-Bothwell match in April 1874 and 'many ladies' a match between Stirling and Perthshire the following November (*Stirling Journal*, 1874, 6 February, 10 April, 27 November). Direct evidence on the presence of middle class females in the crowds at regattas, highland games and horse races is sparse. In view of the large attendances attracted to such events and the common practice of constructing grandstands to cater for spectators of higher social status, however, upper and middle class women must often have attended in considerable numbers, a conclusion confirmed by such fragments of specific, contemporary comment as do exist. The 24th annual gathering of the Stirling and Bannockburn Caledonian Society in Stirling in 1846, an occasion deliberately restricted by high admission charges to the social elite of the town, attracted 'numerous ladies'. The Strathallan Highland Games at Bridge of Allan in 1877 were viewed from the grandstand by some six hundred patrons and patronesses drawn from the social elite of the neighbourhood (*Stirling Journal*, 1846, 26 June; 1877, 10 August). Whenever sport was watched and played by upper and middle class males their women were frequently present in not inconsiderable numbers.

Females of upper and middle class background were also extensively involved in sport as patrons or sponsors. In addition to the patronage provided by officers of the Stirling Garrison and 41 individual male patrons, the Strathallan Games of 1868 received financial assistance from eight patronesses, the Countess of Kellie, Lady Alexander, Lady Erskine, Mrs Johnstone, Madame Campbell, Mrs Houldsworth, Mrs Cochrane and the wife of Colonel McLeod. Among the patrons of the Bridge of Allan Lawn Tennis Club in 1899 were Mrs Braidwood, Mrs Fraser, Mrs Hall, Mrs Johnstone, Mrs L. Pullar, Mrs E. Pullar, Mrs W.B. Pullar and Mrs J.B. Smith (*Stirling Journal*, 1868, 24 July; 1899, 29 December). In a total of 516 individuals named in the newspapers as officially elected patrons or unofficial sponsors of sports clubs extant within a rough twenty-mile radius of the town of Stirling at one time or another during the period 1820–1900, 96, almost one in five, were women. Of these, 54 were officially elected club patrons, the majority with clubs in the sport of curling. Around one in three of all curling clubs established in the Stirling region during the period boasted an official patroness. By contrast, official female patrons were present in only 5 per cent of all bowling and tennis clubs, 4 per cent of all angling clubs and 1 per cent of all cricket clubs. In other sports they were entirely absent. In some cases women served as an official patron for more than one club and many, like Mrs Blackburn of Killearn House, patroness of the Killearn Strathendrick Curling Club for over a quarter of a century, maintained an official association with the clubs they patronised for long periods. Twenty of the 42 women who supported sports clubs without being elected to an official status also assisted clubs in the sport of curling. The remaining 22 divided their support more or less evenly between clubs in the sports of bowls, cricket, football, golf, quoiting and tennis, a somewhat wider distribution of assistance than was the case among official patronesses.

Whether given in an official or unofficial form, the patronage supplied by upper and middle class women undoubtedly made a significant contribution to the development of organised sport in the second half of the nineteenth century, particularly so in the sport of curling. In the main, this assistance took the form of donations of cups, medals and other prizes to stimulate interest in inter-and intra-club competitions. But it also frequently included the provision of refreshments at matches, ponds on which to curl and skate, ground on which to construct bowling greens, cricket, football and quoiting pitches and, though less regularly, donations of money. Judging from the frequency with which it was sought and the gratitude with which it was received, the assistance provided by female patrons to club sport was by no means solely cosmetic (Tranter, 1989, pp.39–41).

For much of the nineteenth century, in Scotland as in England, women of upper and middle class origins took little active part in sporting activities outside the home and garden. During the later decades of the century, however, the extent of their involvement as players increased.

In southern and south-western counties of Scotland anyway, albeit in limited numbers, upper and middle class females were already participating as players in the sport of curling at the beginning of the Victorian era: at Peebles and Sanquhar in the 1820s: at Penicuik, Loch Ged in Nithsdale and Buittle in Kirkudbrightshire in the 1840s: and at the third annual bonspiel of the Grand Caledonian Curling Club at Lochwinnoch, Ayrshire, in 1850. In the 1850s and 1860s Lady Eglinton and her daughter, Lady Egidia Montgomerie, were among a group of ladies who regularly curled on one of the four artificial rinks in the grounds of Eglinton castle at Kilwinning in Ayrshire (Murray, 1981, pp. 98 and 100; Smith, 1981, pp.158–62). Women were among the founder-members of the first curling club to be established at Blairlogie, in 1866. 'Curling by ladies is no new thing', it was noted of the presence of two female curlers among the players at the Royal Caledonian Club bonspiel of 1899. By February 1899, in addition to two clubs made up wholly of females, twenty-two of Scotland's curling clubs included women on their membership rolls (*Stirling Journal*, 1866, 23 February; 1899, 3 February).

Small numbers of upper and middle class women are also known to have participated actively in the sports of foxhunting, staghunting, beagling and bowls, In 1866, for example, 'a number of ladies on horseback' was reported to have accompanied the pack of beagles kept by officers stationed at Stirling Castle to a hunt on Sherrifmuir near Bridge of Allan. As early as 1860 a match for the Championesses' Belt of the Bridge of Allan Bowling Club attracted as many as twenty female competitors. In 1897 the Doune Castle Bowling Club announced that it was 'the proud and happy possessor of a spirited young lady member' and the secretaries of the Doune Castle and Deanston clubs that they had 'bought new books for the enrolment of ladies'. In February 1912 four of the 41 members of the Polment Bowling Club were women, though the ratio had fallen to 1:54 two years later (*Stirling Journal*, 1860, 12 October; 1866, 15 December, 1897, 20 August; Tranter, 1989, pp. 36 and 47). In none of these sports was the number of active female participants more than negligible. In the sports of archery and croquet, cycling, golf and law tennis, however, it was more substantial.

'Archery is practised as an elegant and pleasant pastime by ladies and gentlemen', it was reported in 1850. Throughout the 1850s and 1860s competitions for women, often attracting champion and ex-champion archers from as far afield as England and Ireland, were regularly included in the programme of events at the annual meetings of the Scottish National Archery Association. So popular were these competitions that when the fifteenth annual meeting of the Association, at Linlithgow in 1869, failed to attract a single female competitor it was thought to have considerably 'detracted from the interest'. As attested by the presence of females in the membership of the Ochil Archery and Croquet Club, archery was 'played by both sexes' (Tranter, 1989, pp.36–47).

By the early 1860s croquet was already a well-established pastime among women of the upper and middle classes. 'Even farmers' daughters are adding it to their accomplishments', it was claimed. By 1867 the game was so popular in Stirling that the Town Council considered adding a ladies' croquet ground to its plans for constructing a skating pond in the Kings Knot. Neither the croquet ground nor the skating pond materialised. But two years later the popularity of croquet was sufficient for Sir Arthur and Lady Hay to institute a Stirling Subscription Croquet Club, made up of a 'goodly number of . . . ladies and gentlemen of the town', and for the editor of the *Stirling Journal* to express the hope that further croquet pitches would soon be established (Tranter, 1989, pp.36–37 and 47; *Stirling Journal*, 1869, 26 March).

Cycling was another activity which ultimately became popular among women from those social groups able to afford the £5 or £10 needed for a new or second-hand bicycle. By the final decade of the nineteenth century female cyclists were commonplace in the Stirling region and elsewhere in Scotland. At Doune 'the number of lady cyclists is rapidly on the increase', it was reported in 1893. At Bridge of Allan in 1896 cycling was 'greatly in evidence among the ladies'. At Stirling, where cycle agents struggled unsuccessfully to meet the demand for machines, 'the craze for cycling among the fair sex is not diminishing', it was noted in May of the same year. For the most part, it is true, women seem to have preferred casual, recreational cycling to a participation in cycling clubs. Attempts to form ladies' cycling clubs at Alva in 1895 and Stirling in 1896 failed. Not until 1900, some ten years after its formation and then only as a result of persistent efforts on the part of its committee, was the Milngavie Cycling Club able to report 'a large' number of female members at its runs (Tranter, 1989, p.37). The Hawick Cycling Club, founded in 1881, did not enrol its first female member until 1892 and four years later still included only three. By 1905, on the other hand, the number had risen to 28 (Smith, Young and Murray, 1981, pp.12–13). In the decade or so prior to the outbreak of the First World War, the female representation in cycling clubs certainly increased. But, on the whole, women continued to prefer casual to formal participation.

This was less obviously the case with two of the other sports that were particularly popular with middle class females, golf and lawn tennis.

Despite the example set by Mary Queen of Scots three hundred years earlier, golf did not become a popular game for women until the final quarter of the nineteenth century. In Scotland the first ladies' club was established at St Andrews in 1867, shortly followed by clubs at Perth, in 1879, Musselburgh, in 1872, Carnoustie, in 1873, and Panmure, in 1874 (Browning, 1955, pp. 120 and 123; Wilson, 1952, pp. 222–23). Indicative of what was as yet only a peripheral involvement is the fact that the *Perthshire Advertiser* expected its female readers to be 'surprised and gratified to learn that a ladies' golf club has been formed at Perth' (*Bridge of Allan Reporter*, 1870, pp.14–15). In the course of the later 1880s and 1890s the popularity of golf among upper and middle class Scottish females increased dramatically. By 1886 the St Andrews club already had five hundred members (Wilson, 1952, p.223). What happened between then and the end of the century can be illustrated from the experience of the Stirling region. Of the 31 clubs extant in the region between 1891 and 1900 at least thirteen are known to have included female members. Compared with the number of upper and middle class female residents in the area, from whose ranks the bulk of female, institutional golfers were drawn, this represents an average of one club for every 677 women aged between 15 and 44. On the not unreasonable assumption that all 31 clubs in the neighbourhood included females the ratio falls to as low as 1:284. In 1894 the Stirling Golf Club had as many as 80 women on its membership roll. Membership of the Stirling Ladies' Golf Club rose from 59 at its inception in 1897 to 69 in 1898 and 70 in 1900. The share of women in the total membership of mixed-sex golf clubs in the Stirling region varied from around one in three at Aberfoyle and Tillicoultry to over one in four at Bearsden, one in six or seven at the Falkirk Tryst and between one in ten and one in twenty at Milngavie (Tranter, 1989, pp.37–38).

The sport of lawn tennis quickly established itself as a popular pastime among women of upper and middle class origins. In June 1880 the courts of the Dollar Lawn Tennis Club were 'crowded everyday with ladies and gentlemen'. On its formation in April 1881 the Dunblane club reported that 'already a large number of ladies and gentlemen have joined' (Tranter, 1989, p.38). Eight members entered the ladies' singles at the first tournament organised by the Stirling Lawn Tennis Club in September 1880 and fourteen women the ladies' doubles competition at the first Bridge of Allan open lawn tennis tournament in August 1884 (*Stirling Journal*, 1880, 3 September; 1884, 1 August). Almost two-thirds of the 42 founder members of the Avon Lawn Tennis Club, formed at Linlithgow in 1880, were female (Tranter, 1989, p.38). In some cases the number of females equalled or even exceeded the number of males in club memberships. In 1895, for instance, the Edinburgh Braid club comprised sixteen men and sixteen women. By 1912 the number of men had risen to 32 and the number of women to 67 (Borthwick, no date, p.14). At least one club, the Stirling Irvine Place, specifically committed itself to a policy of maintaining an equal balance of the sexes. At the peak of the sport's popularity, in the 1880s, the Stirling region boasted one tennis club for every 431 upper and middle class females aged fifteen to 44 resident in the area (Tranter, 1989, p.38).

Despite a not insubstantial presence as spectators, patrons and players in an ever-widening range of sports, the participation of upper and middle class Scottish women in sport must not, of course, be exaggerated. With the possible exceptions of croquet and lawn tennis, organised sport remained overwhelmingly a male pursuit, with men forming the vast majority of its official and unofficial patrons, its directors, shareholders and officebearers, its players and spectators.

Except in the case of golf, where they often ran their own clubs or independent sections within men's clubs, females rarely figure in the lists of sport club directors, shareholders and officebearers. In none of the handful of clubs in the Stirling region which adopted company status before 1914 was there a single female director. Typically, the number of women with shares in publicly-owned sport clubs ranged from zero in cases like the Crieff (1889) and Kirkintilloch (1889) bowling clubs and the Bathgate (1904, 1914), Bo'ness (1907, 1913) and Stirling Kings Park (1919) soccer clubs to just three per cent in the case of the Leith Athletic Football Club (1893: West Register House, Edinburgh, BT2 2540) and four per cent in the case of the Stenhousemuir Football Club (1905). Only in a minority of instances were the proportions marginally higher: 3 per cent and 7 per cent for the Polmont Bowling Club in 1897 and 1914: three per cent and 16 per cent for the Callander Recreation Company in 1893 and 1908: 11 per cent for the Bridge of Allan Curling and Skating Company in 1889: and 20 per cent in the case of the Pitlochry Golf Club in 1908 (Tranter, 1989, pp.34–35).

Even in those essentially male sports clubs and organisations in which women were reasonably well represented as spectators, patrons and players, female officebearers were rare. Apart from two clubs made up entirely of women, excluding official patronesses only one of Scotland's five hundred or so curling clubs in 1897 was reported as having a female among its elected officers. Of the numerous cricket clubs established in the Stirling region in the course of the nineteenth century only one, the Dunmore Cricket Club, claimed the 'unique distinction' of possessing two female officials – Miss Claudia Hamilton, its secretary, daughter of the owner of the estate for the benefit of the employees of which the club was instituted, and a Miss Sutcliff, its treasurer. Neither clubs like the Bridge of Allan and Stirling lawn tennis clubs nor organisations like the Strathallan Highland Games included women in their lists of officebearers and committee members (Tranter, 1989, 35). Not until 1954 did the Hawick Cycling Club appoint its first female captain (Smith, Young and Murray, 1981, p.13). The sole function of the ladies' committee established by the Edinburgh Braid Lawn Tennis Club in 1896 was to provide refreshments at matches. Attempts to elect women to the club's general committee in 1899 and 1907 foundered on a rule, not abolished until 1913, that the main committee should be made up solely of men (Borthwick, no date, p.15).

In relation to both the absolute and relative extent of middle class male participation and to the size of the middle class female population as a whole, the number of middle class women who took an active part in organised sport was small. Of the five hundred or so Scottish curling clubs affiliated to the Royal Caledonian Curling Club in 1899 only 24 included women among their members. Until the construction of indoor ice rinks in the 1930s the number of female curlers remained modest (Murray, 1981, p.155). Among the 600 cyclists who attended a meeting of the Scottish Cyclist organisation in Edinburgh in June 1884 there were no more than 'several ladies' (*Stirling Journal*, 1884, 20 June). From the evidence of the Polmont Bowling Club, where in the years 1911–14 women comprised only between two per cent and ten per cent of the total membership (West Register House, Edinburgh, BT2 3344), there must have been very few females among the 25,000 or more bowlers active in Scotland in the early 1890s. In the Stirling region the solitary reference to an active participation of middle class women in cricket is to a match at Dunblane in 1890 when a ladies' team, captained by a Miss Blair, played a gentlemen's team whose members battled left-handed. Significantly, the match was described as 'novel' (*Bridge of Allan Reporter*, 1890, 8 March). Other than for an occasional involvement in tilting at the ring competitions at highland games gatherings, the middle class female population of central Scotland appears to have taken little or no active part in athletics or in the sports of angling, boating, pitching, quoiting, rugby and soccer. Overall, the number of upper and middle class women who indulged in sporting activities outside the privacy of the home and garden never amounted to more than a small minority of the number eligible by age to play. At a rough estimate, evidence for the Stirling region suggests that the number of upper and middle class females actively involved in one or other of the sports favoured by women rarely exceeded one in five, or more probably one in ten, of the total number of females in the age-groups from which the great majority of players came.

Primarily responsible for this limited involvement of middle class women in sport, it is often argued, was an attitude towards women which emerged in the early decades of the nineteenth century and which in the male-dominated world of Victorian and Edwardian Britain successfully restricted the functions of the woman almost entirely to the confines of the household and family. Central to the philosophy of nineteenth century elite and middle class society, we are told, was the notion that, with few exceptions, whenever and wherever possible men and women ought to inhabit their own 'separate spheres', the former in the public world of business, politics and leisure, the latter in the private world of the home where they would bear and raise children and establish a haven of tranquillity and moral rectitude to which men might escape from the inevitable pressures and corruptions of public life (Burstyn, 1980, pp.18–22, 30–33; Davidoff, 1974, pp.406–28; Duffin, 1978, pp.57–91; Dunbar, 1953, pp.17–22; Dyhouse, 1986, pp.27–38; Summers, 1979, pp.33–63; Vicinus, 1972, pp.vii–xv). In the context of the new world of public, organised sport the strength of this 'ideology of domesticity' was sufficient to restrict women to a subordinate, minor and persistently derided role. To middle class Victorian and Edwardian men sport in general, and competitive, team-based and mixed-sex sport in particular, was an unsuitable pursuit for women, a threat to the masculinity of the male and to the femininity, domestic and procreative responsibilities of the female and thus to the prevailing belief that, for biological, cultural and social reasons, the functions of the sexes should be kept largely separate. Confronted by such attitudes, the argument goes, it is little wonder that few middle class women actively participated in sport (for example, Brailsford, 1991, pp.131; Branca, 1978, pp.193–94; Browning, 1955, pp.123; Duffin, 1978, p.39; Hargreaves, 1987, pp.130–34; Holt, 1989, pp.8; Mangan and Park, 1987, pp.3–4, 5–6; McCrone, 1987, pp.97–99, 100–02, 116–17, 121; Mrozeck, 1987, p.286; Park, 1987, pp.59, 61, 76, 86–87; Smith-Rosenberg and Rosenberg, 1987, pp.38–57; Williams and Woodhouse, 1991, p.88).

That the 'separate spheres' ideology played some part in restricting the involvement of women in sport cannot be denied. There is, however, a growing body of evidence to suggest that its significance can easily be over-stated. As more recent work has demonstrated, in practice the attitudes and behaviour of upper and middle class Victorian and Edwardian females, and the reactions of men towards them, by no means always conformed to what we are led to believe was the desired ideal (Burstyn, 1980, pp.11, 34–35; Copelman, 1986, pp.175–176; Degler, 1974; Jalland, 1986, pp.94, 130, 133–136; Petersen, 1984). As Jane Lewis has noted, 'it is possible that the fabric of middle class women's lives bore little relation to that presented for the angel of the home and even that the divergence from the ideal did not necessarily produce tensions' (Lewis, 1986, pp.x–xi). On the whole, it has been suggested, middle class females were not 'functionless, helpless, insipid and unhealthy' nor should middle class men always be accused of being their 'exploiters and conquerors' (Branca, 1975, pp.152–153). More specifically, a similar reassessment is already under way in relation to the extent and nature of women's involvement in sport. In their participation in over 30 different sports during the period 1880–1914 English middle class females displayed a desire for competition, physical exertion and risk far in excess of that supposedly insisted upon in the emphasis of the ideal on recreational, passive and decorative involvement (Parratt, 1989, pp.144–48). In the evidence for Scotland, too, there are clear indications of the need to reassess the nature of the relationship between women and sport and, in particular, of the attitudes adopted by men towards this relationship.

In the character, as well as in the extent of their participation in organised sport, Scottish middle class women often behaved very differently from the requirements of the supposed ideal and, moreover, were often positively encouraged to so do by middle class men. One of the most striking and, in view of the emphasis supposedly placed on their domestic priorities, surprising features of female sporting activity was the extent to which married women participated. Because of its relatively energetic nature and thus the comparative youth of its players, lawn tennis was predominantly a game for unmarried females. In sports such as croquet and golf, however, married female players were common, sufficiently numerous in the case of clubs like the Stirling Ladies Gold Club for regular matches between married and unmarried members to take place. Married or widowed women were particularly prominent among sport club patronesses, in the Stirling region comprising all but two of the 54 patronesses of known marital status (Tranter, 1989, pp.41–42, 47).

A second notable characteristic displayed by Scottish middle class females in their participation in sport was the obvious enthusiasm of at least some of them for competitive rather than simply recreational, forms of play. Except in the case of cycling which they seem invariably to have preferred as a casual, non-competitive recreation, Scottish middle class women frequently showed a keen interest in formally organised, competitive types of sporting activity, an interest abundantly reflected in the frequency of prize competitions for women in sports like archery, bowling and swimming and of inter- and intra-club team matches in sports like golf and lawn tennis. In the year ending March 1900, for example, the Stirling Ladies Golf Club played as many as seven matches against other clubs. Between 1897 and 1904 its fixture list included regular matches, in teams of from six to ten players a side, against the ladies of the Alloa, Dollar, Dunblane, Falkirk Tryst, Lenzie and Perth clubs. Indeed, so keen was the Stirling club to promote inter-club competition that in 1903 its members voted to use club funds to meet part of the travelling expenses of those chosen to represent it in away games. All golf clubs ran regular fortnightly or monthly championship tournaments and, on a less regular basis, other forms of prize competition. In season 1897–98 the Stirling Ladies Club organised 22 separate competitions for members, attracting an average of twelve entries: in season 1899–1900 eighteen, with an average entry of thirteen. As indicated by their presence in teams representing the Stirling and Crieff clubs in 1884, the Stirling and Alloa Marshill clubs in 1891 and the Stirling and Bridge of Allan clubs in 1896 and by the numbers who entered tournaments organised by the Stirling and Bridge of Allan clubs in 1880 and 1884, middle class females were also frequent participants in inter- and intra-club lawn tennis matches and competitions (Tranter, 1989, p.42).

It is, however, in the attitudes of middle class males to the participation of women in organised sport that the existence of a firmly entrenched, all-pervasive ideology of 'separate spheres' is most questionable. The clear implications of the Scottish evidence are that men did *not* always regard the public world of institutionalised sport as an exclusively male preserve, to be jealously and fiercely protected from female encroachment. On the contrary, the participation of women as patrons and players as well as merely spectators was often welcomed and even, at times, strongly encouraged. One indication of this is the frequency with which wives and daughters participated as patrons and members in the same clubs as their husbands and fathers. Another is the obvious popularity of mixed sex competitions in sports such as croquet, golf and lawn tennis. Mixed foursomes and mixed-sex individual handicap tournaments, in golf, and mixed doubles matches and mixed-sex club teams, in tennis, were commonplace. A leap-year foursome tournament run by the Bearsden Golf Club in 1892, at which women were allowed to select their partners, attracted an entry of nineteen couples. In June 1895 a Miss Baillie Hamilton was runner-up in a mixed-sex handicap competition organised for members of the Callandar Golf Club. In May 1900 twenty couples took part in a mixed foursome tournament run by the same club. Annual tournaments organised by the Bridge of Allan Lawn Tennis Club in the 1880s included mixed doubles events as well as separate events for men and women. At the time, indeed, much of the popularity of tennis was thought to depend on the fact that males and females could participate in the same game (Tranter, 1989, p.43).

No less indicative of the sympathetic attitudes often adopted by men towards the participation of women in sport is the frequency with which the former attempted to persuade the latter to become more fully involved. The establishment of the St Andrews Ladies Golf Club, we are told, was 'greatly encouraged by men who provided it with prizes for competitions' (Wilson, 1952, p.223). The men of the Scottish Mountaineering Club made a signifi-cant contribution to the formation of a Scottish Ladies Climbing Club in 1908 (Keir, 1966, p.527). In 1864 the promoters of the annual meetings of the Scottish National Archery Association were reported to be 'active in encour-aging women to overcome their natural shyness and compete'. In the same year the male editor of the *Stirling Journal* urged the development of croquet on the grounds that it was 'the best attempt yet to provide a game in which both sexes can join'. The presence of women at soccer matches was a 'desirable element', the *Journal* insisted in 1881. On the formation of the Stirling Amateur Boating and Swimming Club in 1894 the editor of the *Stirling Observer* expressed the hope that 'ladies (too) would take part in boating' : five years later the editor of the *Stirling Journal* also expressed the hope that efforts to establish a ladies' curling club in the town would prove successful. Cycling clubs were particularly anxious to encourage active female participation. In 1887, for example, women were 'especially invited' to attend the third annual meeting of the cyclists of West Perthshire at Dunblane. In 1896 and 1898 respectively both the Clackmannanshire and East Stirlingshire bicycle clubs instituted separate ladies' sections. In 1897, albeit unsuccessfully, the *Stirling Observer* pressed for the establishment of a ladies' cycling club in Stirling. In 1899 the Balfron Strathendrick Cycling Club made a special point of reminding female cyclists that they were eligible for membership while the Milngavie club began a sustained, and ultimately successful, campaign to persuade women to join its newly formed ladies' section.

In their attempts to increase female participation, sports clubs frequently offered women free admission to matches and preferential subscription rates. Throughout the 1870s and early 1880s, when middle class males were charged 6d and artisans and youths 3d, female spectators were admitted free to home games of the Stirling County Cricket Club. Senior soccer clubs in the Stirling region, which charged adult males between 3d and 6d depending on the importance of the fixture, also often admitted female spectators free of charge. In 1896 the Stirling-based Scottish Central Cycling Club offered women free annual subscriptions in an attempt to persuade them to join. At the Alva Golf Club in 1900 subscription rates were £1 for men and 10s–6d for women: at the Polmont Bowling Club between 1912 and 1914 15s and 7s–6d respectively (Tranter, 1989, pp.43–44).

There were, no doubt, numerous occasions when the relationships between men and women in sport were remote and strained. But this was by no means always the case. Within five years of its foundation in 1895, for example, the predominantly male Bridge of Allan Golf Club had sufficient respect for its female members to allow them to elect a separate committee to manage their own affairs (*Bridge of Allan Reporter*, 1900, 27 October). As the minute books of the Stirling Ladies' Golf Club indicate, relationships between it and the Stirling Golf Club were generally amicable, so amicable indeed that at its annual general meeting in 1900 the ladies' club agreed to allow men to join as associate members (Stirling Ladies' Golf Club, Minute Book 1897–1905, Central Region Archives, Stirling, PD 22 January, 1900 1 March).

To suggest, as some do, that middle class Victorian and Edwardian males were *always* opposed to the involvement of women in the public world of organised sport is to overlook a growing body of evidence to the contrary. Admittedly, the willingness of men to encourage female participation did not extend across the whole range of sports. Some sporting activities, particularly those of a physically robust kind like soccer and rugby, were considered unsuitable for active participation by the female sex. It does, however, bear emphasising that the debate about the suitability of sport was not restricted solely to the issue of women's involvement. On the contrary, it was conducted with no less vigour for men. As the editor of the *Stirling Journal* noted of golf, 'boys are beating their fathers. This is not how it should be. So long as we have football in winter and cricket in summer, golf should be forbidden to all males under 25 or 30 . . . Let the young not be middle-aged too soon' (*Stirling Journal*, 1896, 17 April). In his attempt to define the age-groups most suited to individual sports and his efforts to separate the 'professional' from the 'amateur' in his advocacy of physical activity for the white-collar worker and artisan and physical repose for the labourer, there is abundant evidence that the Victorian and Edwardian male was not singling out women for special treatment when he considered the question of what kind of sport should be permitted. Depending on their age and backgrounds, for men as well as women some sports were acceptable and others not.

Although more work needs to be done, the evidence presented in this chapter confirms that current orthodoxy on the involvement of middle class females in organised sport is a distortion both of reality and of what was at least sometimes actually desired by males. To judge from the extent of their participation as players, patrons and spectators, the frequency with which they shared this participation with men, their enthusiasm for competitive forms of play and the extent to which married as well as single women took part, the relationship of middle class women to organised sport does not always sit comfortably with the view of women portrayed in early, crude versions of the 'separate spheres' thesis. Nor, to judge from the frequency with which they supported female sport, their willingness to participate in mixed-sex events and their practice of offering women preferential admission and subscription rates, do the attitudes often adopted towards women's sport by middle class men. Whether the presence of females in sport was seen as a means of raising male standards of morality and social behaviour, of increasing opportunities for contact between the sexes or simply as a means of improving the quality of life for women themselves, the middle class Scottish male not infrequently acted to promote the cause of women's sport, at least in those sports deemed physically and aesthetically suitable. In Scotland, anyway, the middle class female should not be too readily dismissed as frail and housebound or the middle class male as always her exploiter and conqueror (Tranter, 1989, pp.44–45).

To the extent that the involvement of middle class females in public sport remained limited the explanation probably has less to do with the strength of male hostility than with decisions taken by women themselves (Park, 1989, p.10; Parratt, 1989, p.155). Even if, as it is usual to assume (McCrone, 1987, p.99; McCrone, 1988, pp.6–7), middle class females in nineteenth century Britain were less involved in sport, and less encouraged in this involvement by men, than had been the case in earlier centuries the influence of an ideology of exclusion imposed by men may turn out to be less significant than has sometimes been suggested. If assumptions about the relative vitality of middle class female sport in pre-modern times themselves prove to be wrong, and these assumptions certainly require more rigorous testing than they have so far received, the significance of a male-inspired philosophy of 'separate spheres' will need to be reduced still further. Given that in thirteenth century

England physical recreations were also predominantly a male pursuit (Carter, 1988, p.171), perhaps the numbers of women who participated in sporting activities outside the home had *always* been relatively small.

BIBLIOGRAPHY

Bailey, P., 1978, *Leisure and class in Victorian England: rational recreation and the contest for control, 1830–85*, Routledge, London
Borthwick, A., *Braid Tennis Club, 1890–1990*, Edinburgh
Brailsford, D., 1991, *Sport, time and society. The British at play*, Routledge, London.
Branca, P., 1975, *Silent sisterhood. Middle class women in the Victorian home*, Croom Helm, London
Branca, P., 1978, *Women in Europe since 1750*, Croom Helm, London
Browning, R., 1955, *A history of golf*, J. M. Dent, London
Burstyn, J. N., 1980, *Victorian education and the ideal of womanhood*, Croom Helm, London
Carter, J. M., 1988, Sports and recreations in thirteenth century England: the evidence of the Eyre and Coroners' rolls, *Journal of sport history*, 15, (2), pp.167–73
Copelman, D. M., 1986, A new comradeship between men and women: family, marriage and London's women teachers, 1870–1914, in Lewis, J., (ed.), *Labour and love. Women's experience of home and family, 1850–1940*, Basil Blackwell, Oxford, pp. 175–93
Davidoff, J., 1974, Mastered for life: servant and wife in Victorian England, *Journal of social history*, 7, pp.406–28
Degler, C., 1974, What ought to be and what was: women's sexuality in the nineteenth century, *American historical review*, 79, pp.1467–490
Duffin, L., 1978, Prisoners of progress: women and evolution, in Delamont, S. and Duffin, L., (eds) *The nineteenth century woman. Her cultural and physical world*, (eds), Croom Helm, London, pp.57–91
Duffin, L., 1978, The conspicuous consumptive: woman as an invalid, in Delamont, S. and Duffin, L., *The nineteenth century woman*, (eds). Croom Helm, London, pp.26–56
Dunbar, J., 1953, *The early Victorian woman. Some aspects of her life*, Harrap, London
Dyhouse, C., 1986, Mothers and daughters in the middle class home, c.1870–1914, in Lewis, J., (ed.), *Labour and love*, Basil Blackwell, Oxford, pp.27–47
Fittis, R. S., 1891, *Sports and pastimes of Scotland*, Edinburgh, reprinted 1975, E. P. Publishing, East Ardsley
Guttmann, A., 1986, *Sports spectators*, Columbia University Press, New York
Hargreaves, J., 1987, Victorian families and the formative years of female sport, in Mangan, J. A. and Park, R. J., (eds), *From 'fair sex' to feminism. Sport and the socialization of women in the industrial and post-industrial eras*, Frank Cass, London, pp.130–44
Hill, J., 1986, The development of professionalism in English league cricket, c., 1900–1940, in Mangan, J. A. and Small, R. B., (eds), *Sport, culture and society. International historical and sociological perspectives*, E. and F. N. Spon, London, pp.109–16
Holt, R., 1989, *Sport and the British. A modern history*, Oxford University Press, Oxford
Jalland, P., 1986, *Women, marriage and politics 1860–1914*, Clarendon Press, Oxford
Keir, D., (ed.), 1966, The city of Edinburgh, in, *The third statistical account of Scotland*, xv, Collins, Glasgow

Lewis, J., (ed.), 1986, *Labour and love. Women's experience of home and family, 1850–1940*, Basil Blackwell, Oxford

Mangan, J. A. and Park, R. J., (eds), 1987, *From 'fair sex' to feminism. Sport and the socialization of women in the industrial and post-industrial eras*, Frank Cass, London

Marshall, R. K., 1983, *Virgins and viragos. A history of women in Scotland from 1080 to 1980*, Collins, London

McCrone, K. E., 1987, Play up! Play up! and play the game: sport of the late Victorian girls' public school, in Mangan and Park, (eds), *From 'fair sex' to feminism*, Frank Cass, London, pp.97–129

McCrone, K. E., 1988, *Sport & the physical emancipation of English women*, Routledge, London

McCrone, K. E., 1990, Emancipation or recreation? The development of women's sport at the University of London, *International journal of the history of sport*, 7, 2, pp.204–29

McCrone, K. E., 1991, Class, gender and English women's sport, 1890–1914, *Journal of sport history*, 18, 1, pp.159–82

Mrozek, D., 1987, The Amazon and the American lady: sexual fears of women as athletes, in Mangan and Park, (eds), *From 'fair sex' to feminism*, Frank Cass, London, pp.282–98

Murray, W. H., 1981, *The Curling Companion*, Richard Drew, Glasgow

Park, R. J. 1987, Sport, gender and society in a transatlantic Victorian perspective, in, Mangan and Park, (eds), *From 'fair sex' to feminism*, Frank Cass, London, pp.58–93

Park, R. J., 1989, Sport, dress reform and the emancipation of women in Victorian England. A reappraisal, *International journal of the history of sport*, 6, 1, pp.10–30

Parratt, C. M., 1989, Athletic womanhood: exploring sources for female sport in Victorian and Edwardian England, *Journal of sport history*, 16, 2, pp.140–57

Petersen, M. Jeanne, 1984, No angels in the home: the Victorian myth and the Paget women, *American historical review*, 89, 3, pp.677–708

Prochaska, F., 1980, *Women and philanthropy in nineteenth century England*, Oxford University Press, Oxford

Scott, F. T., 1984, The tradesmen's handicap (1884–1984), *Transactions of the Hawick Archeological Society*, pp.10–19

Smith, A., Young, J. and Murray, A., 1981, Hawick cycling club 1881–1981, *Transactions of the Hawick Archaeological Society*, pp.12–14

Smith, D. B., 1981, *Curling. An illustrated history*, John Donald, Edinburgh

Smith-Rosenberg, C. and Rosenberg, C., 1987, The female animal: medical and biological views of women and their role in nineteenth century America, in, Mangan and Park, (eds), *From 'fair sex' to feminism*, Frank Cass, London, pp.38–57

Summers, A., 1979, A home from home: women's philanthropic work in the nineteenth century, in Burman, S., (ed.), *Fit work for women*, Croom Helm, London, pp.33–63

Tod, A., ed., 1988, *Elizabeth Grant of Rothiemurchus. Memoirs of a Highland lady*, vol. 1, Canongate, Edinburgh

Tranter, N. L., 1989, Organised sport and the middle class woman in nineteenth century Scotland, *International journal of the history of sport*, 6, 1, pp.31–48

Tranter, N. L., 1990, The chronology of organised sport in nineteenth century Scotland: a regional study. I Patterns, *International journal of the history of sport*, 7, 2, pp.188–203

Vamplew, W., 1988, Sport and industrialisation: an economic interpretation of the changes in popular sport in nineteenth century England, in, Mangan, J. A., (ed.), *Pleasure, profit and proselytism. British culture and sport at home and abroad, 1700–1914*, Frank Cass, London, pp.7–20

Vamplew, W., 1988, *Pay up and play the game. Professional sport in Britain, 1875–1914*, Cambridge University Press, Cambridge

Vicinus, M., 1972, *Suffer and be still*, Indiana University Press, Bloomington

Walvin, J., 1978, *Leisure and society, 1830–1950*, Longman, London

Williams, J. and Woodhouse, J., 1991, Can play will play? Women and football in Britain, in, Williams, J. and Wagg, S., (eds), *British football and social change. Getting into Europe*, Leicester University Press, Leicester, pp.85–108

Wilson, E., 1952, Women's golf, in, Darwin, B., (ed.), *A history of golf in Britain*, Cassell, London, pp.222–45

4

SPORT AND THE SCOTTISH STATE

Chris Harvie

I typed part of my first draft while watching Celtic trying to push past Borussia Dortmund into the UEFA Cup Final. And failing. The German commentator praised the game and the hosts. 'Die Schotten sind immer fair', and this reputation seemed to weigh on the fans themselves. Scotland's position in international football is both so important and so perilous that being football's *cognoscenti* seems essential. There is no alternative, as the lady said – though one remembers with gratitude the sense of impending *hubris* which enveloped her descent on a Scottish cup-tie.

Scotland and Wales might in late 1992 fail to qualify for, respectively, the football and rugby world cups. The sport-nationality set-up in both countries depends on institutional lethargy in tackling the over-representation of the United Kingdom in international sport, a consequence of the early establishment of the national leagues. 'Uneven development' for once operates in Scotland's favour, an ironic and deceptive British concession towards a 'Europe of the Regions' in sport.

Some market liberals and even Marxists regard demotion as enforcing *real* priorities – economic development, technical training, literary culture, and sexual equality. This condemnatory line was not just inherited from Victorian divines who 'were especially jealous of football, for it above all aroused exactly the heart-warming zeal and total devotion which they themselves had tried, so painfully and so totally unsuccessfully to arouse for God' (Smout, 1986, p.202).

It also emerged in 'bourgeois' social critiques such as Thorstein Veblen's *Theory of the Leisure Class (1899):*

> The culture bestowed in football gives a product of exotic ferocity and cunning. It is a rehabilitation of the early barbarian temperament, together with a suppression of those details of temperament which, as seen from the standpoint of the social and economic exigencies, are the redeeming features of the savage character. (Veblen, 1899, 1925, p.262)

I would have to plead guilty myself. In *Forward! Labour Politics in Scotland 1888–1988* (1989) football goes unmentioned. Nor does it appear, for example, in the index of Stuart Macintyre's study of militant socialist communities, *Little Moscows* (1980), although sport resurfaces prominently in the text.

Yet within the national intellectual tradition the interminable discourse on sport, football in particular, does not seem a case of substance-abuse, misplaced patriotism, or part of some rampant false consciousness. Football is *diplomatically* as important to Scotland as the Olympics were in 1992 to Catalunya, 'a country *in* Spain'. Without football, could the country avoid international obscurity, 'Glasgow who?' greeting the usual tentative attempts at self-identification? The emotion generated by Wallace Mercer's project in 1990 to amalgamate the two Edinburgh teams implied that such commercial consolidation, carried out by a Tory magnate, would end in an all-British league (Linklater and Denniston, 1992, p.350). This, along with any move to exclude Scotland from international competitions, could provide a more powerful propellant towards full independence than any number of Constitutional Conventions.

'1905 AND ALL THAT'

This matrix of sport-and-nation relationships was formed between 1880 and 1920, when sport both enhanced and frustrated political mobilisation on the British periphery. In Ireland the rise of the Gaelic Athletic Association after its foundation in 1884 was to provide a role for such nationalist youth (most of it) disinclined to the evening classes of the Gaelic League. It helped create a scheme of values which included a disciplined approach to fitness. In 1919–21 the military exploits of former GAA men such as Michael Collins, whose physique kept him on several occasions a vital few yards ahead of the Black and Tans, seemed to justify the discipline of its approach. The revival of the Tailteann Games in 1924 was in a sense a founding ceremony of the Free State (Mandle, 1987, pp.218ff). The Games didn't survive the Free State, but even such a sceptic about Irish nationalism as Joe Lee has written that:

> The success of the Gaelic Athletic Association, based on the co-option of intense local loyalties into a wider sense of national identity, reflected a capacity for organisation and a sense of communal coherence more developed than that in much of Mediterranean and eastern Europe. (Lee, 1989, p.80)

In Wales, Rugby Union *was* a conscious 'garrison game', promoted by clergy of the Church of Wales as a means of keeping youth out of the chapels as well as the pubs. A fiercely intellectual non-conformist-nationalist establishment kept it at a distance. For David Lloyd George in 1896 'The English were a nation of footballers, stock exchangers, public house and music-hall frequenters' (Mason, 1980, p.ix; Williams, 1991, p.16). Yet a decade later things had changed. The defeat of the otherwise triumphant All Blacks at Cardiff Arms Park on 16 December 1905 united nationalists with the 'new' Welsh of the valleys – and kicked the last great religious revival into touch. To the editor of *Welsh Outlook* in 1914, that same Tom Jones who was to become Lloyd George's private secretary, and pivot of countless Welsh committees:

> Rugby is . . . the game of the Welshman. The international records of the past twenty years show that the Principality can hold an equal if not superior hand in the game . . . The Association code in Wales is new and alien and comes in on the back of its popularity elsewhere: it is the game of the alien of the valleys whose immigration and de-nationalising tendency is one of the major problems of our country (and) the social context of the game (is) cosmopolitan . . .
> Wales possesses in Rugby football . . . a game democratic and amateur – a unique thing to be cherished and . . . the concern of thinking men who value the complex influences making for higher levels of citizenship. (Smith, 1984, p.35)

In Scotland sport also became a constitutive part of national identity – but of a peculiarly fractured sort. Football was the obsessive topic of most of male society; but this was qualified by internal divisions – of skill and of religion – as well as the complex border between the working and middle classes in a society of achieved rather than ascriptive status (Littlejohn, 1963, p.194). The roles of Lord Kinnaird, W. H. Gladstone MP and Quintin Hogg, all of whom represented Scotland in the 1870s, ensure that the upper-class early Association game had a Liberal and reformist ethos, which it never altogether lost (Hossack, 1989, pp.53–55). Cricket and rugby union, organisationally biased towards the anglicised middle class, still managed to acquire regions of working-class support, the first among coal-miners in the 1860s, the second among the textile workers of the Border burghs in the 1870s (Fraser and Morris, 1990, p.252; Williams, 1991, pp.22–23).

And yet certain elements of Veblen's 'barbarian' model were also salient. The 'normal and characteristic occupations' of the barbarian elite, 'government, war, sports and devout observances', were disproportionately present (Veblen, 1899, 1925, p.40). The Scottish post itineraries of the 'upper 10,000' were in the post-Balmoral period (i.e., after 1848) governed by hunting, the shooting of grouse and deer and the catching of salmon, accompanied by the various not-totally-phoney rituals of Highland Games. From the 1880s the milder rituals of golf became important in the daily life of elite and middle class alike. When H. H. Asquith visited St Andrews in 1876, 'golf was then so little developed that he and his modest-living student companions were able to hire the services of the British open champion to carry their clubs'. In 1907, when he took, as Prime Minister, an East Lothian house with its own nine-hole course, facilities ranged from countless local courses to the huge railway-owned projects of Turnberry, Gleneagles and Cruden Bay (Jenkins, 1964, p.26), perhaps a reflection of lower upper-class incomes because of agricultural depression, and consequently a drop in the cost of land for golf courses. In 1938 thirty-seven per cent of a sample of entries in *Scottish Biographies* golfed, 17.5 per cent fished. Between 1902 and 1914 Britain was literally governed in summer from North Berwick. Before Asquith took Archerfield, the donnish aristocrat Arthur Balfour, at Whittinghame, was the first premier to use the socialisation involved in golf and tennis as an instrument of political discussion, ritualising an informality and approachability, which was in his case thoroughly deceptive (Dugdale, 1939, vol. 1, pp.146–47). 'Fear may ride behind the horseman, he does not walk with the caddy' was one of Balfour's *mots*. The fellowship of the links did not, however, keep the enemies of Liberal Britain at bay. Another recreational innovation, the bicycle, became, in the hands of the Clarion Cycling Clubs, an instrument of radical propaganda, and bicycle-borne suffragettes caused unpleasant things to happen between tee and green.

In 1938, in *Homo Ludens*, the Dutch historian and philosopher Johan Huizinga argued, against Veblen, that sport facilitated the equilibrium of the physical and the mental, the social and the individual. With their conventions and rules, games could be a structure for socialising mass-society; they could also be a means of promoting the co-ordination and communication of elites which controlled, or sought to control it. The rationalisation of the nineteenth century, which Marx and Veblen examined, was a distortion, not the main line of development (Huizinga, 1938, pp.312f).

The national revivalists of the Scottish Renaissance were decidedly unhappy about sport's surrogate politics. Hugh MacDiarmid was – for a Langholm man – a dead loss, and contemplated Ibrox transformed into a vast lecture hall. Compton Mackenzie, who had attended the Tailteann Games in 1924, made the autobiographical John Ogilvie in *The North Wind of Love* deeply critical:

> A nation which thinks that the news of the world in the six o'clock bulletin is a tiresome postponement of the football results is marching in blinkers along the road to ruin. (Mackenzie, 1944, 1949, p.30)

He proposed the abolition of all professional sport, indeed of 'all idle games after childhood . . . (substituting) walking, forestry, shooting and sailing, according to the locality and the season' (Mackenzie, 1949, p.28).

For one more sympathetic nationalist, Eric Linklater (born in Barry and surely conscious of the *annus mirabilis* of 1905, when he would be six) the rugby-football distinction emphasised a line of division between working and middle class inimical to the creation of a national community. He wrote flatteringly of a rugby international crowd in Edinburgh:

> To see them walking in clear spring weather is almost as exhilarating as the game itself, for their shoulders are straight, they are tall and lithe, they are square and strong, their eyes are bright, and their skin is toughened and tanned by the weather . . .

By contrast, the supporters of Hearts and Hibs seemed another nation, predestined to frustrate the romantic nationalism of Linklater's *homo ludens* Magnus Merriman:

> To look at them it seemed obvious that work was a perversion, for it had not given them the upright bearing and the swinging stride that play had bestowed on the others, but rather it had kept their faces pale, and though it had toughened them it had not given them grace. (Linklater, 1933, 1959, pp.128–129)

Scottish sport simultaneously offered and withdrew the possibility of the full and balanced life, the 'mens sana in corpore sano' (of healthy mind and body). To adapt Marx, sport made the Scots 'of a nation' but not 'for a nation': conscious that they were 'agin' others, but also that they were internally divided by class and religion.

In this chapter I want to explore these contrasting patterns of sport and social mobilisation by examining the highly-politicised pattern shown in Ireland, and the reasons why it was not emulated in Scotland. But these also demand that sport be located within a tradition of social interpretation which was uniquely strong in Scotland.

GAMES AND SOCIOLOGY

Closer to Huizinga than to Veblen, the post-enlightenment Scottish politico-intellectual tradition merged sport and political activity, seeing games not just as deliberate forms of social control exercised as a result of class hegemony, or conversely as the random choices of consumers, but as socially constitutive rituals. Moreover, such philosophising about sport was peculiarly infective in the epoch of print-capitalism. In the 1880s historical and anthropological enquiry intersected with the commissioning of the 'social overhead capital' of modern sports. At one level local antiquarians set out to give rugby in the Scottish Borders or South Wales a historical pedigree, linking it to 'hand-ba' or 'cnappan' (Williams, 1991, p.80). At another the great anthropologist Sir James George Frazer argued that the rough field-games which were played by whole communities at Lent were connected with ritual purgation and scape-goating (Frazer, 1936, p.184).

But Frazer was part of a tradition already influential in 'homogenising' a games culture. In his *Essay on the History of Civil Society* (1767), Adam Ferguson dwelt on the persistence of hostility between communities as a means of conferring an identity on them, and of the continuity between the military virtues and the respect granted to sporting prowess:

> Every animal is made to delight in the exercise of his natural talent and forces. The lion and the tyger sport with the paw; the horse delights to commit his mane to the wind, and forgets his pasture to try his speed in the field; the bull even before his brow is armed, and the lamb while yet an emblem of innocence, have a disposition to strike with the forehead, and anticipate in play the conflicts they are doomed to sustain. Man too is disposed to opposition, and to employ the forces of his nature against an equal antagonist; he loves to bring his reason, his eloquence, his courage, even his bodily strength, to the proof. His sports are frequently an image of war; sweat and blood are frequently expended in play; and fractures or death are often made to terminate the pastimes of idleness and festivity. (Ferguson, 1767, 1967, p.24)

Sport was not just a means of passing non-work time, but a necessary component of civic life. Casting back to the Greek games, and anticipating William James' *Moral Equivalent of War* (1911), Ferguson saw sports as a substitute for the exercises of militarism: both a means whereby the youth was disciplined and organised, and a type of collective ceremony in which the solidarity of the community was demonstrated.

Ferguson was born on the Highland line, at Logierait, and had been as a Gaelic speaker a chaplain in the Black Watch, 1745–54. So when he inserts an ironic description of classical Greece, the similarities to his own highlands are all too palpable:

> They come abroad barefooted, and without any cover to the head, wrapt up in the coverlets under which you would imagine they had slept. They throw all off, and appear like to many native cannibals, when they go to violent sports and exercises, at which they highly value feats of dexterity and strength. Brawny limbs and muscular arms, the faculty of sleeping out all nights, of fasting long, and putting up with any kind of food, are thought genteel accomplishments. They have no settled government that I could learn; sometimes the mob, and sometimes the better sort, do what they please: they meet in great crouds in the open air, and seldom agree about any thing. (Ferguson, 1767, 1967, p.197)

There's more than a foretaste here of George MacDonald Fraser's description of a post-1945 Scottish regimental football team in 'Play up, Play up, and Get Tore In':

> From the moment when the drums beat *Johnnie Cope* at sunrise until it became too dark to see in the evening, the steady thump-thump of a boot on a ball could be heard somewhere in the barracks. It was tolerated because there was no alternative; even the parade-ground was not sacred from the small shuffling figures of the Glasgow men, their bonnets pulled down over their eyes, kicking, trapping, swerving and passing, and occasionally intoning, like ugly little high priests, their ritual cries of 'Way-ull' and 'Aw-haw-hey'. The simile is apt, for it was almost a religious exercise. . . . (Fraser, 1970, p.36)

For Adam Smith, as later for Bentham and Marx, sports were either recreation or pleasure; emotional releases which could also be secured by card-playing or shove-ha'penny. For Ferguson (and for that matter for MacDonald Fraser) they were constitutive of *Gemeinschaft*, the goings-on of a community aware, however intermittently, of the 'unanticipated consequences' of its conscious actions in developing its complex solidarity.

The expression of this took two forms. For the first, Ferguson, demobbed, deployed his enthusiasm for Machiavellian civic *vertu* in the attempt to secure a militia for Scotland in the agitation of 1760–61 (Lenman, 1981, pp.30–31; Robertson, 1985, passim). This awoke little resonance outwith the *literati*, and when a militia was set up in the 1790s the Scots rioted against it. But, after political reform came in 1832, few areas of Britain flocked more energetically to the Volunteer movement of the late 1850s (Cunningham, 1975 pp.46–47) and what Harry Hanham calls 'radical militarism' bore heavily on the various religious organisations which in the early 1870s and subsequently developed the amateur football game, not to speak of a multitude of formal and casual local athletic bodies (Neill, 1977, p.63f).

The old philosopher was still alive – and his son Sir Adam was almost certainly present – when Sir Walter Scott patronised folk-football at Carterhaugh on 14 December 1815, in the famous match between his Selkirk team and the Earl of Home's men, organised by James Hogg; an occasion which helped revive the Common Ridings of the Border Burghs. Given his popularity in translation, Ferguson may also have had a direct influence on the role played by gymnastics in national revivals in Europe. The German contribution came after the Napoleonic invasion in 1806, especially through Friedrich Ludwig Jahn's (1778–1852) Liberal and nationalist *Turnvereine*, first organised after 1811, in which outdoor exercises were linked to an appreciation of folklore and history. Such organisations were developed on the left and the right, and replicated in other national movements, most notably the Czech *Sokol* (Falcon) movement founded in the 1860s (Koralka, 1992, p.89).

The second looming presence was Thomas Carlyle. On the face of it, no one was more remote from organised sport, which he would doubtless have dismissed with an oath or two. But Carlyle's social thought was deeply influenced by Ferguson in its criticism of the reduction of society to a 'cash-nexus' in 'Signs of the Times' (1829) or 'Characteristics' (1831). In *Heroes and Hero-Worship* (1841) he lauded the cult of effort, something to be transformed into 'muscular Christianity' by his Christian Socialist acolytes Tom Hughes and Charles Kingsley. 'From the cradle to the grave' wrote Hughes in *Tom Brown's Schooldays* (1857), 'fighting, rightly understood, is the business, the real highest, honestest business of every son of man' (Norman, 1989, p.90). Hughes combined radicalism and support for trade unionism with 'fighting, rightly understood' in the Volunteers and sports clubs.

Finally, in *The French Revolution* (1837) Carlyle perfected a style of descriptive writing able to capture fast-moving events: the pabulum of that under-researched performer, the sports journalist:

> See Huissier Maillard, the shifty man! On his plank, swinging over the abyss of that stone Ditch; plank resting on parapet, balanced by weight of Patriots, – he hovers perilous: such a Dove towards such an Ark! Deftly, thou shifty usher: one man already fell; and lies smashed, far down there, against the masonry; Usher Maillard falls not; deftly, unerring he walks, with outspread palm. The Swiss holds a paper through his porthole; the shifty Usher snatches it, and returns. Terms of surrender: Pardon, immunity to all! Are they accepted? – '*Foi d'officier*, on the word of an officer', answers half-pay Hulin, – or half-pay Elie, for men do not agree on it, 'they are!' Sinks the drawbridge, – Usher Maillard bolting it when down; rushes-in the living deluge: the Bastille is fallen! *Victoire! La Bastille est prise!*. (Carlyle, 1837, 1907, p.152f)

Carlyle was, as Young Ireland's magus, as much behind T. F. Meagher's invocation of Celtic games as a challenge to the Anglo-Saxons, as he influenced Almond of Loretto's apotheosis of the rugger captain (Edwards, 1968, p.21; Harvie, 1992, passim; Mandle, 1987, pp.16 and 154; Williams, 1991, p.22).

The European resonances of 'radical militarism' and Carlyleian hero-worship give Scottish individual and team sports a much denser context than stereotypes of the urban *untermensch* as gawping spectator, or the educated paragon embodying physical fitness and social unity. Their formative years as a mass-movement, in the 1890s, coincided with the *Wandervogel* in Germany, the nationalistic Central Committee for the Promotion of National Youth Games of the 'Carlyleian' 'cultural pessimist' Julius Langbehn, with Pierre de

Coubertin's propaganda in France for the revival of the Olympic games, and an overall concern about 'degeneration' as a result of the move to a mass urban society (Stern, 1960, p.172; Weber, 1991, pp.207–12). Not to speak of such Scottish peculiarities as Sir Hugh Munro of Lindertis making up in 1891 his celebrated list of 276 peaks above 3,000 feet, and James Bryce MP doing his bit for Munro-bagging by presenting his Access to Mountains Bill in 1888, and a resolution on the same lines in 1892 (Fisher, 1928). This unsuccessful project was itself symbolic, since it directly conflicted with the shooting and stalking which had earlier defined field sports in the highlands.

Coubertin, though like Langbehn from an ultra-conservative, clericalist background, was liberalised by English muscular Christians, Tom Hughes in particular. After a visit to England in 1883, he set up the Committee for Physical Exercises in Education in 1887. The Olympic spirit, only just set in motion by the 1896 games in Athens, effectively promoted a version of Ferguson's medication for a mass-society. Common games, competitively undertaken, proved to be an effective formula for reconciling co-existence and aggression.

But Coubertin's was not the only sport-political formula. His republican rival Paschal Grousset, cycling publicist, and nationalist promoter of *barette*, also developed links with British education. This was more inflected towards the child-centred 'learning through play' of the 'progressive school' tradition. Robert Muirhead, Fabian socialist and, like his more famous brother Roland, ardent Scottish nationalist, was prominent here, as was Margaret MacMillan (who had started as a preacher in the Bradford Labour Church) was similarly influential on the evolution of Board of Education policy under Sir Robert Morant, (Smith, 1899, p.81). This informally-organised 'play' element was evidenced by 1902 in the setting-up, rather in advance of the rest of the country, of the Royal Commission on Physical Training (Scotland) in 1902, evidence to which, particularly that of Dr W. L. Mackenzie, the Edinburgh school medical officer, stressed the importance of spontaneous games over drill. Somewhere here lurk John Buchan's Gorbals Diehards, as well as A. S. Neill.

TO THE TAILTEANN GAMES

The success of the GAA influenced some contemporary Scottish nationalists, such as Mackenzie, William Power, and John L. Kinloch, who founded his 'Clan Scotland' youth movement in the 1930s. Grant Jarvie has raised the issue: why did it not become a paradigm for the creation of a national sports movement, playing distinctive Scots or Celtic games? In the 1870s organised shinty made considerable strides in Scotland, with several of the early soccer sides, particularly those of the Vale of Leven, being shinty teams as well (Hutchinson, 1989, p.107; Jarvie, 1992, p.228). Shinty itself was firmly rooted in the counties of Argyll, Bute and Sutherland, not to mention the Islands, at a very early stage. Nationalists and land reformers – John Stuart Blackie, John Murdoch, Captain Chisholm of Strathglass – helped organise the game, and Scotland was actually in advance of Ireland in codifying its rules. Yet after some success in the last two decades of the nineteenth century, shinty retreated to the Eastern Highlands, and was further confined by the damage inflicted by World War I.

The GAA had ostensibly been provoked by the organisation, on a popular basis, of 'English' sports in Ireland. Its patron Archbishop Croke (whose time as Bishop of Auckland, 1870–75) had coincided with the rise of New Zealand rugby, had surely seen what organised sport could do for national prestige) took a line rather similar to that of 'sport politicians' such as Henry Drummond and Blackie in Scotland:

> If we continue travelling in the next score years in the same direction that we have been going in for some time past . . . effacing our national features as if we were ashamed of them, and putting on, with England's stuffs and broadcloths, her masher habits, and such effeminate follies as she may recommend, we had better at once, and publicly, abjure our nationality. (O'Sullivan, 1916, pp.9f)

There are, moreover, paradoxes in the GAA story. Michael Cusack, the GAA's moving spirit, pilloried by James Joyce as 'the Citizen' had himself made a fortune in cramming Irish candidates for the British civil service (Greene, 1960, p.76). Although Michael Davitt wrote to the founding meeting at Thurles to plead for the fostering of 'athletic sports peculiar to the Celtic people' and condemn 'the degenerate bearing of most of our young men at home' (Mitchell and O'Snodaigh, 1989, pp.61f) he would four years later feature as a patron of Glasgow Celtic Football Club. Even the GAA's most notable product, Michael Collins, found it desperately hard work compelling Irish exiles to play Gaelic games in London in the 1900s. All but three teams dropped out when the ban on 'garrison games' was enforced (Coogan, 1900, pp.14–16).

But the real answer to Jarvie's question – why the GAA succeeded while shinty never spread beyond Invernesshire, the Gaelic community in Glasgow, and the universities – was political. As W. F. Mandle's research in government and police archives has shown, the bulk of the organisational input of the GAA at its first peak in 1888–91 came from the Irish Republican Brotherhood. Although it claimed over 600 branches by 1887 (Scotland had only 26 shinty clubs a decade later) the GAA's sporting element at this stage was both attenuated and in national terms vague – 'for its first few years athletics were virtually all the GAA had to offer!' (Mandle 1987, p.204). There was an impulse towards 'national sports', but this remained subordinate to the IRB's desire to maintain its representation in a national struggle largely taken over by the parliamentary and land campaigns headed respectively by Parnell and Davitt. Not only was there no conspiratorial tradition in Scottish nationalism, there was – even more significantly – no Irish conspiratorial tradition in Scotland either (Murray, 1984, pp.66–75).

Three IRB men were among the thirteen who attended the inaugural meeting, while the politicos and clericals restricted themselves to sending letters. The games of hurling and Gaelic football promoted while the IRB remained in the ascendant – until it was engulfed in the split provoked by the Parnell crisis in 1890–91 – seem to have been closer to bando or folk football on one side or to rugby, until codified by R. T. Blade in 1895 (Mandle 1987, p.105). So the camans ritually shouldered at meetings in the 1880s – and at

Parnell's funeral – were at this stage more symbolic rifle-substitutes than evidence of a distinctive sport-culture.

In the decade or so during which GAA nationalism coincided with clerical control and formal 'no politics' rules – between 1896 and the revival of secret society agitation within the GAA around 1910 – Gaelic games developed as impressively as football in England, but without any element of professionalism, and with a far higher degree of county, as opposed to urban organisation. They were patently a godsend to a dense but underused railway system – a major difference with the Scottish highlands – which provided their main challenge cup (Mandle, 1987, pp.147–153). Further, Ireland, out of the port towns, was a relatively cohesive peasant society with a stable middle class of shopkeepers, auctioneers, publicans, teachers and clergy in the market towns. It could sponsor its own internal sporting system – it already did with horse-racing – without it getting out of control and into professionalism. This might curb emigration, while playing 'garrison games' well would simply provide another route out of the country for its most virile young men.

The 'Irish option' was not typical of nationalist movements, with the GAA at one end of a line of calibration, Scottish football in the middle, and English cricket and rugger on the right. It was a unique type of movement in which the conspiratorial and physical force tradition consciously patronised athletics. In fact it coincided with the adoption elsewhere in the empire, almost simultaneously, of 'English' games and anti-English sentiments and organisation – rugby in South Africa, cricket in India, Australia and the West Indies. The GAA is as much a one-off as the fact that, in their inimitable fashion, the 'real' English public school elite continue to play soccer rather than rugby.

THE CIVIC MODE

James and Muir both reflected in 1901 that the discourse of Glasgow working men about football was complex and 'political'. It was perhaps as influential as that of any political party member, as the performance of the team acted symbiotically on the mood of its supporters and their self-respect (Muir, 1901). This elaborated some nineteenth-century sport-political ideals and distorted others: revolutionary discipline for national liberation; ceremonies of community identity; socialisation through collective enjoyment.

Scotland had been influenced by an educational propaganda in favour of games and dancing analogous to that of the *Turnvereine* and *Sokol*. Robert Owen in his *New View of Society* (1816) seems to have copied the – anything but effeminate – dancing of the Scottish regiments. The utility of games in school education was also advocated by the influential David Stow at the Glasgow Normal Seminary in 1836:

> The playground animates, invigorates, and permits the *steam* which may have accumulated to escape, not in furious mischief, but in innocent, joyous and varied amusements, under the superintendence of the master. (Smith, 1899, p.81)

In Europe the division in national physical training organisations tended to lie between advocates of military drill, and advocates of sports. The 'military' element saw drill as a means of instilling discipline and obedience, the 'sportsmen' sought a more flexible, autonomous citizenry. The Volunteer movement combined both, but the attractiveness of drill alone seemed to decline in the 1880s, not just with the rise of commercialised sports, but with the impact of new military technologies and tactics which diminished the importance of the highly-drilled military unit in favour of the 'skirmishing' attack – something which was to gain its expression in the popularity of Baden-Powell's *Scouting for Boys* (1908).

Scotland played a particular role in the transition from the 'military' to the 'civic' mode. The Vale of Leven, the cradle of Scots soccer, had been an important centre of the Volunteers in the 1860s, part of a paternalist tradition represented by the Orr-Ewings and Wylies (Macintyre, 1980, pp.82f). They were Tories, but a strong Liberal element went into the creation of the Scouts' precursor, the Boys' Brigade, founded in Glasgow in 1883 by (Sir) William A. Smith, a Free Church Sunday School teacher and officer in the First Lanarkshire Rifle Volunteers who fielded one of the first Scottish elevens (Cunnison and Gilfillan, 1958, pp.703f; Young, 1968, p.108). In 1873 Rangers had been founded as a club with presbyterian connections: not perhaps the best of precedents for civic tolerance, but in the aftermath of the successful, and highly-ecumenical Moody and Sankey mission of that year Smith, concerned at the inability of Sunday schools to hold youngsters' attention, found that they responded to a physical training programme – parading with wooden rifles – combined with sports. BB companies were set up, invariably linked to churches and missions, but rarely without athletic, swimming and above all football clubs. If in 1910 the bulk of amateur teams in England were linked to churches, then the situation must have been even more apparent in Scotland (Fishwick, 1989, p.12).

The rationale was spelt out by Professor Henry Drummond, scientist, explorer and charismatic Free Church leader:

The wise Officer, the humane and sensible Officer, in short makes as much use of play for higher purposes than parades, and sometimes more. The key to a boy's life in the present generation lies in athletics. Sport commands his whole leisure, and governs his thoughts and ambitions even in his working hours. And so striking has been this development in recent years that the time has come to decide whether athletics are to become a curse to the country or a blessing. (Smith, 1899, p.459)

Drummond had his doubts about commercialised sport, regarding BB football as 'the making moral of what, in the eyes of those who really know, is fast becoming a most immoral and degrading institution'. But he had to admit that the most effective captains were those who coached their teams during the week, and acted as referees on Saturday afternoons. By the 1950s the Glasgow Battalion of the BBs was running 'the largest football league in the world', fielding 200 teams every Saturday (Cunnison and Gilfillan, 1958, p.626).

This elaborate amateur spirit lay behind the SFA's withdrawal from 'British' football in 1887, after a pitch invasion at Preston North End on 30 October 1886, by genteel Queens' Park supporters. But an all-British league, paradoxically, was really only accessible to the better-off – a 100 mile rail journey being necessary to reach the most northerly English ground. These were not the classes, increasingly being attracted as supporters, who would be the mainstay of the professional game (Young, 1968, pp.122f).

It is at this point that the Irish Catholic-Nationalist input does indeed become significant for the development of the game. The Catholic equivalent of the YMCA, the Catholic Young Men's Society, had been responsible for the foundation of Edinburgh Hibernian in 1873 by Canon Hannan. Fifteen years later Glasgow Celtic was founded by another priest, Brother Walfrid of the Marist order, but the motive was quite different. Celtic was from the start the flagship of an entire community, many of whose members were unable to afford to be amateurs, but who took pride in Celtic as a top club and a well-run business, which by 1893 could afford to build a stadium with a 30,000 capacity. As Bill Murray writes, this deliberate challenge, and the Rangers response, gave Scottish football both a sectarian and a gladiatorial aspect which marked it indelibly (Murray, 1984, pp.25–55).

Despite Davitt's planting of a shamrock sod at Parkhead in 1893, the ethos behind Celtic was as far from the GAA as it was from the temperance pietism of Canon Hannan. Not just because six out of its seven directors in 1897 were publicans (Gallagher, 1987, pp.55 and 61). Celtic's backers were home rulers, but the Glasgow variety were orthodox Nationalists. Some may well have been IRB members, but they stuck with the old Nationalist party, and did not, like the GAA, move to Sinn Fein after 1910. The team and the enterprise had put the community on the Scottish map. By 1914 Celtic was patriotic (Murray, 1984, p.126). Celtic's growth was less to do with solidarity than with proving that the Catholic community could create its own niche on a grand scale and assert its claim to equality of esteem in West Central Scotland. By the 1920s this 'Catholic' loyalty counted for more than 'anti-British' sentiment. Glasgow Catholics would be for a further half-century the pillars of Labour unionism.

The career of an archetypal footballer-as-publican, James Kelly, 'the fastest centre half-back that Scotland has produced' was surely emblematic. Kelly was a member of the 1888 Celtic team, and was subsequently capped sixteen times for Scotland; in 1911 he had become JP for Blantyre and a member of the School Board, as well as President of Celtic (Stothers, 1912, pp.226–27). But, as he started his career by playing for Renton, he would in fact have started as a 'soccer-and-shinty' man, with the option of a GAA-type development open to him. Instead, the 'star' soccer of the 'Old Firm' supervened.

And yet . . . the problem with sociological explanations is the assumption that the actors in society are always content with the injunction 'be this' instead of 'do this'. And this is dodgy when applied to that gamut of activities which stretches from 'play' with its anarchic implications to 'organised sport' with its harsh motivators, whether nationalism, personal excellence or money. And probably nowhere else is wayward individuality so well developed as in Scotland. This chapter has been about how organised sport came to exercise a socially constitutive function, but this activity sits mid-way between a primitive, pre-social and possibly destructive individuality, and that post-industrial identity that can create its own conscious balance of body and mind out of the security that civil society gives. At the first level we have the Cromarty tearaway Hugh Miller running wild, pulling knives on his school-fellows, but also geologising and collecting folklore. At the second we have the ingenuity of the Glasgow Catholic community in coming from far behind to capture a position at the top of the soccer scale. At the third? Perhaps another quote from a novel of the thirties sets the tone:

> He was now past the half-way line, a little distance ahead of one of the Clausons, with no colleague near him, and with Charvil racing to intercept him. For one of Jaikie's inches there could be no hand-off, but he had learned in his extreme youth certain arts not commonly familiar to rugby players. He was a most cunning dodger. . . . (Buchan, 1930, 1967, pp.17f)

In *Castle Gay*, that inspired Peacockian comedy of ideas, is also structured like a huge game, in which the forces of a Scottish *Gemeinschaft* reconcile the ideologies which threaten to tear it apart. John Buchan announces this by having wee Jaikie Galt score the winning try against Australia in 1929 by slewing from one mode to another, employing the arcane and unanticipated skills of the Gorbals Diehards – with devastating effect. Just as, five years earlier in the Tailteann Games, Scotland had beaten Ireland in hurling . . .?

BIBLIOGRAPHY

Arlott, John, 1967, *Oxford Companion to sport*, Oxford University Press, Oxford
Buchan, John, 1930, 1967, *Castle Gay*, Pan, London
Carlyle, Thomas, 1837, 1907, *The French revolution*, Chapman and Hall, London
Coogan, Tim Pat, 1990, *Michael Collins*, Hutchinson, London
Cunningham, Hugh, 1975, *The volunteer force*, Croom Helm, London
Cunnison, J. and Gilfillan, J. B., 1958, *Third statistical account of Scotland: Glasgow*, Collins, Glasgow
Donnachie, Ian, Christopher Harvie and Ian S. Wood, (eds), *Forward Labour politics in Scotland 1888–1988*, Polygon, Edinburgh
Dugdale, Blanche, 1939, *Arthur James Balfour*, Hutchinson, London
Duncan, Robert, 1986, *Wishaw*, Leisure Services, Motherwell
Edwards, Owen Dudley, 1968, 'Ireland' in *Celtic nationalism*, Routledge, London
Ferguson, Adam, 1767, 1967, *Essay on the history of civil society*, Edinburgh University Press, Edinburgh
Fisher, H. A. L., 1928, *James Bryce*, Macmillan, London
Fishwick, N., 1989, *English Football and Society, 1910–1950*, Manchester University Press, Manchester
Fraser, George MacDonald, 1970, *The general danced at dawn*, Collins, Glasgow
Fraser, W., Hamish and Morris, Robert, (eds), 1990, *People and society in Scotland, Vol. II, 1830–1914*, John Donald, Edinburgh
Frazer, Sir James George, 1889, 1936, *The golden bough*, (abridged edition), Macmillan, London
Gallagher, Tom, 1987, *The uneasy peace*, Manchester University Press, Manchester
Greene, David, 1960, 'Michael Cusack and the rise of the GAA' in Conor Cruise O'Brien, (ed.), *The shaping of modern Ireland*, Routledge, London, pp.76–83
Harvie, Christopher, 1992, 'Carlyle and the Scottish Mission' in Priscilla Metscher, (ed.), *Regionalismus in Grossbritannien*, Gulliver/Argument Verlag, Hamburg
Holt, Richard, 1989, *Sport and the British: a modern history*, Clarendon, Oxford

Hossack, Jim, 1989, *Head over heels: a celebration of British football*, Mainstream, Edinburgh

Huizinga, Johan, 1938, *Homo Ludens*, Pantheon, Basel

Hutchinson, Roger, 1989, *Camanachel*, Mainstream, Edinburgh

James, William, 1911, 'The Moral Equivalent of War', in Leon Bramson and George W Goethals, (eds), 1968, *War: studies from psychology, sociology, anthropology*, Basic Books, New York/London, pp. 21–31

Jarvie, Grant, 1992, *Sport, Gaelic nationalism and Scottish politics, 1879–1920*, Warwick University, unpublished paper

Jenkins, Roy, 1964, *Asquith*, Fontana, London

Koralka, Jiri, 1992, 'The Czechs, 1840–1900' in Andreas Kappeler, (ed.), *Comparative studies on Governments and non-dominant ethnic groups in Europe, 1850–1940*, vol. 6, *The formation of national elites*, European Science Foundation, Aldershot/New York University Press, Dartmouth, pp.77–103

Lee, Joseph, 1989, *Ireland, 1900–1985*, Cambridge University Press, Cambridge

Lenman, Bruce, 1981, *Integration, enlightenment and industrialisation: Scotland 1746–1832*, Edward Arnold, London

Linklater, Eric, 1933, 1959, *Magnus Merriman*, Penguin, Harmondsworth

Linklater, Magnus and Denniston, Robin, (eds), 1992, *Anatomy of Scotland*, Chambers, London

Littlejohn, James, 1963, *Westrigg, the sociological of a Cheviov parish*, Routledge, London

Lyons, F. S. L., 1979, *Culture and anarchy in Ireland*, Clarendon, Oxford

Macintyre, Stuart, 1980, *Little Moscows: communism and working-class militancy in inter-war Britain*, Croom Helm, London

Mackenzie, Compton, 1944, 1949, *The north wind of love*, Chatto and Windus, London

Mandle, W. F., 1987, *The Gaelic athletic association and Irish nationalist politics, 1884–1924*, Christopher Helm, London

Mason, Anthony, 1980, *Association football and English society*, Harvester Press, Sussex

Mitchell, Arthur and O'Snodaigh, Padraig, 1989, *Irish political documents , 1869–1916*, Irish Academic Press, Dublin

'Muir, James Hamilton', 1901, *Glasgow in 1901*, William Hodge, Glasgow

Murray, Bill, 1984, *The old firm*, John Donald, Edinburgh

Neill, A. S., 1977, *Neill! Neill! orange peel!*, Quartet Books, London

Norman, Edward, 1989, *The Victorian christian socialists*, Cambridge University Press, Cambridge

O'Sullivan, T. F., 1916, *The story of the Gaelic athletic association*, Purcell, Dublin

Robertson, John, 1985, *The Scottish enlightenment and the Militia issue*, John Donald, Edinburgh

Scottish Biographies 1938, E. J. Thurston, London

Smith, Dai, 1984, *Wales! Wales?*, Allen and Unwin, London

Smith, Dai and Williams, Gareth, 1980, *Field of praise: the official history of the Welsh rugby union 1881–1981*, University of Wales Press, Cardiff

Smith, George Adam, 1899, *The life of Henry Drummond*, Hodder and Stoughton, London

Smout, T. C., 1986, *A century of the Scottish people*, Collins, Glasgow

Stern, Fritz, 1960, *Varieties of cultural pessimism: a study in the German ideology*, Knopf, New York

Stother's Glasgow, Lanarkshire and Renfrewshire Xmas and new-year annual, 1911–1912, n. p.

Sugden, John and Bairner, Alan, 1993, 'National identity, community relations and the sporting life in Northern Ireland' in Allison, L. (ed.), *The changing politics of sport*, Manchester University Press, Manchester, pp.171–206

Tomlinson, Alan, 1984, 'De Coubertin and the Modern Olympics' in Tomlinson, A. and Whannel, (eds), *Five-ring circus: money, power and politics at the Olympic Games*, Pluto, London, pp.84–97

Veblen, T., 1899, *The theory of the leisure class*, Macmillan, New York

Weber, Eugen, 1991, 'Pierre de Coubertin and the Introduction of Organised Sport' in *My France*, Belknap, Harvard, pp.207–12

Williams, Gareth, 1991, *1905 and all that*, Gomer Press, Llandyssul

Young, Douglas, 1971, *Scotland*, Cassell, London

Young, Percy, F., 1968, *A history of British football*, Stanley Paul, London

5

THE KING OVER THE BORDER:
DENIS LAW AND SCOTTISH FOOTBALL

Richard Holt

'The First Twenty Million Pound Footballer?' runs another transfer rumour, this time concerning the young Dutch star Dennis Bergkamp. Why 'Dennis' for a Dutchman? 'Why don't we call him after Denis Law? his father, an Amsterdam electrician and 1960s football fan, had suggested. 'How good is Bergkamp?' Bobby Robson was asked. 'He's like Law, Greaves or Maradona' came the answer (*Independent on Sunday*, 22 November 1992). Denis Law turned 50 a couple of years ago and is alive and well in football legend. If heroes are more than stars, if being a hero requires a player to outlive his own time and to embody something greater than himself, then Denis Law was, and is, a hero, arguably a key heroic figure in the recent Scottish past. But what is his place in the mythology of Scottish sport?

So much of the serious study of sport in recent years has been about the economic, social or political context of events that the performance itself has been almost overlooked. Historians fight shy of the drama of sport, its emotional extremities; dismissive of most journalistic prose, understandably anxious not merely to describe or celebrate but to analyse and explain, rightly aware of the danger of hagiography, the social history of sport has steered away from the great moments and the great men. This may have been sensible, even necessary, at first, but it is a pity to continue to neglect what most sports fans consider so important. There is a particular problem with football. If Steve Bloomer or Dixie Dean had been a batsman there would be no shortage of the kind of good writing about them that there is for Hobbs or Hutton. Football has been the dominant sport in Scotland and its great players are folk heroes. But their wider significance remains unclear.

By the same token serious social cum stylistic analysis of a performer has been rare in sporting journalism which has avoided such comment as too divisive, too intellectual, too pretentious. 'Cultural analysis' has been left too much to the Left Bank, which at its worst airily dismisses the need for evidence, experience and even clarity of expression. Stranded between impenetrable jargon on the one hand and instant gossipy, ghosted biography on the other, good writing about football has been all too rare; recently, however, Eamon Dunphy has shown how a former player can draw on a profound knowledge of the game to write well about it and Dave Hill's study of John Barnes 'stakes out radical sensibilities, forcing you to confront the irrational, elemental forces'; people behave at football matches in ways they don't behave elsewhere; they express feelings of identity and hostility more fiercely and openly – in Barnes' case this exposed the residual racism beneath the cosy image of 'working class culture'; (*New Statesman*, 17 November 1989). In Scotland in the 1960s these 'radical sensibilities', this public display of extremes of sentiment, took the form of the vaunting of national feeling by the 'Tartan Army'. During a decade when for the first time a mass political movement based on Scottishness came to the fore, it was still 'The King' and the princes of football who shaped the debate over what a Scotsman really was or ought to be.

What follows is an attempt to do for a Scottish football hero what, for example, Tony Mason has done for Stanley Matthews and the idea of Englishness (Mason, 1990); to build on the work of Moorhouse and Murray to discover something of what was distinctive about Scottish football (Moorhouse, 1987; Murray, 1984); to look at how the increasingly strident press of the 1960s treated football and nationalism, and to do this through their treatment of Denis Law, 'The King' of Old Trafford and, intermittently, of Scotland too; I want to focus on the marked ambivalence of the press towards the legend they helped to create and the seemingly contradictory attitudes of Scots to one of their most gifted sons. What was there about the style of a certain player that had special meaning for the public or a certain moment? Can this illuminate shifting notions of national identity? If we accept the concept that nations are in some sense 'imagined communities' where people who really know little of each other come to believe they are profoundly alike, the way these identities are disseminated in print becomes very important (Schlesinger, 1987, pp.247–49); and the printed media in Law's case was especially important as he only occasionally played in Scotland and television restrictions on English games limited his exposure on the screen. The Scottish press helped to create a myth of Denis Law; they made him an 'emblematic figure' in the national male community; and an image can take on a life of its own.

That something of this kind happened to Denis Law in Scotland in the 1960s is the theme of this chapter. Through discussing him, the Scots obliquely discussed themselves and their muddled historical relationship to England; the English 'Other', the distorting mirror, through which they defined themselves. In the course of a Scottish career, which lasted from 1958 until 1974, Denis Law broke both the record for the number of international appearances and the number of goals scored at international level for Scotland. He was the youngest player to represent Scotland for 60 years; he broke records for transfer fees, and could have broken his neck in a spectacular car accident in Italy at 22; he argued with officials and could lash out at other players; he was blond and had 'style' – not the full 'El Beatle' pop star glamour that came to Best – but a toned down late 1950s rebelliousness; coming to prominence just as the maximum wage was abolished, he had money too; this Scot was a star even the English respected, especially youngsters; 'Denis Law was the first player I saw who made me almost afraid with anticipation. He came back from Italy (in 1962) with boots cut so low that the white foot of his all red socks shone off his feet' (Williams 1990, p.64). He played in a forward line with Best and Charlton that would have satisfied even the most extravagant dreams of a Berlusconi; Busby's last great Manchester United side who won the League, the FA Cup and the European Cup with a panache that made them world famous, even in Scotland.

For Denis Law Scottishness was crucial, never forgotten or minimised, absolutely central to his sense of himself; he was a model patriot who was always fiercely proud of playing for Scotland. He was typical of many Scots in the way he defined his sense of national identity. He did not dwell on distinctiveness of dress or language, religion or politics. For him anti-Englishness at a crude cultural level, the fierce commitment to beat England at football, was the proof of true Scottishness. Law was fairly typical in his ability to be anti-English from time to time without questioning the wider validity of the Union. Indeed the Union was accepted; it was a long-standing reality; it was practical, making it easy to work in England and to gain financially from the larger and richer neighbour whose dominance could be ritually challenged on the field of play but never seriously threatened in the real world (Harvie, 1977; Nairn, 1981).

This 'subcultural nationalism' was quite separate from the mainstream of political nationalism in Scotland – most football fans were Labour voters like the majority of the urban working class in Scotland. It is nonetheless significant that the 1960s also saw the emergence of a new style of nationalist politics in Scotland. For this majority of the urban working class, although they voted Labour, were sympathetic to greater Scottish control over their own affairs. Although political pressures did not touch Scottish football directly, which fed a cultural nationalism above and beyond party political loyalty, the changing national atmosphere may have been important, if unrecognised, for football. The reality of a new, more student, kind of nationalism was a feature of the public response to Denis Law both as an emblem of Scottish pride and a source of national exasperation. For it is the emphatic love/hate response to him, the sixth child of an Aberdeen trawlerman, which is especially interesting. Law was no common uncomplicated hero, universally admired by his public. Why was this?

A great deal of cultural conflict and confusion lay beneath the surface of what appeared to be the simple business of representing Scotland, especially in the annual match against England. For Denis Law as for the rest of the Scottish footballing public this was the supreme event of the year. Some might say that World Cup football was undermining the importance of the England-Scotland fixture by the 1960s. But *The Scotsman* would have nothing of this vapid internationalism. The annual match at Hampden Park or at Wembley, it declared, 'is the most serious game of football played in Britain each year and when it ceases to be just that, then the game in these islands is really finished' (*Scotsman*, 11 April 1964). Scots took the fixture so seriously that ever since the 1920s tens of thousands – the 'Tartan Army' – would save in special 'Wembley Clubs' in order to travel four hundred miles for a weekend in London (Moorhouse, 1989, p.87). He described England's 9–3 victory of 1961 as 'the blackest day of my life' in his first autobiography published in 1964 (Law, 1965, p.94); but later 'the blackest day' became the afternoon England won the World Cup – the English victory that prompted the well-known story that he went off to play golf at his home near Manchester rather than watch the game, only to be assailed by jubilant English members when he got to the final green (Law, 1979, p.102). When Scotland beat England the following year at Wembley he was overjoyed to have been part of the team and scorer of a goal. This was the highlight of his professional career.

It was not just statistics and patriotic fervour that should have made Denis Law the true Scottish hero, the embodiment and representative of a people who considered themselves the founders of modern professional football; a country whose small population of five million in proportional terms supported a larger professional game than any other footballing nation; for a long time the vast crowds – 120,000 or more – at Hampden Park for the England match were unprecedented in the football world. Denis Law felt himself to be unlike the English type of international footballer, who in the 1960s was held by many Scots to be lacking in natural talent; 'Ramsay's Robots' may have won the World Cup in 1966 – at home without having to qualify as Law himself liked to say – but had destroyed football in the process by suppressing instinct and outright attack down the wings in favour of a dull, machine-like organisation (Law, 1979, pp.102–03). This was the sporting expression of the wider pity and contempt of the minority for the cultural impoverishment of the majority, which was a feature of Anglo-Scottish relations; there was no 'inferiorism' in football, the Scots genuinely thought they were better; the record between the two countries was about even; they had the Wembley Wizards of 1928; they had a tradition of brilliant forwards from Jimmy Quinn and Patsy Gallacher, Alex James, Hughie Gallacher, Alan Morton, Jimmy McGrory and Alex Jackson between the wars; in the 1950s there was the 'famous five' from Hibs, Smith, Johnstone, Reilly, Turnbull and Ormond – 'a forward line that surely had no superior in the entire life span of British football' (Pawson, 1978, p.122); then come the Scottish sides of the 1960s, which included Jim Baxter and Jimmy Johnstone who with Law made up Scotland's trio of inspirational players. They were seen by Scottish journalists and spectators as 'naturals', who passed on the torch of football genius, embodying the passion and creativity of their nation (Crampsey, 1978, pp. 56–64).

Law's talent was for sudden flashes of pure speed near goal both on the ground and in the air. Both Busby and Shankly – who with Stein made up that extraordinary trio of similarly inspirational managers, all Scottish, all from the same mining area around Belshill that produced Hughie Gallacher and Alex James as well – thought he was the best player in the penalty box they ever saw. This supreme quality moved Scottish football writers to superlatives; his combination of swiftness and sheer aggression delighted the crowds and the press; this was purveyed as part of an ancient tradition of raiding across the English border, of lightening strikes against a bigger and less mobile neighbour. Law was 'fiery' – the most frequently used adjective about him – and so were the Scots, forceful, potent, a celtic theatricality balanced by industriousness and determination; the performance could always be manipulated to suit the desired national self-image, even if the result could not. For most of the time the Scottish press were willing to forgive Denis his bouts of bad behaviour; it was his 'Scottish' nature, and in any case Scots had the right to fight back against the superior economic power of English football as best they could. Even a respectable Edinburgh-based middle class newspaper, commenting on Law's performance in Scotland's 1–0 victory over England in 1964, was prepared to condone some of his fouling for 'in this instance one remembered that it was not quite sporting to set spokes in Bannockburn field' (*Scotsman*, 13 April 1964). For in Scotland the language of football was steeped in references to medieval battles with the English. After Scotland's victory over England in 1967, *The Scotsman* again remarked 'Now we know how William Wallace felt after his success at Stirling?' (*Scotsman*, 17 April 1967). If Law was an angry player, was his not the righteous anger of the Scots who had been patronised and dominated by the English for so long?

This brings us to the paradox at the heart of this chapter. For Denis Law was *not* as popular in Scotland as his talent or his fervent Scottishness would suggest. Indeed, he was often extremely unpopular, especially in the press where he was regularly criticised both in terms of his playing skills and his attitude. Obviously, any national press can be fickle and no footballing hero ever escapes some unfair criticism; moreover his career coincided with the advent of televised football and the need for journalists to find new and more sensational human interest angles for their stories. All the same, this does not properly explain their response to 'The King' as he came to be known to the Manchester United fans. In Scotland, at least, his was a strange kind of reign. He was blamed almost every time Scotland was defeated in an important game. He was selected for special punishment by the press, who launched a series of campaigns between 1961 and 1967 to have him dropped from the Scotland team, several of them successful. He faded from the scene in the late 1960s, partly but not entirely through injury, and was then brought back in 1972–73 to help Scotland qualify for the World Cup. At the height of the criticism of Law, he was in fact at his peak, performing at the highest level for his club with 81 goals in 104 games for Manchester United in the three seasons 1962–65. He was voted European Footballer of the Year in 1964 (Green, 1978, pp.130–32).

Foreigners could hardly believe the intermittent hostility of the Scots towards arguably their greatest player. Denis really was worthy of the overused tag 'world class'; the Scots certainly had something to shout about when he was selected with Jim Baxter to play alongside Eusebio, Di Stefano, Kopa, Puskas and Gento for the Rest of the World against England for the centenary of the Football Association. Law even scored his team's only goal, but was predictably unhappy that the ageing Rest of the World side did not take the game as seriously as England, who won 2–1. Anything that meant the greater glory of England did not please Denis, despite the fact that he liked living in England and had plenty of English friends. That was, of course, a familiar, even typical, expatriate Scottish reaction.

Sometimes this endeared Law to the Scots living in Scotland; sometimes he was a victim himself of the same resentful, grudging, suspicious, 'Jack's as good as his master' mentality; this was the petty side of a Scottishness, which at its best enshrined equality, self-respect, endeavour, courage and inventiveness. When Law was dropped for a crucial World Cup qualifying match against Italy in November 1965 the Italian press literally refused to believe it; 'many of the squad of 60 Italian journalists . . . sent back a story that Law would play and that around 7.00 pm his blonde figure would bounce into Hampden'. 'This', they predicted, 'is to be the masterstroke of Stein' (*Scotsman*, 9 November 1965). The truth was more banal. Law had been dropped because he had been playing in the side which had narrowly lost to Poland the month before. He had had no particular part in the loss of two late goals – in fact the *Daily Record* had 'sighed with relief when Denis Law saved a certain goal with a hand off that any rugby three-quarter would have envied' – yet it concluded 'Law must accept much of the blame' (*Daily Record*, 14–15 November 1965). Having announced on 29 May 1965 that 'the accent on choosing teams will from now on be on . . . CLASS', the *Daily Record* abandoned 'the idea that a corps d'elite should carry the banner' and demanded on 15 October in capital letters that 'LAW MUST BE LEFT OUT OF THE SCOTLAND SIDE TO PLAY ITALY', adding for good measure that 'no man, no matter how famous is bigger than a Scotland team'. Like the English, Denis had to be brought down a peg or two.

After a narrow victory and a predictable round of self-congratulation, the press became increasingly worried about the return game to be played in Naples upon which the fate of Scotland's World Cup hopes would depend – a World Cup to be played in England and which offered the supremely satisfying prospect of knocking England out of the event on their own territory. There was a groundswell of opinion for the return of Denis Law. When Herrera, the coach of Inter-Milan said 'I have only one fear for Italy's chances – and that is Denis Law' even the more parochial Scots began to listen (*Daily Record*, 3 December 1965). Law's selection became the major talking point in Scottish football as the match approached and on 4 December 1965 the *Daily Record* changed its mind again. 'It would be mad to forget Denis Law' ran the headline beneath which were printed readers' letters on the issue, most of which favoured his inclusion. In the event he was injured a few days before the game. Busby took the telling precaution of inviting Scottish journalists in to inspect the damage and protect Law from press gossip that he was refusing to play because he had been dropped earlier.

None of this was really new. The love/hate syndrome whereby Law was praised to the skies only to be ferociously torn from his pedestal, and later recalled before being dropped again was established almost from the beginning of his international career. For example, there had been a particularly shrill demand for his scalp after the infamous 9–3 defeat at the hands of England in 1961, for which the defence and the unfortunate replacement goalkeeper surely ought to take most of the blame. But it was not as simple as that; there was another explanation. 'The records of post-war football show that in most cases the men who have let us down are the Anglos. I SUGGEST WE THROW THEM OVERBOARD AND DEPEND ON ENTIRELY HOME BASED PLAYERS. LET US STAND OR FALL BY AN ALL-TARTAN COLLECTION'; as a result of playing in the English League

'Denis Law's attitude has changed. I SUGGEST THE SELECTORS FOR-
GET ALL ABOUT HIM' the article concluded (*Daily Record*, 18 April
1961). Small wonder Law remarked a few years later that 'I sit at home on a
Sunday morning looking at the newspapers, wondering which one will call for
my head and which will demand my exclusion from all Scottish teams' (Law,
1965, p.118).

The reason Law was blamed so often only to be desperately recalled to the
side after a couple of matches in the end had less to do with the kind of
football he played and more to do with where he played it. For Law left
Scotland at fifteen to play for Huddersfield, progressing to Manchester City in
1960 and then to Torino in 1961 and back to Manchester United in 1962.
There he stayed until 1973 – his glory years – moving briefly back to
Manchester City before retiring the following year. In other words, he never
played club football at any time in Scotland. He only played 28 internationals
in Scotland and the SFA's television restrictions meant that he was not even
seen on the screen all that much. Although born and brought up in Aberdeen,
he settled down happily and permanently in Manchester. This was his fatal
flaw. More than any other player Law paid the price for his ambition to earn
high wages and play top club football in England. There was speculation in
the press about how much he was being paid and probably resentment among
other players, who in Scotland were still on what would have been Second
Division wages in England. No wonder there were complaints about lack of
team spirit. Keeping the 'Anglos' out may have had a certain logic from that
point of view, if from no other.

Scotland's ambivalence to Law's success reflected a wider difficulty in
coming to terms with the realities of her own economic dependence on
transfers to the English league (Moorhouse, 1990, pp.182–83). The constant
departure of many of the best players from Scotland to England made
Scottish football feel second class no matter how much it protested to the
contrary and fed the endless debate about whether Scottish professional
football was of equivalent standard to the Football League. This in turn may
have brought to the surface a deeper sense of grievance and concern about
the extent of migration from Scotland, especially of the more talented Scots.
The awakening of Scottish nationalism in the 1960s may have focussed
attention more sharply on the problem of expatriate players, although expatriate stars had never been without some problems at home. The record for
the number of 'Anglos' playing in a Scottish national side goes back to the
1906 England-Scotland game when there were nine and there were a good
few Anglos among the Wembley Wizards of 1928. In other words, it was not
so much the numbers but the extent of the public debate about the 'Anglos'
which seemed to be new in the 1960s.

The sin of being an 'Anglo' was forgiven when the team was doing well.
When the team was winning the Scottish press and public revelled in 'Denis
the Menace', 'Law and Disorder', the 'fiery one' who could turn a game
instinctively in a couple of seconds near goal. These it was claimed were the
true Scottish qualities that commanded respect in England and elsewhere.
After all, 'who is more patriotic than the exile', especially when high earnings
in England make the match fee a paltry sum in comparison with an 'enthusi-

asm which reaches beyond monetary rewards' (*Scotsman*, 1 April 1965). But this was exceptional. For most of the time a different and less tolerant view of the 'Anglo' prevailed. When Scotland failed twice to qualify for the World Cup in 1961 and 1965, it was the selfish and undisciplined individualism of Law and the other 'Anglos' that was blamed. 'Individualism' was now a fault rather than a Scottish virtue bred by centuries of self-reliance and struggle with the English. The trouble was that these self-important, overpaid expatriates would not play for the 'jersey'; they were not 'triers', they had been corrupted by big money and the eulogies of English football writers. 'IF ONLY THEY COULD FORGET THEIR SUPERIORITY COMPLEX', complained Scotland's most popular daily paper in 1965 after Scotland had only managed a draw with an England side reduced to nine men; 'Why can't they stop being prima donnas? Why can't they play the game naturally? Why can't they stop acting all the time? (*Daily Record*, 12 April 1965).

When Scotland won an important match with 'Anglos' in the side these arguments were turned on their head. Take, for example, the reporting of the famous victory of 1967 against England's World Cup winning team. The press revelled in the individual genius of Jim Baxter and Denis Law. What had earlier been unprincipled selfishness suddenly became a supreme display of the native genius of the Scottish footballer. *The Sunday Post* was only too willing to excuse Law and Baxter, both playing in the English League, for being 'over-cocky at times' as they rubbed salt into the wound of the English defeat (16 April 1967). 'I shall cherish for a long time the memory of Baxter slowing the game up almost to walking pace, insolently juggling the ball with instep, forehead and knees, while Stiles, no more than a couple of yards away, bobbed up and down unsure whether to make his challenge at ground or head level', enthused the football correspondent of *The Glasgow Herald*, who also smiled benignly on 'the impertinent genius of Law' (17 April 1967). Scotland had beaten the World Champions at home; they were, by celtic logic, the 'Unofficial World Champions'.

So the pattern was established. When the national side did well the 'Anglos' escaped criticism and the individualistic, impudent style of star Scottish players was openly celebrated. But when the team failed, scapegoats had to be found. At the heart of the problem was the fact that football had become too culturally important to the Scots; lacking other popular national institutions – the Law, the Church of Scotland, and the Civil Service could hardly be called popular – football, especially the Scotland side, just had to bear too much of the weight of national pride. Burns and whisky were not enough. To admit that defeat was not the fault of the 'Anglos' but the logical result of a small nation trying to compete on equal terms with much larger ones who had a bigger pool of top class players flew in the face of the footballing myth that sustained the Scots : namely that great players were born not made and more of them were born in Scotland than anywhere else. When Tommy Docherty previewed the England-Scotland game in 1965 he cheerfully insisted that Scotland would win because of her natural class. 'We have five players in our team who are world class or touching world class', he enthused. 'They are Billy McNeill, Willie Henderson, Davy Wilson, Eddie McCreadie and Denis Law. England have NOBODY in their team who reaches that rating' (*Daily*

Record, 7 April 1965). The England team he was referring to included Bobby Charlton, Bobby Moore, Jimmy Greaves and Gordon Banks. All this was said and done with absolute seriousness. Self-deception was taken to be one of England's characteristics. As John Hughes wrote in the *Daily Record* in the run-up to England's 1966 World Cup campaign, 'it amazes me how the English keep kidding themselves' (11 December 1965).

Scotland's confused blend of Calvinistic and celtic elements made up in vehemence what it lacked in coherence. Urban Scotland did not know if it was a nation of 'triers', distinguished by the work ethic as embodied in the massive solidarity of a George Young, Rangers and Scotland captain in the 1950s and an idol of the young Denis Law; or were the Scots really 'celts', brilliant individualists like the Glasgow Celtic of Stein who won the European Cup and preferred to think of themselves as putting style above safety? When Scotland won with one style it continued until it was beaten, and then turned back to the other. Scotland was not unique in this; there was, for example, a similar debate over the 'national style' in Argentina; and football may always more or less oscillate between these poles; what is distinctive about Scotland is the volatility of such swings and the particular kinds of meaning attached to particular players or techniques. Perhaps this oscillation from effort to inspiration and back again represents a way of trying to define different kinds of Scottishness, which has been overlooked by intellectuals like Nairn for whom 'a London pub on international night was intolerably vulgar . . . unbearable, crass, mindless philistinism' (Nairn, 1981, p.162): yet the dismissal of so large a part of Scottish popular male culture as merely 'tartanry' or 'an extraordinary blatant super-patriotism . . . a kind of dream nationalism' means that significant divisions within working class culture and meanings attached to popular heroes do not come to light (Beveridge and Turnbull, 1989, pp.58–60).

The heart has its own logic and it is that pattern of national feeling which an analysis of a star player's public reception can reveal. In this case it is the plainly contradictory nature of the different accounts of what Scotland's strengths are, or should be, which is interesting. Some journalists, and no doubt many others, felt no need to be consistent at all. 'WE NEED MEN WHO PUT GUTS BEFORE GENIUS' wrote Ken Gallacher in the *Daily Record* on 2 April 1966. On the facing page of the same issue Hugh Taylor stated the alternative creed. 'I believe in FREEDOM for the individual. I believe the FLASH OF GENIUS is more likely to win a match than any plan'. These views were not, however, presented as alternatives; there was little debate about opposing strategies between two camps. Rather they were simply two sides of the same national coin. Having nailed his colours to the mast by backing Scotland's 'instinctive stylists versus Ramsay's robots' on the eve of the 1966 England-Scotland game, Taylor underwent a Pauline conversion after the result. 'The way ahead for Prentice and Scotland is clear', he insisted on the Monday following the 4–3 defeat, 'THERE MUST BE A METHOD' (*Daily Record*, 4 April 1966).

This confusion about how Scotland ought to play led to a distortion of Law's actual qualities as a player. He was not really the classic kind of Scottish individualist, the 'tanner' ball player, like Jimmy Johnstone, who never beat a man once when he could do it twice. Law even criticised Baxter for 'knocking the ball about instead of hammering home our advantage' at Wembley in 1967 after his notorious ball-juggling antics during the game (Law, 1979, p.111); it is all very well for Cairns Craig and literary nationalists to revel in Baxter's marvellous eccentricity – 'can you see the slightly hen-toed saunter, the florid gallus expression . . . his sense of theatre, his exact awareness of how we Scots felt about winning and the English' – but this did not impress Denis, for whom the margin of victory was more important than the manner of it (Jenkins, 1983, p.3). On his own admission his desperation to win partly came from a longing to go back to Old Trafford and gloat over Charlton, Stiles and the other England players at Manchester United, still basking in their World Cup glory. Substance, another goal at least, was more important than style when the stakes were so high. England, after all, only lost 3–2. Unlike Baxter, a Protestant but perhaps the most truly 'celtic' hero – this adjective goes beyond the sectarian division though it is easily confused with it – Law did not seem to relish danger for its own sake. Denis's Scottish cheek did not extend to taking the chances 'Slim Jim' was prepared to take and perhaps in the end Baxter, the more beautiful but less effective player, was closer to Scottish hearts; not only had he played his best football in Scotland but, unlike Law, he followed 'the primrose path' to the pub as a true poet of the Scottish game. He seemed closer to the long line of wayward football geniuses than Denis Law, who resembled them more in his quick temper than in his style of playing or style of life.

If Law was in reality less 'celtic' than he was made out to be, the Scottish press always refused to see him in anything other than a sensational light. Take the case of the 1965 England-Scotland match; this was the game where England managed a 2–2 draw despite being reduced to nine men at the end, and where Law became Scotland's highest international goal scorer at the age of 25. Congratulations were exceedingly thin on the ground; as the Scottish press smarted under the taunts of the English, Law was predictably singled out for special criticism. Denis was to blame, but for surprisingly different reasons depending on the paper concerned. For *The Scotsman* Law seemed 'strangely short of energy, and after a burst would disappear for a rest' whilst *The Daily Record* (12 April 1965) complained that 'I FEEL HE WANTS TO BE A NEW DI STEFANO, WANTS MAY BE TO DO TOO MUCH, TO CONTROL DEFENCE AS WELL AS ATTACK'. The point here is not whether or not the team or Law had a particularly good game; it seems they were disorganised and perhaps Law untypically drifted between two roles – as the *Glasgow Herald* remarked 'there he was in the number ten jersey taking throw-ins in the right half position'. The point is that his real achievements were overlooked because the result was seen as disappointing; expectations were too high and prejudices too strong. Yet Scotland had drawn at Wembley against a very good side – and as all reasonable football people ought to know a depleted squad can play exceptionally well, especially defensively.

But the Scottish press would have none of it. It was not amenable to reason. This was a disaster; it had exposed Scotland to the worst fear of all – the scorn of the English; better to be heroically defeated than to scramble a messy draw. The fact that the European Footballer of the Year had broken

Hughie Gallacher's 30 year record of goals for Scotland at 25 scoring almost a goal a game was glossed over. Had the match been won by a late goal, the story would no doubt have been completely different. The nine man opposition would probably have faded from the picture; instead of being attacked for trying to be Di Stefano, he might have been praised for the scope of his ambition. As Law commented much later, 'in the mid-sixties the Scottish press were violently anti-Anglo. Any non-resident Scot had to be twice as good as a player playing in Scotland to win their approval . . . the knives were out in a big way' (Law, 1979, p.96).

Law's own later version of the 1965 England-Scotland game inadvertently gives an entirely different – and more convincing – account of the match. Reflecting on his team-mates at Manchester United, Denis recalled how he and Nobby Stiles, with whom he was 'quite good friends', lined up in the tunnel just before the kick-off. 'But "Happy", as we nicknamed him at Old Trafford, apparently didn't realise the significance of the event' and committed what to the Scots was the unpardonable sin of pretending it was just another game, even calling out 'Hi Denis, good luck – a typically patronising English ploy, downgrading the importance of the fixture and of Scotland too. So Denis played the tough, taciturn Scot. 'Instead of replying, I just looked through him, then turned away. He must have wondered what the hell was going on. It turned out to be the worst thing I could have done, because Happy spent the rest of the afternoon kicking me from one end of Wembley to the other' (Law, 1983, p.53). Denis's fate in the spring of 1965 was the same that awaited Eusebio in the World Cup the following year. As Eamon Dunphy has remarked, 'the public caricature of "Nobby the Destroyer" was an outrageous underestimation of his true talent . . . given a man-marking job to do rather than physical, and concentration was the key. Break his spirit, not his leg'. Busby used him as Ramsay did, to do a job on the key opposition player and for a change 'The King' himself was the victim (Dunphy, 1991, p.305).

This at least makes some sense of the confused and contradictory press accounts none of which gave much credit to Stiles, who seemed a clumsy English buffoon with a vicious streak. To the *Scotsman* Law simply 'played the most silly game tactically that one could imagine' and the *Glasgow Herald's* verdict of the same date was that 'Law's part in the proceedings passed all understanding' (12 April 1965). In fact, it passed only the understanding of those who could not see how he was trying to get away from his marker and would not give any credit to the 'auld enemy'. The Scots would not acknowledge that Nobby had done to Denis what an eighteen year old Law in only his second international for Scotland had done to Danny Blanchflower in 1958 – a tough marking job on a great player that prompted John Rafferty in *The Observer* to remark that 'it does seem all wrong that a youngster of no more than school age should be roughing up a world celebrity and football master'; 'If that is him at eighteen', remarked Blanchflower, 'I wouldn't like to play against him at twenty-four' (Hamilton, 1992, p.132). He wasn't called 'Denis the Menace' just for his goalscoring.

The Stiles episode is revealing not just for the way Scottishness got in the way of good judgement, or for the compulsive scapegoating of the 'Anglos'. It says a good bit about Denis himself and the way he acted up to being a Scottish hero. 'My heart pounds when I pull over my shoulders the dark blue jersey of Scotland. This is the proudest moment of all, the prelude to 90 minutes which represents more than a game of football. It is an expression of one's deepest loyalties and convictions, a giving of oneself wholly to the task of proving Scotland's everlasting greatness' (Law, 1963, p.23). Even allowing for the stilted style of the 'ghost' writer – who also credited the young Aberdonian with being deeply moved at playing before the Queen and ashamed of having committed a foul (on Bobby Robson) right in front of her – the patriotic sentiments seem authentic enough. International football heightened the dramatic instincts that permeated his ordinary play, 'the hunched shoulders, sleeves pulled down his hands as he trotted toward the action' that precede the furious attacking bursts which had the crowd chanting his name more than any other – 'to him their blood warmed', Mancunians or Scots 'he embodied the dream of the heroic in all of them'; 'I've always been two different people on the park and off it. Its like looking at a stranger and I can hardly bear to watch', he told Hugh McIlvanney. 'It seems such an extravagant way to go on. And yet when I'm out there it's the most natural thing in the world' (Pawson, 1978, p.119).

Law had an image to keep up, the tough Scot, the 'No Surrender' attitude of the Rangers team that he had idolised as a boy whilst, as an Aberdonian, happily avoiding the narrow sectarianism that went with it. Law was a Protestant but not in the activist Old Firm sense; he was managed by a Scottish Catholic and his best friend, Pat Crerand, was a catholic from Celtic. Despite playing all his life in England, he lived in a strongly Scottish environment. He had been 'spotted' as a scrawny lad with a squint by a neighbour whose brother happened to be the manager of Huddersfield; his next manager at Huddersfield was Bill Shankly. Law embodied the English stereotype of the great Scottish player, edgy, hungry, clever and unpredictable; like many performers what was really him and what was a persona was never quite clear; 'I occasionally act it up a bit on the field', he admitted with nice English understatement (Law, 1965, p.31).

Off the field Law had not yet developed into the jocular, much-loved, media-friendly pundit of today. 'In the main his private persona is very private indeed', remarked McIlvanney (Pawson, 1978, p.119); Dunphy speaks of his personality during his playing years as 'privately taciturn, self-possessed, watchful . . . an Aberdonian, canny, unlike Crerand the genial Glaswegian, or Busby off-duty who enjoyed the gregarious company of the Cromford Club on a Saturday night . . . Even in the dressing room he left the talking to others. He was his own man, popular but of no faction' (Dunphy, 1981, p.302). There were no antics off the field to match the ones on it. He married in his early twenties. Diane was a solicitor's secretary from Aberdeen whom he met after his flight from Torino in 1962. They were a quiet, nice, respectably married couple, raising five children. Here were two sides of the Scottish male, especially of the East coast sort – the divide that tends to get forgotten in the overwhelmingly Glaswegian ethos of Scottish football; and even in the east of Scotland, Aberdeen was a place apart, with its own dialect, rigour and sense of isolation. There was Law the serious, private, sensible man, the responsible parent who would never drink or gamble too much, not a creature of self-conscious modesty like English heroes such as Charlton or Matthews, or a Hobbs or Hutton – 'cricket's a game I've never seen' he said in a telling aside – but a man of few words, who knows his worth and will bow to no one (Law, 1963, p.90). This side could, however, quickly turn into the other; the street fighter to whom nothing was given; football was a jungle and you had to have sharp elbows in the penalty box and outside it. Here was a man who was quick to feel an insult or an injury and could dish out both without compunction; the struggle for respect and success was a hard one – Law had watched his father and mother work their whole lives just to keep food on the table – 'meat was a luxury my family rarely saw. Our meals consisted of soup and pudding' (Law, 1979, p.12).

It is easy to forget the real poverty that was the lot of many people who grew up just before Britain became an 'affluent society'; there were few Christmas or birthday presents, not even any decent shoes, let alone proper football boots – he got his first pair just two years before he turned professional; this was Christmas 1953; his mother broke the father's rule against credit to buy the boots, which were duly hidden when Dad came back from fishing. He practised in the back lanes with old balls or with a ball of wool strung up from the clothes pulley in the kitchen on winter evenings (Law, 1979, pp.14–16). Law began his paying career just as one epoch ended and he became inextricably associated with the new age. Within a couple of years he had been transferred for £55,000 from Huddersfield to Manchester City, then for a record fee for a British player to an Italian club of £110,000, and then back again to Manchester United for £115,000 – another record. He was suddenly showered with money; Italy showed top players what they were worth and the abolition of the maximum wage opened the way for the best players to earn what seemed big salaries. But Law, the 'canny' Scot – money was another way he slotted into the stereotype – realised Manchester United were still paying way below what the top players could earn elsewhere. Scottish realism and toughness showed when he tried to get Busby to increase his wages – Best and Charlton hardly bothered. But Busby, with his reputation for managerial 'thrift' to consider, was not going down that road. He forced Law to climb down publically while privately giving him half of what he wanted, making him the highest paid United player; the details were secret – Charlton understood that no-one was to be paid more than him – but rumours of Denis's wages circulated freely and this provoked its share of jealousy north of the border.

All this was a long way from the world of post-war austerity. New wealth was combined with reserves of spiky resilience and pride – his mother, for example, he remembered had refused to ask for the free school meals they were entitled to. The fact that Denis had a bad squint in one eye was an added burden to him, making him both self-conscious and a bit of a fighter; he played schoolboy football with one eye closed; his success on the field was a way of dealing with the taunting – 'children can be cruellest people in the world' he later remarked; he became a brilliant schoolboy footballer in spite of all this; when he had the operation to cure the squint shortly after joining Huddersfield, his self-esteem got a massive boost; Law himself felt this was the turning point of his life, personally and as a player; 'After my operation I threw away my glasses and felt a different, self-confident person' (Law, 1963, p.18); suddenly he was wearing tight jeans and Italian suits, a bit of a rock and roller with a blond quiff. The sense of struggle, the aggression remained, shaping his fiery persona on the field and as he grew taller and stronger he acquired the knack of seeming to hang in the air that is a feature of the great as opposed to the merely good headers of a ball. He now had self-belief. All the effort bore fruit, even turning down a place at a grammar school in favour of a secondary modern because they had a football team – in football a working rather than a middle class background could be a positive advantage.

Busby, despite the generation gap did not have such a different early life, and seems only occasionally to have criticised Denis; privately his antics were tolerated; as Matt's respected wife Jean remarked, 'many, many marvellous players have worn the Manchester United shirt but there can only ever be one Denis' (Pawson, 1978, p.119). In his brief period as Scotland manager when the Blanchflower incident occurred and for longer spells with Manchester United when Law had a 28 day suspension in 1963 for kicking an opponent, another 28 days in 1964 and six weeks in 1967, Busby quietly remonstrated but that was all. 'Try to change him, to tone him down, and he'll be ruined as a player' as John Rafferty had presciently remarked after watching him hustle and kick Blanchflower out of the game in 1958 (Hamilton, 1992, p.132). Busby had kept faith with him then and later. It was this intuitive understanding, the shared memories perhaps of hard playground 'fitba', the 'human' touch – not too indulgent not too censorious – that worked between Busby and Law.

It was the breakdown of this trust when Tommy Docherty took over and broke a private agreement to let him retire with dignity after a testimonial that distressed him – high level failure, blasted across the headlines, is peculiarly hard for great players. He had struggled with injury since the late 1960s and knew he could not go on at the top level for much longer despite appearing for Scotland seven times in 1972; but for Docherty, a fellow Scot, a former Scotland team-mate who he had recommended for the United managership, publicly to put him on a free transfer – the news broke as he was watching the Saturday lunchtime football programme in an Aberdeen pub with a few pals – was the hardest moment in a long career. Sensational to the last, he went across to Manchester City and scored the infamous backheel goal in the last game of the season which put United into the Second Division. But he was visibly unhappy to have done so – like Charlton he was really always a 'one team' man – and never played another League match. Happily, he made a comeback for Scotland in their World Cup qualifying run in 1973, playing in the match against Zaire in the World Cup itself, though not being picked for the crucial match against Brazil where Scotland failed to score. As with Best, World Cup success was the one major disappointment. Perhaps this was partly why Charlton and Law, while respecting each other, were never close. Bobby was the quintessential understated English sporting hero who had the good fortune to win the ultimate prize; Denis was the Scottish counterpart with the opposed temperament who missed the chance to show his greatness on the world stage.

There is clearly a risk in reading too much into the acts, utterances and images of one individual, however 'emblematic'. Yet Law's career does seem to offer a peculiarly good vantage point from which to observe the complexities of Scottishness. If, like Nairn for all his brilliance, you choose to ignore football a whole dimension of the Scottish male community is closed off; for football has been a singular passion of Scotsmen give or take parts of the Borders, the Highlands and the former pupils of private schools mostly around Edinburgh. Of course, the discussion here has been based upon press responses to a famous player that few had seen in the flesh. What most fans really thought of Denis we just don't know. All we know is something of what the press wanted them to think and even here the sample is far from complete. We know that Law's career coincided with a period when television began to pose a serious threat to sporting journalism and the writers accelerated the process of 'star-making and breaking', which sells copies and has now reached such extravagant proportions (Holt, 1989, pp.306–26). This shift in the approach to writing about sport, and about football in particular, was universal and coincided with the 'youth revolution' of the 1950s and 1960s when young people suddenly had some money in their pockets and a range of consumer industries emerged to clothe and amuse them.

Such forces found different forms of expression depending on specific historical circumstances; a new nationalism appeared in Scotland at this time but for the most part national identity continued to be expressed non-politically through figures in entertainment or sport, like Denis Law, fresh from Italy, the kind of Scot who was sufficiently traditional to be recognisable and strikingly new enough to make an impact; 'he was describing Denis Law but it could have been his era' wrote Stuart Cosgrove of an early profile of Law by John Rafferty, part 'old pro', part the new 1960s man 'expensive, aggressive, big-headed, eccentric, moody and petulant' until marriage in that same year soon turned him towards semi-detached decency like Matt Busby and put an end to the exuberant posturing, rebelliousness of his Italian adventure except when he was on the field (Cosgrove, 1991, p.24).

What apart from his conventional, even in later years jokey, anti-Englishness made him a 'true Scot' in terms of the press? Perhaps it was that at his best he briefly united the two sides of Scottishness that were usually opposed to one another. Of those who saw Law and wrote about him only Hugh MacIlvanney really seemed to grasp his wider importance for Scotland: 'Denis Law may be regarded, after all, as a representative rather than a violator of the tradition. He was a paradox, a player whose style of goal-scoring was a unique blend of economy and theatricality . . . he had a compelling sense of his singularity, a conviction of his own irrepressibility that seemed to radiate from his lean, electric presence. In him Scottish football, for once, resolved its central dilemma, satisfying the national hunger for panache while at the same time meeting the practical demands of the game' (Pawson, 1978, p.119).

NOTE

This chapter is a revised and expanded version of a paper first presented at the colloquium on Sport, Culture and Nationalism at the European University Institute, Florence, in October 1989, and later at the 'Colloque sur Sport et Anthropologie' at the University of Paris (Sorbonne) in 1991; however, not surprisingly, the most informed discussion took place within Scotland at the Arts Seminar at the University of Stirling which brought literary as well as historical and media specialists together, and I must particularly thank Rory Watson, Alisdair Macrae, Philip Schlesinger, Mike Hopkinson and Ian Gow for their comments. Finally, I am indebted to Bert Moorhouse for his criticisms of the first draft and for his own work in this area. Bill Murray's *The Old Firm* first got me interested in football and Scottish cultural identity and I am grateful to him for it. Law has proved almost as prolific – and provocative – in the seminar room as he was on the pitch. 'The Gods don't answer back' someone said of a baseball star and at the time of writing so it has proved with Denis Law. Getting hold of those on the celebrity circuit is not so easy as the BBC and public figures naturally protect their privacy. So this chapter was written without the advantage of an interview or comments from Law himself, which is a pity. However lest someone should object that this is Hamlet without the Prince it should be remembered that my theme was the Scottish reaction to Law, not Law's reaction to Scotland or his view of their image of him. My chief press sources were the relevant match reports of *The Scotsman*, *Glasgow Herald*, *Daily Record* and *The Sunday Post* as cited directly in the text; finally, Patrick Barclay and Hugh MacIlvanney of *The Observer* shared some thoughts on Scottish football with me at different times.

BIBLIOGRAPHY

Beveridge, C. and Turnbull, R., 1989, *The eclipse of Scottish culture*, Polygon, Edinburgh
Cosgrove, Stuart, 1991, *Hampden babylon: sex and scandal in Scottish football*, Canongate, Edinburgh
Crampsey, Bob, 1978, *The Scottish footballer*, Blackwoods, Edinburgh
Crampsey, Bob, 1990, *The Scottish football league: the first 100 years*, The Scottish Football League, Glasgow
Dunphy, Eamon, 1991, *A strange kind of glory: Sir Matt Busby and Manchester United*, Heineman, London
Green, Geoffrey, 1978, *There's only one United: the official centenary history of Manchester United (1878–1978)*, Heineman, London
Hamilton, Ian, (ed.), 1992, *The Faber book of soccer*, Faber, London
Hanham, H., J., 1969, *Scotland and Nationalism*, Cambridge University Press, MA
Harvie, C., 1977, *Scotland and nationalism*, George Allen and Unwin, London
Hayter, Reg, (ed.), 1970, *Soccer stars of today*, Pelham, London
Hill, Dave, 1989, '*Out of his skin: the John Barnes phenomenon*, Faber, London
Holt, Richard, 1989, *Sport and the British: a modern history*, Oxford University Press, Oxford
Jenkins, R., 1983, (ed.), with an introduction by Cairns Craig, *The thistle and the grail*, Paul Harris, Edinburgh

Lamming, D., 1980, *A Scottish internationalist's who's who*, Edinburgh

Law, Denis (with K. Wheeler), 1963, *Living for kicks*, Stanley Paul, London

Law, Denis, 1965, *Denis Law's book of soccer*, Pelham, London

Law, Denis, (with R. Gubba), 1979, *Denis Law: an autobiography*, Futura, London

Law, Denis, 1983, *Denis Law's soccer special*, Willow Books-Collins, London

Mason, Tony, 1990, 'Stanley Matthews' in Richard Holt, (ed.), *Sport and the working class in Britain*, Manchester University Press, Manchester, pp.159–78

Matthews, Tony, 1985, *Manchester United: who's who 1945–1985*, Breedon, Derby

Moorhouse, H. F., 1987, Scotland against England: Football and Popular Culture, *International Journal of the History of Sport*, 3 (2), pp.189–202

Moorhouse, H. F., 1989, 'We're off to Wembley!' The History of a Scottish event and the sociology of football hooliganism', in McCrone, D., Kendrick, F. and Straw, *The making of modern Scotland: nation, culture and social change*, Edinburgh University Press, Edinburgh, pp.207–27

Moorhouse, H. F., 1990, Shooting Stars: Footballers and working class culture in twentieth century Scotland, in R. Holt (ed.), *Sport and the working class in modern Britain*, Manchester University Press, Manchester, pp.201–32

Murray, Bill, 1984, *The old firm: sectarianism and sport in modern Scotland*, John Donald, Edinburgh

Nairn, Tom, 1981, *The Break-up of Britain*, Verso, London

Pawson, Tony, 1978, *The goalscorers: from Bloomer to Keegan*, Cassell, London

Schlesinger, P., 1987, On national identity: some conceptions and misconceptions criticised, *Social science information*, 26 (2), pp.219–64

Webb, K., 1978, *The growth of nationalism in Scotland*, Penguin Books, Glasgow

Williams, J., 1990, 'Albert Stubbins knew my father', *Offside*, WSC Publications

Williams, J. and Wagg, S., 1991, *British football and social change: getting into Europe*, Leicester University Press, Leicester

6

GOLF AND THE MAKING OF MYTHS

John Lowerson

In early 1992 a Scottish Tourist Board advertisement included a Victorian picture of Mary Queen of Scots' playing golf shortly after the murder of her husband, Lord Darnley (*The Times*, 28 March 1992). Once again Scotland was portrayed as 'the home' of golf. Where better to go to play? Such advertising has become a major component in the projection of a national image, an identity at least for external consumption. It is 'Scottishness' in the marketplace. In Scotland alone, if the myth is to be believed, golf can really be played – on proper courses, rich in historical association, according to rules suitably agreed, and, above all, as a 'people's game', democratic in its appeal. The country is, in hackneyed journalese, the 'Mecca of Golf', to which the really dedicated (and suitably affluent) player must make pilgrimage. This chapter will examine some components of that myth and ask to what extent is it an outside imposition or whether some elements of Scottish society have colluded in its creation.

It is worth stating here the sense in which 'myth' is being used. It is usually seen as falsehood but in most societies, especially primitive ones, myth is used to express deep truths which bond the culture together. At this level the historian's difficulty lies in attempting to disentangle the projected and received images from some of the more measurable phenomena they encapsulate.

THE ANCIENT AND NATIONAL GAME OF GOLF

In a recent exercise in demythologizing the influential golf journalist Peter Dobereiner wrote a piece called 'How Golf Invented Scotland'. In reviewing the oft-told stories of golf's antiquity he suggested that it was introduced into the country by medieval soldiers returning from European campaigns. He went on to suggest that its adoption by the Scots had been accompanied by the lauding of national and individual virtues with all the marks of 'the music-hall cliche' (Dobereiner, 1973, p.41). Victorian *genre* painting, such as that of Mary Stuart, had created an unwarranted sense that Scotland owned golf.

Dobereiner's understanding of the cultural underpinning of the nationalist claim is perceptive but his treatment of the early historical development is less persuasive. The difficulty partly lies in the dependency of writers on limited archival references to the game before the mid-eighteenth century. Late medieval royal bans on playing (to encourage archery) were followed by an embracing of the game by Stuart monarchs. For instance Charles I was said to have been playing on the Leith links in 1641 when the news of Irish insurrection reached him (Sitwell and Bamford, 1984, p.166). According to myth Charles pocketed the dispatch and then holed the putt. He certainly played on regardless and there is an implication that this was an omen of his downfall, in sharp contrast with the English assumption that Drake's playing bowls in the face of the Spanish Armada was a demonstration of national phlegmatism. One might speculate as to why so much weight has been put, in Scottish culture, on the stories of failure.

Students played in late medieval St Andrews and the involvement of the Montrose family is well-attested. Most of these stories owe their currency to one key volume on the game's history. In 1875 Robert Clark, an Edinburgh printer of antiquarian tastes, produced *Golf: the Royal and Ancient Game*, a disjointed and bulky compendium of doggerel, stories and archival reprinting. It listed the significant chronological points and virtually every writer since has depended on its accuracy. Its main influence has been in the less historically clear argument over golf's origins. Was it Dutch or Scottish? Did ancient Romans and Renaissance Frenchman play variations on it? Published in the wake of the Caledonian medievalism of Sir Walter Scott the book fed into a stage nationalism as Scotland was caught up in, and risked being subsumed by, an English – dominated economic and imperial expansion.

The value of the antiquarian claims and the debate over invention have allowed subsequent authors, amid interminable squabbling, to concede the possibility of an early crude importation while claiming that Scotsmen refined the game as the 'national pastime'. This strand of writing is deeply rooted in what Murray Pittock has castigated as both 'sham celtification' and 'the fancy-dress school of history largely pioneered in Scotland' (Pittock, 1991, pp.100–03). Much of it has depended on the invention or reiteration of 'traditional' elements of a folk culture. In 1894 the new Edinburgh magazine *Golfer*, eventually absorbed by an English publisher, offered the following 'GOWFF SANG', its banality typical of a widely printed *genre* (*Golfer*, 18 August 1894):

> Wi' a club an' a ba',
> A club an' a ba',
> The load of existence is lichter tae draw,
> An scourin' a grenn, wi' a cronie' or twa',
> Is proof o' the worth o' a club an' a ba'.

Social bonding, the gregariousness required for organisation, were often at odds in such a telling with the ascribed, determined individualistic dourness of the journalists' stock Scottish character.

A similar affection for national quaintness emerged in the enthusiasm with which both English and American consumers of exported golf in the later nineteenth and early twentieth centuries took up arcane Scottish terms suggesting quasi-religious rituals in play. Describing implements as 'cleek', 'mashie', 'niblick' and so on survived until some time after the Second World War – a new range of clubs carrying James Braid's name in 1950 still used them – before they succumbed to technician-dominated numbering (*Golf Illustrated*, 8 June 1950). As a Scot of the 1890s observed, it was to English writers 'that our national sport' had come to owe much of its best writing (Dalrymple, 1894, p.20). Horace G. Hutchinson's *Badminton Series*, volume, 'Golf', of 1893 was the key text in this process. It acknowledged a dependence on Clark but it set a pattern of fine writing on golf which has largely come from outside. This ascribed debt to Scotland survived easily a small rearguard attempt at de-nationalisation in the 1890s and will long outlast Dobereiner's account (Fittis, 1891, p.149).

Dourness has been mixed in this tradition with an almost indiscriminate romanticising dependent on a stock of hybrid national characteristics. Although golf was restricted for much of its history before the late Victorian boom to a small part of the Eastern Lowlands, the playing Scot depicted by writer, cartoonist and advertiser has often been dressed as a displaced Highlander. This often mingled with an equally popular assumption that 'the essential Scottish manner . . . (was) wholly devoid of thrills', that the game was played in unadorned simplicity (*Golf Illustrated*, 6 February 1920). The blend came fully into its own between the two World Wars. In 1932 the Silvertown Golf Ball Company advertised its products using photographs of characters owing more to Harry Lauder than to St Andrews (*Golf Illustrated*, 19 August 1932). When the quality of Scottish tournament play appeared to be emerging from deep doldrums in the same year a journalist suggested that, 'it calls for a waving of the balmorals and glengarries, and a whirling of the kilt in a dance of jubilation' (*Golf Illustrated*, 9 December 1932).

Such writing imposed on the game an image sharply at odds with its actual playing and a weight as a bearer of national aspirations that it was singularly ill-equipped to bear. Everyone was supposed to be involved in this – 'The sportsmanship and golfing knowledge of the Scottish race is proverbial' (*Golf Illustrated*, 15 June 1928). Occasional attempts at debunking have only reinforced the myth. From being just the place where the game developed practically, 'North Britain' became 'the spiritual home of golf', hand in hand with a 'frank and sturdy nationalism'.

This became the stock language of tourist promoters, selling a remarkable meld of apparently contradictory features. The English corporate entertainment firm of Keith Prowse offered visitors to the 1992 Open Championships at Gleneagles and Muirfield, 'Hospitality – A Scottish Tradition', at £119 a head plus VAT per day. The hospitality included that traditional Scottish entertainment of champagne, with food and television to watch the game, inside a pavilion (*Scottish Golf Magazine*, July 1992). Collusion with this pattern at one level has, as we shall see, depended on assumptions about golf's role in the national economy. But there is still some uncertainty about how far it is something imposed by English needs for entertainment and travel and by a cultural hunger for 'otherness' stemming from south of the Borders. That can be seen in such a claim as 'With such deep traditions everyone, it seems, (in Scotland) plays and plays without fuss' (Steel, 1982, pp.17–18).

THE NATIONAL GAME –
EVERYONE UNDERSTANDS IT AND THE MAJORITY PLAY IT

Because of its essential individualism golf seems an unlikely base on which to pile the nationalistic symbolism attached to team games in much modern sport. The team in golf, where it emerges, is distinctly of secondary importance to the individual player. It is necessary here to examine briefly the historical development of Scottish golf, particularly in the light of claims that its 'national' character involved near-universal participation and a suspension of social differences sharply at odds with the mainstream experiences of the rest of the modern nation.

The much-repeated key ascription is that Scottish golf is egalitarian and pan-class; the *Glasgow Herald's* claim of 1929 that golf, 'must be regarded as a thoroughly democratic pastime, appealing to youth of all ages' is typical of a vein of writing that had rarely been questioned since the 1890s (*Glasgow Herald*, 11 December 1929). In simple numerical terms the claims for universalism are easily dismissed; Tranter has recently demonstrated that golf was rarely likely in the late Victorian boom to attract as much as five per cent of its potential male cohort (Tranter, 1989, p.62). More recent estimates of active participants do not suggest a much greater involvement.

Historically there has been considerable growth, but largely as an ancillary to the leisure needs of an industrial and service society, led both by Scottish middle-class recreational aspirations and, particularly important for Scotland, the tourist fancies of outsiders. The 450 or so clubs and courses (the former exceeding the latter because of the extent of shared facilities) which exist at the time of writing are the survivors of those which went under because demand was insufficient to sustain them or alternative pressures on the land killed them off.

Of the 406 whose founding dates can be readily traced some 40 were started before 1870. Founding rates were sporadic thereafter, the greatest spurts coming in the 1890s, with 111 new clubs and the first decade of this century, with 79. The 1920s added another 38 but only 28 have opened since 1961.[1] Golf is proverbially land-hungry, occupying some 32,000 Scottish acres by 1939, 'more or less the size of Clackmannan' (*Glasgow Herald*, 9 May 1939). Scotland does seem, however, to have a higher incidence of nine-hole courses than its southern neighbour so the overall landscape impact is less obtrusive than in England.

The story of this growth reveals not so much the emergence of a cohesive national pattern as one of social tensions, the identity problems of particular classes and a searching for exclusiveness at odds with the pressures to play. Golf in Scotland does have a marginally wider social base than its English counterpart and there are plenty of well-attested individual instances to suggest a thinly-spread trans-class following. But this is not pan-class in any sense that might be applied to horse-racing and it rarely deserves the 'democratic' model which has been so widely imposed upon it. Nor is there much evidence to suggest that the English observers who have fostered this image have ever regarded it as a desirable import into their own country alongside the rest of the game's paraphernalia to which they took with such enthusiasm. It could be left safely across the Borders.

The well-trodden early history does suggest, however, that there was some 'popular' participation before the eighteenth century formalization began to shift it towards being a middle-class preserve. Playing on common land, particularly the seaside 'links', put golf in the same category as other pre-industrial recreations, except that it was rather less violent than most. When the Duke of York played alongside the Edinburgh shoemaker John Patersone for a wager in 1682 it marked less of a 'democracy' than the readily-satisfied whim of a grandee.

The formation of clubs and playing societies in the mid-eighteenth century represents both emergent middle-class ambitions, expressed through associational bonding, and the beginning of a process of privatisation. In many cases it led eventually to a withdrawal from public space. Some recent writers have suggested, but with no clear evidence, strong links with rampant Freemasonry in the emergence of the new clubs in both Edinburgh and St Andrews. Certainly heavy drinking, wagering, secretive selection and initiating procedures as well as picturesque uniforms played considerable parts in the early history of both the Edinburgh Burgess Club (1735), the (Honourable) Company of Edinburgh Golfers (1744) and the Society of St Andrews Golfers (Royal and Ancient from 1834) (1754) (Pride, 1962, pp.90–91; Stirk, 1987, p.64).

Tranter has seen this as the emergence of a sporting cult well before the public school-driven boom of the later Victorians (Tranter, 1989, p.57). It was, but it must also be seen as signalling a new trans-European *bourgeois* self-awareness and patterns of association (Nenadic, 1988, p.109ff). The Scottish contribution was unique in its apparent objective of playing this particular game but its ancillaries differed little from those of most other clubs. In Edinburgh they added to a growing range of common-interest societies reflecting varied political allegiances and to internal professional hierarchies that are often quite difficult to reconstruct now. In Scotland generally their membership patterns reiterated the position of local dominant classes. Edinburgh tended to attract lawyers and other professionals, with printers coming in later, St Andrews local lairds and major academics, Glasgow (1787) commercial and later industrial magnates (Smout, 1970, p.364). As smaller towns were added to the numbers the range within each club reflected the local oligarchies. Inevitably, ministers of the Church of Scotland appeared in most of them.

The leading artistic expression of all this is one of the country's best-known, and most frequently reproduced paintings, Charles Lee's 'Grand Match' of about 1850. It is like one of those pictures of a great Parliamentary debate, in which every member can be seen, placed in positions which allow for clear identification and maximum discomfort. Set on the Old Course at St Andrews, it includes one caddie and a servant girl – the rest is all gentry. It offers an interesting contrast with the pan-class Englishness of Frith's 'Derby Day'.

When the great boom came after 1870 Scotland had a significantly wider base for expansion than did England, where growth was essentially *de novo*.

But this can be overstated. What triggered Scotland's boom was much the same as in England – newer sections of the middle classes found themselves sufficiently affluent, with disposable time and income, but insufficiently secure socially. They sought healthy, ethically acceptable recreations which would strengthen their class perceptions, provide attainable targets for aspiration and control over those with whom they wished to mix. With their selection procedures, and the possibility of blackballing for exclusion, golf clubs fitted the moment admirably.

Thus, by 1899 Glasgow had some twenty private clubs reflecting this, easily paralleling Edinburgh. The Port Glasgow Club (1895) had a reputation as favouring shipbuilders (*Golfer*, 8 November 1895). The eastern capital's social distinctions continued to grow and survived well through the First World War. Neighbouring clubs often shared little more than geographical proximity – of the Corstorphine and Torphin clubs it was reported, 'Relations between these two clubs do not exist for one is a suburban product and the other is associated with the Printing Federation (*Golf Illustrated*, 12 December 1920).

Social differentiation was at its most pronounced in smaller towns with more than one club, particularly where they followed familiar practice in sharing a common course which none of them owned. In North Berwick the original club (1832) was a closed shop of some 50 gentry, 'one of the most aristocratic clubs in Scotland' (*Golf Illustrated*, 10 September 1920). It eschewed a club house until well into the present century, erecting a tent for two days a year for business and social meetings, rather like the pavilion at older chivalric tournaments. In 1879 a New Club was formed, for local professional men. They united in 1963 (Houghton, 1967, p.118ff).

It was at Carnoustie that division within the middle classes was at its clearest. The first club, formed in 1835, catered very much for local gentry and professionals. In 1868 businessmen from nearby Dundee formed the Dalhousie Club, which 'remained more or less a recreation centre for the magnates of jute, jam and journalism' (*Golf Illustrated*, 14 December 1928). A Ladies' club followed in 1873 but the next step was the founding of the Mercantile in 1880 for those men unable to join the other two. In addition there was the Caledonia (1887). Such was the pressure on play that a common management committee between some of the clubs and the local council was formed to oversee the links in 1901 (*Golf Illustrated*, 29 April 1939).

Such stories of founding can be repeated time and time again in smaller Scottish towns. The impetus to middle-class play grew particularly because the country was caught up in a parallel late Victorian boom, that of holiday-making and tourism. The romanticisation of the Highlands in the wake of Scott was pushed further by the royal patronage of Balmoral and Deeside. In the wake of the monarch came an aristocracy and plutocracy wanting to shoot and fish. Alongside and behind them came the English and indigenous middle-classes.

The latter were driven as much by the need to cluster as to admire hills and glens. It was the opening up of Scottish seaside reports by the railway networks that gave golf its greatest impetus – Dunoon and Largs on the West Coast and Elie on the East were, in the words of Christopher Smout, 'as exclusively the domain of professional men, tradesmen and shopkeepers as the Highland grouse moor was of the rich' (Smout, 1986, p.157). Canny local entrepreneurs saw and proclaimed their opportunities and obligations. As Provost Philip of Bridge of Allan said, 'It is a duty to give ample facilities for bowling, cricket, curling, golf, etc., so as to induce visitors to come and bring prosperity to the town' (Tranter, 1989, p.60).

In this, golf was just one part of a package of attractions, but it was one linked with a sense of opportunity. When Bridge of Weir developed as a small spa in the 1880s, a local doctor, W. F. Mudie, persuaded some of his fellow townsmen to found a nine-hole club, the Ranfurly Castle (Crampsey, 1989, pp.1–2). Visitors and players enjoyed reduced fares on the Glasgow railway. Exercise, health and profit went closely together in many of these enterprises. For a modest outlay the Scottish middle classes could enjoy a 'Golfing Season' in their favourite resorts, such as Dunbar (*Golfer*, 18 January 1894). Visiting English players were the cream on top. It was estimated that the rateable value of Dornoch doubled in the early 1890s, due largely to golf (*Golfer*, 27 October 1894). Kingarth opened up at the same time, a place where, 'one may putt or potter, play a match or bathe or picnic, or pass from tee to tee through a summer day' (Mosley and Thain, 1967, p.472). It set a pattern for much of Scottish middle-class golf, seasonal and not overly-competitive, which had considerable influence on the country's eventual ranking in international competition.

Some resorts benefitted also from their convenient closeness to larger towns. In the summer this allowed professional and businessmen to get in an evening's golf, making the most of the legendary extended northern daylight; they played at courses such as North Berwick, using the convenient 'golfing' express from Edinburgh (*Golf Monthly*, January 1930). This close dependence on trains gave Scotland some golfing developments which owed a great deal to their placing and a reputation that eventually moved a long way indeed from the rough seaside links dominating the story so far. At Turnberry in Ayrshire, golf by the sea was started in 1902. It stepped into a very different class two years later when the Glasgow and South Western Railway built a huge hotel, dominating the links which it took over (Houghton, 1967, p.95). By the 1920s it had become the core of a golfing 'package', when the company offered two days combined fares and hotel accommodation, with all meals, for seventy-two shillings on any weekend (*Golf Monthly*, December 1925). But Turnberry was far outclassed by a very 'un-Scottish' inland development. Planned before the First World War as a combined parkland hotel and golf complex, the scheme was held up by hostilities. In 1919 James Braid designed a course to offer 'the best possible inland golf for those who are comfortably well-off' (Houghton, 1967, p.17). It was sited in Perthshire at what used to be Croft Junction, renamed as Gleneagles after a cleft in the hills to the south (*Golf Illustrated*, 21 January 1927).

Essentially it was developed by the London Midland and Scottish Railway and became 'The most pushful course in Scotland, a railway-cum-commercial enterprise, as keen to get and keep in the limelight as some golf courses seem to be anxious to hide in the background' (*Golf Illustrated*, 6 February 1920). It offered to plutocratic golfers the same sort of prestige as they might have found by renting shooting in the Highlands During the interwar period it stood out as a sharp reminder that not all Scotland, and its consumers, were affected by recession. It also prompted other resorts to rethink their attractions, particularly when it obtained sponsorship for a big prize money annual tournament from the *Glasgow Herald* (*Golf Illustrated*, 26 November 1920). In 1927 Carnoustie replied with its new Open Tournament, offering its solid silver Craw's Nest Tassie as a prize (*Golf Illustrated*, 6 May 1927). The country was generating an income from golf increasingly dependent on external wealth, attracted very largely by the game's mythical place in a national heritage. And that was largely fostered for and by the middle classes.

The rapid spread of inland golf brought pressures which, even where it existed, the much-vaunted 'democracy' of the Scottish game found increasingly difficult to bear. If anything, as the game prospered among the middle classes, the claims for a pan-class following flourished even further. One recent writer has pointed to a national 'tendency to seek an escape in the historical past', for the middle classes in particular to revel in the belief of an egalitarian 'Open Society' prompted by popular Presbyterianism (Maclaren, 1976, pp.1–2). Most English as well as Scottish commentators on golf in its heyday of expansion accepted this readily enough – 'Democratic as it may have been in its indigenous Scottish soil, where the duke stood aside for the dustman on the dustman's medal day . . .' (*Golf Illustrated*, 18 February 1927).

Much of the evidence suggests a somewhat different picture, however, Scottish golf never quite reached the near-universal class exclusiveness of its English counterpart but there were clear social tensions as it spread, with a strong tendency towards snobbery and privacy in some of its leading groups. The 'pre-industrial' game, disorganised and using rough seaside land, had allowed for play by all classes, which was not the same as enjoying a universal following. Tobias Smollett's eighteenth-century 'multitude of all ranks' on the links was perhaps kept together as much by drink as by play (Grant, III, p.262). Knocking an old ball about with makeshift clubs on common land on public holidays, even when exalted by the prize given to the best-scoring fishwife by the Musselburgh Golf Club in 1810, was a long way from the etiquette and club-dominated game which had emerged by the 1850s (Fittis, 1891, p.154).

Although working-class men could be found in some clubs, actually providing a majority in Bruntsfield Allied in 1869 (Gray, 1976, p.104), the story is one of their steady marginalisation, belying *The Golfer*'s claim of 1894 that, 'Golf is a great social force, which levels mankind with the impartiality of an epidemic' (*Golfer*, 8 September 1894). Smout and Wood have pointed out that expensive playing costs took the game away from informal working-class pursuit (Smout and Wood, 1990, p.185). When workers did play it was largely outside club organisation and in growing competition for scarce and overcrowded open spaces. Even where, as on some of the older seaside links, a wider class mix could be found there was considerable pressure from visitors and middle-class new residents for precedence on the tee.

Furthermore, in passing it should be noted, that many golf clubs in Scotland have had a long history of excluding Jews and Catholics. Such was the anti-Jewish feeling that the Jewish community in the West of Scotland had to purchase its own course at Bonnyton Moor in order to make the game more accessible to the Jewish community. Having purchased the course in the early 1940s the new owners then heaped coals of fire on establishment golf in Scotland by instituting an open admissions policy.

Scottish golf has experienced demands on playing space which have favoured the affluent and relatively leisured. Even though it now has a larger proportion per head of 'public', i.e., municipal, courses than any where else (totalling 71) some of these are dominated by prestigious clubs. Many clubs have located themselves on private ground, to escape both the crowds and the ordinary players, with their questionable playing styles and their threat to exclusiveness. Yet the myth lingers on. A history of Edinburgh's Royal Golfing Society claimed in 1987 that, 'They walked with Kings and yet retained the common touch.' Some pages later, with no sense of contradiction, it asked, 'How does one become a member of this distinguished society?', and answered that well-mannered participation was necessary to guarantee acceptance (Royal Burgess, 1987, p.1, p.11). That is the history of Scottish golf writ small.

The small number of seaside commons on which the older game was played were inadequate for the new late Victorian demand. When the key cities, Edinburgh and Glasgow, expanded provision for golf became both an issue for would-be players and a source of some contention over the shared use of public land. By the 1890s Glasgow had two public courses, with 27 holes between them but another twenty private links around the city; there it continued largely as, 'very much the business man's game' (Cunnison and Gilfillen, 1958, p.268; M'Dowall, 1970, p.97).

It was in Edinburgh that the social tensions showed most openly. It is not always clear how far down the social scale the demand went but there is some indication that an urge to play among clerks and prosperous artisans was important in the drive towards exclusiveness by more affluent groups. When Braid Hills was opened in 1890 by the municipality, the game was initially free but demand was so great that a penny green fee was soon introduced as a partial deterrent (Keir, 1966, p.532). Within five years some 5,000 players a week were using the Braids; there were often 200–300 golfers prepared to queue for up to three hours each morning to tee off (*Golfer*, 18 August 1894, 15 September 1894). The impact of 'uncomfortably crowded' facilities drove the Burgesses and Honourable Company from links they had regarded virtually as private property – 'A race of independent golfers was . . . arising who refused to recognise these autocratic claims' (*Golf Monthly*, May 1911).

The justification of both old-established and newer ambitious bodies was that they wanted peace and places to play which were not damaged by overuse. But they also sought to maintain social distance. In some senses their departure freed more space for the less wealthy but it also initiated a competition for scarce land near the towns which many authorities found expensive to enter. It is to the credit of many Scottish burgh councils that they did provide some land for less-favoured individuals rather than clubs to use. But it is also true, at Carnoustie and elsewhere, that some clubs virtually monopolised public land by collaborating with the authorities and paying for improvements for their own purposes. There were pleas for private link-owning clubs to allow some access at minimum rates and 'have the comfortable feeling that they were doing good and profiting thereby' (*Golfer*, 5 January 1895). The frequency of repetition suggests a limited compliance. St Andrews has long stood out against the trend to selfishness, despite intense pressure on its courses, and Dornoch maintained a reputation for democracy (Houghton, 1967, p.71). With a few others they have sustained the external reputation for widespread participation belied so much elsewhere in the country.

Occasionally, the issues became more open. In the 1860s Kilspindie golfers played on land near Gullane, leased from a local landowner for a shilling a year. In 1894 he withdrew that right when club members refused access to his tenants and workers; much of the club moved elsewhere, to stay uncontaminated (Houghton, 1967, pp.100–01). The trend towards the private grew with the sport, justified by one patronising writer in 1920 as fleeing from 'some of the weirdest styles that I have ever seen in my life', shown by players who would have been embarrassed in private clubs (*Golf Illustrated*, 30 January 1920). Stylistic purity did not stem a continued demand for play underpinned by 'municipal socialism'.

In 1927 Aberdeen opened a much-vaunted new course at Hazlehead, enjoying national media coverage. The Lord Provost praised 'the people's golf course . . . planned for them . . . owned by them . . . maintained by them' (*Aberdeen Press and Journal*, 4 July 1927). No mention was made at the civic dinner of its construction by the local unemployed, who got an extra seven shillings and sixpence on their dole; in the words of one of the families, 'The Hazlehead golf course was built with sweat and tears', exhaustion and the risk of rheumatism (Smout and Wood, 1990, pp.211–12). At least one local paper pointed out that it would be unlikely to benefit local workers, 'for a shilling a round and fivepence in return fares soon mount up to considerable proportions' (*Aberdeen Press and Journal*, 4 July 1927). Its rival printed a cartoon showing a henpecked golfer being told by his wife she was going to buy him a knickerbocker suit, to suit the social tone of the new municipal course (*Aberdeen Evening Express*, 4 July 1927).

Golf commentators still continued to claim that this was a town where 'any artisan can have the maximum amount of pleasure at the minimum amount of expense (*Golf Illustrated*, 8 June 1928). Yet there were places where artisans, in the fullest meaning of that word as a 'labour aristocracy', did organise themselves to play. These were usually 'Thistle' clubs, such as Edinburgh's, playing on municipal courses (*Golf Illustrated*, 20 February 1920). There they were largely kept to themselves; a match between 'the horneyhanded sons of toil' with the younger members of the Panmure club was held to be remarkable because 'the artisan has seldom crossed a lance with the well-to-do golfer' (*Golf Illustrated*, 17 December 1920). In general the evidence suggests that the class divide in golf widened during the interwar years. In the larger cities in particular the situation was still the same some 30 years later, when an estimate put Edinburgh's club membership at around 20,000 but claimed that a further 25,000–30,000 unattached players used the public courses (Keir, 1966, pp.530–32). In the smaller towns there was often not even this chance if the course was in the hands of an exclusive local oligarchy. There were exceptions; at Gladsmuir a writer of the 1950s pointed out with an economic tartness, 'There are three golf clubs, one for men, one for women, and one mixed. The last is known as the Artisan's Club' (Snodgrass, 1953, p.237). The Scottish manual worker did have more opportunities for play than did his English equivalent, but they have proved far from sufficient to bear the weight of the label of 'democracy' attached to them.

If artisans fared indifferently, however, they seem to have done rather better than women. For the Scottish middle-class man modern golf was as much a refuge from the home as it has proved to be elsewhere in the world (Smout and Wood, 1990, pp.48–49). St Andrews, never quite typical, founded a Ladies' Club in 1867 and women formed a substantial part of some other clubs but this was far from common (Tranter, 1989, p.64). Women were restricted in number, Carnoustie had 60 members in 1894, in times when they could play and in their access to club facilities (*Golfer*, 18 August 1894). The municipal links were hardly an acceptable alternative; at the best less than ten per cent of players on them seem to have been female.

Scottish women were penalised very much by their tendency to play amongst themselves and by their general lack of professional tuition (*Golf Illustrated*, 11 February 1927). It was some time before they produced a player of major quality in the person of Jessie Anderson (later Valentine), 'The Fair Maid of Perth'. She became British Girls' Champion in 1933, British Champion in 1937, 1955 and 1958, played internationally in the later 1930s. But to achieve real freedom and recognition she had to turn professional (Houghton, 1967, p.14ff). Despite this rare model and a stream of lesser local champions women's role in Scottish golf has been marginal indeed. Attempts to rouse social concern and offer the game to 'artisan women' in the 1920s failed (*Golf Illustrated*, 6 April 1928). Forty years later women were still excluded from the Troon clubhouse, barred from Muirfield and firmly separated at the Royal Aberdeen. With its emphasis on mixed and family play, the 'New' at North Berwick offered a rare exception (Houghton, 1967, passim). One writer in 1990 estimated some 34,000 women golfers in the country, still very much the poor relation of male players (Lowe, 1990, p.171).

IT'S GOOD FOR TRADE . . . THEY LIKE A SCOT TO BE REAL SCOTTISH . . .
IT MAKES THE PROFITS SOMETHING EXTRAORDINARY

The canny appreciation of his own value by Jim Glennie, the exiled professional to a pretentious English club in A. G. MacDonell's witty 1930s novel, summed up much of what golf had come to mean. There was a clear contrast between many of its domestic features and the way it was, quite literally, 'sold' abroad. The components of this selling were people, real and caricatured, a sense of moral virtue in the game and good government.

The growing numbers of Victorian middle-class players spawned a dependant whose lampooning in picture and print has added much to the lore of golf and disguised some of its more exploitative social features. Caddies, wretchedly clad, underfed, but rich in sarcastic observation, were a product of wealth and the absence of local knowledge among many players (Smout and Wood, 1990, p.183). In their thousands, these poorly-rewarded club carriers of all ages swelled the stream of casual labour on which seasonal leisure provision depended. Few clubs did more for them than allow their employment. The depression of the interwar years increased their numbers and their predatory swarming around arriving trains at St Andrews and elsewhere was well-documented, reminiscent of the beggars who still beset European travellers in the Third World (*Golf Illustrated*, 11 January 1935).

Caddies depended on accumulated local folk knowledge. Some were able to acquire playing skills in off moments, with cast-off implements. A very few, beginning as boy labour, moved on to skilled apprenticeship and work as a professional. It was a career more to be found in myth than actuality – most exiled Scottish golf professionals seem to have begun their work with other skills, not least joinery in the days of wooden clubs. With a few carefully retained exceptions, kept to add some character, the breed has largely died out since the Second World War, 'a diminution in the pageantry of golf' (Royal Burgess, 1987, p.89).

Glennie, with other fictional counterparts, illustrated a major part played in the game's general growth by exiled Scots. For the keen artisan, employment in golf at home was difficult. Even today, only about a third of Scottish clubs employ a teaching professional – generally those with relatively low retaining fees (Lowe, 1990, p.104). When the English boom started Scots were imported virtually wholesale and another large number found ready employment across the Atlantic. It has been Carnoustie's proud boast that it has sent some 250–300 (the figure varies with the telling) to the United States and Canada (*Golf Illustrated*, 14 January 1927, 29 April 1939). But, in the early days at least, employment there was as seasonal as at home, and they returned like migrant birds to winter in Scotland (*Golf Monthly*, January 1925). Most were competent players, but more likely they would earn money making clubs. Hence the Scottishness of much professional sales advice. A few used their memories of links back home to lay out new American courses with an amalgam of the best native features (*Golf Illustrated*, 11 January 1929).

Their presence did much to boost the 'homeland' myth, as did the early records of a handful of key tournament players. The legendary Tom Morrises ('Old' and 'Young', father and son) of St Andrews have been credited with creating championship golf by their performance before the 1880s; the tale was much re-told in print and commemorated in 'Staffordshire Ware' (Steel, 1982, p.28). After them the St Andrews clubmaker, William Auchterlonie, the last home-based Scot to win the Open, in 1893, enjoyed prominence (*Golfer*, 19 January 1895). He was followed briefly by an amateur, the lively Black Watch Officer Freddie Tait, whose death in the Boer War was for many the symbolic end of great Scottish amateur play (*Golf Illustrated*, 19 April 1935). The Parks, father and son, became the first real Scottish tournament professionals, clubmaking and designing new courses, independent of club employment (Stirk, 1987, p.104). The son proved a better designer than businessman, touching bankruptcy before the First World War.

They epitomised a canny Scottishness, the eye for a good playing space.

But one man more than any other since the Morrises came to represent Scottish golf. James Braid, a joiner who migrated from St Andrews and Edinburgh to England as clubmaker and professional to Walton Heath, formed the third member of the great 'Triumvirate' with Vardon and Ray, winning the British Open five times. As a player he peaked before the First World War and he spent most of his very long working life (he died in 1960) in England, designing courses and making clubs (Darwin, 1991, passim). For many, the standard of play in and for Scotland has declined steadily since. In the 1960s R. D. B. M. Shade, an amateur, brought new glory but the country has produced no one to match its turn-of-the-century giants (Keir, 1966, p.532). The paradox seems to have lain in the fact that most Scots have played for pleasure rather than ruthless competition (Houghton, 1967, p.135). Attempts to breed up new champions of international status, such as the golf scholarships offered by a number of universities, including Stirling and St Andrews, since the 1980s have yet to reveal the sort of results of the American models on which they are based (*Scottish Golf Magazine*, September 1991, February 1992, see also Lowe, 1990, p.134).

If Scotland has long lost international hegemony in tournament play it has managed to maintain a more than nominal one in regulating the game. The Royal and Ancient Golf Club of St Andrews is still regarded as the final arbiter on key matters, not least the rules of play. Given the financial clout of such national bodies as the United States Golf Association this is somewhat surprising but the R and A is more of a constitutional monarch than an absolute one. The wholesale exporting of the game in the later nineteenth century coincided with a hesitant codification of practice much on the lines of other contemporary sports. The R and A found itself being approached for guidance. Then, as it has so often since, it hesitated in making its mind up, producing various versions of the *Rules of Golf* in the 1880s and 1890s and dithering for years over formulating a definition of an 'amateur'.

The choice of St Andrews was perhaps surprising but, with its strong local tradition of 'democratic' play, it offered a greater image of integration and conciliation than did the more obviously divisive Edinburgh clubs. In the long term it has developed a remarkable international membership, with 1800 members coming from a number of countries. Effective control has been maintained through consultations with the major associations of the key golfing countries. This was won at hard cost – the English demanded 'rational-isation' (i.e., English control), 'something more practical than tradition', repeatedly in the 1890s; the United States threatened schism, new Scottish clubs demanded a share in power (*Golfer*, 13 May 1896, 21 October 1896).

The R and A has sidestepped such demands by repeatedly giving in graciously at the last minute, although that process has sometimes taken decades. The standardisation of ball sizes in 1921 and the legalisation of steel-shafted clubs in 1930 were as much the result of industrial pressure on an international scale as of innovation in St Andrews (*Golf Illustrated*, 2 August 1929). The club's role has largely been reflective and responsive rather than innovatory, although it has frequently managed to give the impression of the latter since it took over the management of the British Open and Amateur Championships in 1919. Despite repeated claims on the lines that it should join 'with the flowing tide of enterprise and popular opinion', its chief role has been as a fountainhead of honour for an oligarchy of the main international interests in golf (*Golf Illustrated*, 20 July 1950). For many, however, it offers more importantly the 'indefinable something' that still attaches to its part in managing the St Andrews links, particularly the 'Old Course' (*Golf Monthly*, March 1939). Unlike most other sports, golf's 'Mecca' is open to the ordinary visitor as much as to the tournament star, reinforcing an image of accessibility which is not entirely applicable to the rest of the country.

. . . SURELY THE INVENTION OF GOLF MUST BE CONSIDERED ONE OF THE MORE NOTABLE SCOTTISH CONTRIBUTIONS TO THE ADVANCEMENT OF CIVILISATION

Golf is perhaps the only sport of British origin and codification to have been transplanted readily to much of the rest of the world. It lacks the internal divisions of football and its 'Scottishness' has never produced the ethical crises and nationalism that 'Englishness' has bequeathed to cricket. In many ways it is as much a child of the British Empire as both of those games but it has spread much wider, allowing Scots to claim a moral superiority, invariably over the English.

It is worth finishing by reflecting on two aspects of the game's continued impact on its homeland.

It has existed for centuries in an uneasy symbiosis with religion, reflected in the as yet under-explored tensions over Sabbatarianism. Virtually every popular history of golf has included well-told stories of the Kirk's post-Reformation suppression of Sunday play. The new bourgeois clubs of the formalising years, with their distinctly non-Calvinistic social rituals, never challenged the dominance of the ministers. But a slowly creeping secular demand became obvious with the late Victorian middle-class drive. A number of attempts at Sunday play in the 1890s were prevented, leading to resignations of members of the Burgess Society (*Golfer*, 18 October 1895, 10 January 1896). Some golfers played surreptitiously on Sundays at out-of-town courses in the early 1900s but even after the First World War few clubs would openly admit to allowing Sunday play (Darwin, 1910, p.200). To the Kirk's strictures were added the almost as sacred views of Old Tom Morris that courses need a rest as well (*Golf Illustrated*, 7 September 1928). Despite pressure from English visitors and local liberals, over half the country's clubs still forbade Sunday play in 1939 (Lowerson, 1984, p.218). After 1945 that number diminished rapidly but popular Presbyterianism (not necessarily linked with kirkgoing) still prevented Sunday morning play in many areas (Houghton, 1967, p.129).

It is in golf as business that Scotland has seen some considerable recent changes. The years of boom produced a wide range of craft-based club and ball manufacture which provided some legendary names – Nicoll of Leven, the Auchterlonies of St Andrews, and Robert Forgan, also of St Andrews (Houghton, 1967, p.30ff). The small workshop image beloved of the homely national myth needs, however, to be modified in the case of the latter; by the 1890s he was holding enough timber stocks for two years' production, some

100,000 clubs (*Golfer*, 11 November 1896). Many such makers went under during recessions but some survived until after the Second World War. Since then many have disappeared or become parts of international conglomerates. Yet the new masters still see advantages in locating part of their production in Scotland, as if a mystical value is added to the economic one of their goods. Lynx Golf of the United States moved into East Kilbride in 1986, and Mizmo of Japan into Cumbernauld in 1991, where it produces using imported pre-fabricated components (*Scottish Golf Magazine*, February 1992).

Scottish golf is sold internationally, through association and much more directly, as a tourist attraction. Although a 1960s survey showed that only 8.2 per cent of visitors played golf they were very much concentrated on the few internationally-known and hyped locations (Hunt, 1964, p.137). Its most obvious role as an economic generator emerges with the major international tournaments. A survey of the 1979 Open Championship at St Andrews which attracted 56,000 spectators and 233 outside firms calculated that it brought the equivalent of a week's income, although very unevenly divided, for every household in the district (Blake et al., 1979, p.31). For Bell's, the whisky firm, who 'took the Open by the scruff of the neck' in 1986 – the tournament drew 109,000 spectators in 1991 – the sponsorship seems amply justified (*Scottish Golf Magazine*, July 1992).

It is this modern, high-cost and high-profile game which is seen by many as that to which obeisance and pilgrimage are due and few opportunities are lost in its marketing. Glossy books on the 'great courses' abound. In 1991, recognising a new market sector, Columbia Tristar issued a home video, *Great Golf Courses of the World; Scotland*. It is lyrically shot on the few great courses which are regarded as 'typical' of the country, St Andrews, Gleneagles and so on. The narrator is probably the best known of the country's amateur golfers, although an exile, the actor Sean Connery. The script is propped up by many of the hackneyed elements of media Scottishness – a piper, the poetry of Burns, a minister of the Kirk and a craggy old caddy. It also gives the addresses and telephone numbers of the courses. It is pilgrimage for the affluent.

Such golf remains a long way from much of the contemporary Scottish experience. Popular demand, before the recession of the late 1980s, matched its growth elsewhere. At one point it was estimated that 70 per cent of local clubs had a waiting list for membership (Lowe, 1990, p.113). The opening of a dozen low-cost driving ranges merely fed demand. Yet most developments tended to mirror the up-market image. Turnberry fell into financial crises and was rescued eventually by Japanese investors, who spent almost £30,000 ,000 on redevelopment (*Golf World*, October 1992). An attempt to create a 1990s rival to Gleneagles on Loch Lomond had difficulties in attracting investment – it needed more than a romantic setting to make it marketable (*Golf World*, August 1992).

Scotland may not have invented golf, but it has refined it and encouraged its development along lines which have exploited ascribed national identity to such an extent that it has distorted much of what really happens in the homeland. In so doing, though, it reflects an ambivalence in Scottish society as to what Scotland and its people really are.

NOTE

1. These figures are based on various editions of the *Golfer's Handbook*.

BIBLIOGRAPHY

Blake, D., McDowell, S. and Devlen, J., 1979, *The 1978 Open Championship at St Andrews: an economic impact study*, Edinburgh
Clark, R., 1875, *Golf: The Royal and Ancient Game*, Edinburgh
Crampsey, R., 1989, *Ranfurly Castle Golf Club; a centenary history*, Bridge of Weir
Cunnison, J. and Gilfillan, J. B. S., 1958, *Glasgow*, Glasgow
Dalrymple, W. H., 1894, *Golfer's guide to the games and greens of Scotland*, Edinburgh
Darwin, B., 1910, *The golf courses of the British Isles*, London
Darwin, B., 1991, (ed.), 1952, *James Braid*, London
Dobereiner, P., 1973, How golf invented the Scots, *The glorious world of golf*, London
Fittis, R. S., 1891, Sports and pastimes of Scotland, Paisley
Grant, J., n.d., *Cassell's old and new Edinburgh*, vols I–III, London
Gray, R. Q., 1976, *The labour aristocracy in Victorian Edinburgh*, Oxford
Houghton, G., 1967, *Golf addict among the Scots*, London
Hunt, A., 1964, *A survey of Scottish tourism*, Glasgow
Keir, D., 1966, *Edinburgh*, Glasgow
Lowe, D., 1990, *The Glasgow Herald book of club golf*, Edinburgh
Lowerson, J., 1984, Sport and the Victorian Sunday; the beginnings of middle class apostasy, *British journal of sports history*, I
Maclaren, A. A., 1976, *Social class in Scotland, past and present*, Edinburgh
M'Dowall, J. K., 1970, *The people's history of Glasgow, 1899*, Glasgow
Mosley, H. A. and Thain, A. G., 1967, *Renfrew and Bute*, Glasgow
Nenadic, S., 1988, The rise of the urban middle class, in Devine, T. M. and Mitchison, R., *People and society in Scotland, I, 1760–1830*, London
Pittock, M. G. H., 1991, *The invention of Scotland*, London
Pride, G. S., 1962, *Scotland from 1603 to the present day*, London
Royal Burgess, 1987, *Chronicle of the Royal Burgess Golfing Society of Edinburgh, 1936–1985*, vol. II, Broxburn
Sitwell, S. and Bamford, F., 1984, *Edinburgh*, London
Smout, T. C., 1970, *A history of the Scottish people, 1560–1830*, London
Smout, T. C., 1986, *A century of the Scottish people, 1830–1950*, London
Smout, T. C. and Wood, S., 1990, *Scottish voices, 1745–1960*, London
SMT, 1945, *SMT Magazine and Scottish country life book of Scottish golf courses*
Snodgrass, C. P., 1953, *East Lothian*, Edinburgh
Steel, D., 1982, *The Guiness book of golf facts and feats*, London
Stirk, D., 1987, *Golf, the history of an obsession*, Oxford
Tranter, N. L., 1989, Sport and the economy in nineteenth and early twentieth century Scotland, *Scottish historical review*, LXVIII
Young, D., 1969, *St Andrews, town and gown, royal and ancient*, London
Young, J. S., 1981, Golf, in Daiches, D., *A companion to Scottish culture*, London

7

FAITH, HOPE AND BIGOTRY:
CASE STUDIES OF ANTI-CATHOLIC PREJUDICE
IN SCOTTISH SOCCER AND SOCIETY

Gerry P. T. Finn

INTRODUCTION

Most historical accounts of the football clubs established by the Irish-Scots have assumed that these organisations, and the motivations for their establishment, were very different from other Scottish clubs (Docherty and Thomson, 1975; Mckay, 1986; Murray, 1984, 1988; Watson, 1985; Wilkie, 1984). Edinburgh Hibernian, Dundee Harp and Dundee Hibernian, with the much more influential Glasgow Celtic, are held responsible for the ethnic, political and religious factors that are now recognised to have had considerable influence on the development of Scottish football.

However, the foundation of Irish-Scottish football clubs mainly indicated a willingness to participate in Scottish life, to meet with other Scots and to demonstrate their competence to the disdainful majority community: Irish-Scottish football clubs were very like those in the majority community. Clearly there were differences. The majority community did not have the need to prove themselves as equal to the minority as a motivation in the foundation of football clubs although, with the passage of time, the success of the minority's clubs became yet another source of irritation for those already prejudiced against the Irish-Scots. A belief that the Catholic Irish-Scots were so different has meant that the history of other Scottish clubs has been incomplete (Finn, 1991b). The potential religious and political influences acting on other Scottish clubs have been ignored, with the result that there has been little attempt to explore the nature of other clubs.

Two case studies will be presented in this chapter. Both reveal much about the role of anti-Catholicism in Scottish football and society. The first examines the role of Protestantism and anti-Catholicism in the earliest days of Scottish football by examining the history of Edinburgh's first soccer club, the Third Edinburgh Rifle Volunteers (3rd ERV), established by John Hope in 1874. It reveals the extent to which religion, nationalism, militarism, politics and anti-Catholicism had a potent influence on Scottish football before the entry of the first Catholic Irish-Scots club into the game. The second case study examines the failure of David Hope to become chairman of Glasgow Rangers in 1973. This example reveals the extent to which anti-Catholic prejudice was at the very centre of the club in the 1970s and shows how sections of Scottish society accepted or colluded with this prejudice.

JOHN HOPE AND NO-POPERY!

The 3rd ERV was very much the creature of John Hope, its originator and its commanding officer. The biography written by his admirer and protege, the Reverend David Jamie, is an invaluable source and the following extract usefully illuminates and summarises Hope's life-work and the importance of the 3rd ERV and its football club in his thinking (Jamie, 1900, p.473):

> Very frequently Mr Hope received, by way of a complaint, a photograph from individuals, or groups of individuals, in whom he took an interest. Among these are photographs of a 3rd ERV football club; of the band of the 3rd ERV Corps . . . Not the least interesting of these relics is one which describes itself as 'The Friday Anti-Popery Bible-class, under the patronage of John Hope' . . .

Hope's involvement in anti-popery was not some minor interest. Indeed, recently, John Hope has been described as 'the quiet bureaucrat behind the anti-popery movements in the Scotland of the last half of the nineteenth century' (Bruce, 1985, p.36). Anti-Popery was one of Hope's two great crusades. The other was the temperance cause. Hope saw educational and missionary work as the key to achieving his ends. It was necessary to inform people of what he judged to be the twin evils of the Pope and Catholicism, and alcohol, and to convince them of the benefits of both true Protestantism and absolute temperance. His own anti-popery work was strongly directed against the apathy about Catholicism that he detected in the Protestant population, but he did help finance the employment of Irish-speaking missionaries to convert Catholics in the Irish community in Edinburgh. Opposed to Home Rule in Ireland, he saw all problems there as the result of Catholicism. When elected, as an unopposed Tory in 1857, to the Edinburgh Town Council, he had in his campaign made his views clear as 'an out-and-out Protestant, educationist, and abstainer', who would extend the franchise to Protestants, but not to 'Papists', and who stood for the conversion of 'the Roman Catholics and the heathens at home and abroad' (Jamie, 1900, p.333).

At first Hope had attempted to keep his temperance and anti-popery activities apart, but they eventually became thoroughly intertwined. Hope started the British League of Juvenile Abstainers in 1847. The League revealed some imperial considerations in its object: 'The Union of the youth of the British Empire on (the) principle (of total abstinence)' (Jamie, 1900, pp.165–66 and 240). Hope had carefully avoided linking the League too closely with the Sabbath schools movement, as he wished to extract as wide a group of children as possible. He wished neither to have the League too tied to any particular variant of Protestantism nor, ideally, to appear to be associated with religion at all. Despite this desire, even at the beginning the

League's rules insisted that all League meetings were opened and closed with prayers, and within two years Hope overtly increased the religious influence upon the organisation. He created new Sabbath schools for those League members not already attending one, began evening schools for apprentices and took the first steps towards instigating the British League Anti-Popery Crusade. He believed in the importance of education, but it had to be an education antagonistic to Catholicism. In a letter to his sister in 1840, he complained about the attendance of a local knight at the funeral of a Catholic bishop:

> Suppose Sir Thomas's young children see him showing respect to a Papist, will not the edge of their hatred of Popery, in which I trust they have been educated, be blunted by such an exhibition? These children will be more easily converted than children who have seen Popery, like sin, kept at a distance.

Hope's Protestantism demanded that Protestant children and youth be safe-guarded from the dangers of contact with Catholics. By 1845 he was urging the establishment of a children's anti-popery movement. In 1848 he wrote: 'I have thought of teaching the children to avoid the mass-house as the public-house, and Popery as alcohol' (Jamie, 1900, p.240). By 1851 the work of the League inextricably linked anti-popery and temperance campaigns. The religious classes run by the League now featured No-Popery lessons, and the British League office now contained a Protestant library along with the books on temperance. Hope's apprentice classes also featured No-Popery strongly, and he had initiated an essay competition on Popery for Scottish divinity students as well as for his own British League members. The successful essayists from within the League were then used to extend the number of anti-Catholic classes available for League members. From then on, the British League was an anti-Catholic organisation as well as one promoting Hope's ideas on temperance. It was important, argued Hope, to communicate the No-Popery message to the widest audience possible. He was aware that working class Protestants could ill-afford to buy No-Popery literature, so he would often supply his tracts freely or as cheaply as he possibly could. He also considered how he could maximise the impact of this campaign and he concluded that it was crucial to use all means possible to win people to his cause and, to this end, he recognised the need to give his campaigns as much and as wide an appeal as he could.

INNOCENT, PROTESTANT, LEISURE: DRILLING THE MIND AND THE BODY

Hope saw the provision of leisure activities by his organisations as an import-ant means of maximising his appeal. He had himself been a 'devoted foot-baller', also acting as 'secretary and treasurer for a very select club of young Edinburgh lawyers' (Jamie, 1900, pp.98–99). In 1854, he organised the transformation of some land into a playground. The park, which some called 'John Hope's Park' was opened on the Queen's Birthday with great cere-mony. British League involvement was evident. A loyal address to the Queen was voted, and 'agents of the League' were present that day as on other days

to 'superintend' the games. Hope himself attended and special events were
held on other occasions. A year later the landlord refused to continue the
lease, though some years later another park, also bearing Hope's name, was
developed with his active support elsewhere in the city (Jamie, 1900, pp.302
and 332).

Councillor Hope advocated the provision of grounds, where early versions
of football, and other sports, could be played. Sport to him was enjoyable,
but also an important means by which children could spend their time without
succumbing to temptations. Music and singing, excursions, visits and picnics,
play and sport all became important activities within the British League.
Although these activities were secondary to the main purposes of the League,
they were important in making Hope's movement attractive to would-be
members, and in ensuring the continued interest of members in the activities
of the League itself, once they had joined. So it can be no surprise that the
great popularity of the volunteer movement of 1859 had an immediate appeal
for Hope. Jamie (1900, p.385) writes:

> He deemed it worthy of espousal for many reasons. He was a sturdy patriot; he was
> fond of military display; he saw that the drill would afford healthy exercise and
> healthy recreation for office-lads and working-men; and he believed that there
> would be many social benefits through the bringing together, for a common
> purpose, of various classes of men.

Hope viewed the volunteer movement as a means of educating and exerting
some social control over the working classes: volunteering was an innocent
means of filling their leisure time. Hope had quickly recognised that the
movement would provide him with a means of maintaining contact and
control over those who had passed through the League. Recruitment was easy
since drilling was very popular. Those approached were keen to be involved,
and it is recounted that those still attending his various classes excitedly
demanded that they also be included. Consequently, when he set up the
Abstainers' Volunteer Rifle Company, the sixteenth, in late 1859, with
himself as commanding officer, it also contained within its ranks, a cadet unit
composed of his own British League members. The appeal of drilling varied
with the seasons. The interest of the older volunteers tended to fall away in
the winter months, when they had to drill in the cold and the dark, following
their daytime's exertion. As a result, Hope realised that there was a need to
arrange for other attractions to hold their interest during this time. He
successfully advocated that the Corn Exchange buildings be made available
for groups of volunteers to drill inside. He also argued that volunteers should
be required to drill less often in winter.

Great care was taken to ensure that the potential of the volunteering
movement was maximised: it had to remain attractive to members who should
not be driven away by making unreasonable demands of them. He personally
oversaw every detail of the activities of the company, even down to deciding
on appropriate music to be played by the flute or brass bands. Hope was
especially careful in selecting the company members. Volunteers had to
abstain from alcohol and tobacco and were also selected on the basis of their
'good character'. Complaints were made public by a few of the many who

found themselves excluded but could not understand why. Hope refused to explain publicly the exact principles of selection he employed. However, in a letter, Hope explained the basis on which he judged the character of applicants: they had to be 'church-going and praying young men'. Doubtful cases were given additional opportunities to impress Hope with their good character by having them attend his Sabbath class (Jamie, 1900, pp.390–91). The Protestant and anti-Catholic character of his volunteer company was strengthened in other ways. The officers were chosen from his assistants in the British League. The usual volunteer's motto 'In Defence not Defiance' was judged insufficiently precise by Hope, and replaced by 'God is our Defence'. By 1867, the progress of the original company was such that Hope was determined to establish a full corps, which meant that he could obtain government support for his British League cadets. After some politicking by Hope, the result was the foundation of the 3rd Edinburgh Rifles Volunteers, run on precisely the same principles as before, and with essentially the same personnel involved in its organisation.

It can be no surprise that the character of the 3rd ERV was Protestant. After all, he had advocated that support for the volunteer movement and the extension of the Protestant franchise be achieved by granting the vote to those volunteers with more than two year's service. Indeed, the necessity of maintaining the Protestant nature of political and civil life was a common argument advanced by Hope. Any organisations or institutions that included Catholics within them were not to be trusted. So Hope argued that Catholics had no place in Parliament, questioned their presence in the Edinburgh police force, and implied that they had no legitimate role anywhere within the power of the British State (Jamie, 1900, p.324):

> The preservation of our civil and religious liberty requires the exclusion of Roman Catholics from Parliament, power and place . . . as Roman Catholics are not themselves free agents, but compellable to obey their priests, bishops, and Pope, so, for my enjoyment of my civil and religious liberty, it is needful that the Roman Catholics have no share in making laws for me.

And later Hope was to argue that Catholics be excluded 'from all places of pay and power at home and abroad' (Jamie, 1900, p.274).

In 1854, by which time Hope had formed the Scottish Protestant Association, he chaired a meeting which passed a motion including these last demands and also urged that no public funds support Catholic education or prison chaplains, 'that the Government . . . uphold to the utmost of their power the Protestant faith, as the source, the foundation and the bulwark of our glorious constitution' and 'that the Jesuits be expelled from the country; that nunneries and monasteries by utterly abolished . . .' (Handley, 1947, p.113). Hope's twinned crusades of anti-Popery and temperance, ensured that the 3rd ERV, an offshoot of these efforts, would be restricted to Protestant, anti-Catholic, abstainers. His imperialism and staunch Protestantism inevitably coloured his views on Ireland, which he saw as being the key to the struggle for Britain and Protestantism. 'Ireland', he declared, 'is the battle-field'. He continued: 'Upon Ireland the Pope has laid his hand, and Protestant electors must arise and rend it from his grasp' (Jamie, 1900, p.274). Hope's views continued to influence the 3rd ERV, even after he had departed from the scene. In 1900, the corps, which by then had been first renamed the 2nd ERV before finally becoming the 4th Volunteer Battalion, The Royal Scots, was still commanded by Hope's former proteges and 'still identified with the principles of the British League' (Jamie, 1900, p.540).

THE 3RD EDINBURGH RIFLE VOLUNTEERS FOOTBALL CLUB

On 27 December 1873, Queen's Park, Glasgow and Scotland's very first association football club when formed in 1867, took two teams of club members 'for a missionary game in Edinburgh to popularise the sport there'. One result of this demonstration was that, on 24 February, in the office of the British League, Edinburgh's first football club was set up by the 3rd ERV. Membership of the football club was restricted to the members of the corps and specific rules ensured that it would not interfere with the volunteers' primary duties. Football was to be seen as a useful, additional recreation, rather than as an end in itself. 'The membership was confined solely to members of the corps, and the rules provided that no games should be played during summer or on days when any drills were to take place'.

Hope, as Jamie indicated, was interested in the football club. Certainly the rules strongly suggest his authorship. Within the corps all real authority was invested in Hope alone, and he did oversee all details of the 3rd ERV's activities. A football club would certainly have appealed to his own interest in sport and to his belief that sport was a useful means of retaining the interest of members of the volunteers. The maintenance of interest in volunteer activity had proved difficult over the cold winter months. Hope, who had already identified some potential solutions, would undoubtedly have realised that football could be a big attraction during these times. The club rules indicate that someone in authority was worried that the game could prove to be too attractive, with more appeal than drills, even when the warmth of summer returned. Hope was certainly directly involved with the club at the outset. It is recorded that the opening game began with 'the late Mr John Hope kicking off the ball'. (*Edinburgh Athletic Times*, 23 September 1895).

At first the 3rd ERV football club went from strength to strength. By the time that the first Edinburgh Cup had been established, Hope's club was dominant. The trophy was won by the Third Edinburgh Rifle Volunteers, who beat the Thistle six-nil in the spring of 1876. The next year the same two clubs contested the final again, or to be more precise, one did not. The 3rd ERV, after an abandoned semi-final tie and a convincing five-nil victory over Swifts in the replay, failed to turn up for the final. So Thistle gained possession of the trophy, now renamed the East of Scotland Cup. Although 3rd ERV remained the top team in the East, they were found wanting in games with clubs based in the more competitive West. Soon they were also being overtaken in the East, where the finalists in 1878 were two Edinburgh clubs destined to be rivals to the present day, Heart of Midlothian and Hibernian. Although around this time the 3rd ERV were described as 'the oldest and the best exponents of the dribbling game in the East', they appear to have been in some disarray. The 3rd ERV are reported to have fallen out with the

Edinburgh Football Association, though they did play Hibs in the Scottish Cup. This proved not to be too happy an occasion for them. Three goals were conceded inside half an hour. Two ERV players then made the discovery that they were ill. The game was finished early, but the players did have some further enjoyment as a 'mixed friendly was played until the call of time'.

The 3rd ERV seem to have drifted out of football sometime soon afterwards. It is tempting to conclude that the supremacy of Hibernian, the first Catholic Irish-Scots club, might have had some influence on the decision, but there is no real evidence to support this fancy. Hope's team, despite its short-lived history, did play a significant part in the development of Scottish football. Not only was it one of the first Scottish clubs, the first in Edinburgh, but it was instrumental in founding the Edinburgh Football Association. Early Edinburgh football belied the douce image of 'Auld Reekie'. It was marred by crowd misbehaviour off the field and player misbehaviour on the field. Matches were spoiled by 'the incompetency of the referee', an incompetency which resulted from the partizanship of the official! Often the toss of the coin to decide which team's umpire presided also determined the result of the game. Some of the 3rd ERV players were central to the organisation of the game in Edinburgh, being called upon to arbitrate on decisions about incidents on the field of play and, effectively therefore, they established the framework for the rules of the game. One club member was described as being 'the father of Edinburgh football'. The 3rd ERV became the first club to have their own ground, which inevitably became the location for games involving the Edinburgh Association; and it seems that at least one fundamental principle of the 3rd ERV became a basic principle of Edinburgh football: all after-match entertainments arranged by a home club for their visitors were 'strictly teetotal', with the meetings occurring in various temperance hotels. Nor is this an erroneous boast from a former 3rd ERV player. A Glasgow sporting paper commented that the 'pioneers' of Edinburgh football were 'total abstainers to a man' (*Scottish Umpire*, 12 November 1884; *Edinburgh Athletic Times*, 21 September 1895).

The important role played by 3rd ERV in Edinburgh football may explain why Hibernian's initial application to join the local Football Association was not exactly welcomed. This Irish-Scots club was also firmly associated with temperance. Hibernian was linked to St Patrick's Church, which had, in Canon Hannan, one of Scotland's leading Catholic temperance campaigners in charge. It was this church's Catholic Young Men's Society that 'sponsored' the League of the Cross, the name of the Total Abstinence Society, as well as Hibernian Football Club. Indeed, the League of the Cross followed similar practices to Protestant temperance bodies. The League 'had quite a range of recreational interests, League of the Cross Halls, football and billiards competitions, the principle being that idleness was one of the big factors in intemperance' (Canning, 1979, pp.xvii–xviii and 134–35). Consequently, the Edinburgh FA must have felt itself in something of a quandry. The organisation does appear to have taken its support for temperance very seriously. It may have thought that support should be given even (perhaps especially) to a Catholic Irish-Scots teetotal football team. A Catholic Irish-Scots teetotal team would place even No-Popery, temperance campaigners like Hope in the horns of a dilemma. Hope and his supporters believed that No-Popery and temperance work was allied. From their world-view the pledge of temperance from the Hibernians would be an important break-through; perhaps they entertained a belief in the possibility of the overthrow of what they saw to be an even greater 'evil', that of Popery.

The expectation of greater social tolerance following social contact between different social groups has become known as the 'contact hypothesis' (Hewstone and Brown, 1986). Certainly Hope believed this to be the case, which was why he usually argued against social contact between Protestants and Catholics. The exclusion of Catholics from Protestant company was necessary to safeguard Protestants from what Hope believed to be the malign consequence of this social contact, an increase in Protestant tolerance of Catholics. Yet it is possible that he might have adopted the other variant of the 'contact hypothesis', that it could have benign effects (from Hope's perspective) in certain advantageous circumstances; after all, he did believe in very forceful missionary work among the Catholic Irish by trained missionaries.[1] His volunteers in the 3rd ERV were not naive Protestants, but specially selected Protestants, chosen on the basis of their 'good character', as defined by dual commitment to No-Popery and total abstention. Might not Hope and the 3rd ERV have taken an opposite view on the potential benefits of social contact for No-Popery Protestantism in this situation? Perhaps a breakthrough could be achieved by a more subtle form of No-Popery missionary work than was usual for Hope: a breakthrough aided by sporting efforts and exchanges on the football field. Certainly Hope's self-selection and training of his volunteer corps would have led him to expect that his own followers would be inoculated against the effects of contact with Catholics. Some recognition of these possibilities may have meant that even the 3rd ERV could go along with the eventual decision of the EFA, and organisation which displayed less antagonism to Hibernian than did the Scottish Football Association, to accept Hibernian as a member club (Finn, 1991a; Rafferty, 1973).

One of the reasons for Catholic Irish-Scots participating in Scottish football was that they believed that they would be seen much more positively and that the prejudices against them would be diminished if they had sporting contact with Protestant Scots. Once they were eventually allowed to joint the EFA, Hibs players must have become increasingly convinced that sporting contacts did offer a means of overcoming any anti-Catholic prejudice and anti-Irish racism that they had experienced. The game against 3rd ERV, Hope's anti-Catholic club, which even led to mixed teams continuing a friendly match together, must have seemed to confirm the validity of this viewpoint. Certainly some years later, the writer of the 'Edinburgh Letter' column in the *Glasgow Observer* praised the successes of Hibernian and claimed that (*Glasgow Observer*, 25 April 1885):

> . . . even games and pastimes help the Catholic social revival. Our catholic young men, according to all healthy thinking, do well to take their place in such things as are represented by the cricket and football games of the country. In these as in more important fields, reputation is won, friendship established, and prejudices are broken down.

Nor was this a unique expression of these views. Later the Observer quoted approvingly an extract from a poem published in the Dundee Advertiser which had said that football eased sectarianism and 'a' the evils of life (*Glasgow Observer*, 9 January 1886; 25 April 1885).

It is ironic that members of Hibernian, just like Hope, also believed in the 'contact hypothesis'. As a convinced anti-Catholic campaigner Hope usually wanted to keep Protestants away from the influence of social contact with Catholics. The character of Hibernian was that it was not an anti-Protestant club, simply a Catholic club. So there was the same belief in the effects of social contact, but now it was judged to have positive outcomes. Playing football against Protestant Scots would have the benign effect of diminishing the majority's anti-Catholic and anti-Irish prejudices. Belief in the 'contact hypothesis' is very common and very strong: Hope simply states the belief in one of its more extreme and more negative forms. Yet, the 'contact hypothesis' is much too simplistic and might even be simply wrong. Social contact has a range of outcomes: it can just as easily exacerbate prejudice and conflict (Hewstone and Brown, 1986). It also has a number of unintended consequences.

NO CHARITY: DAVID HOPE, FAITH AND BIGOTRY

After almost another century of contact between Catholics and Protestants, very little magic had been worked, despite the belief in the potent spell weaved by contact: anti-Catholicism still existed, albeit in different forms and to a different extent. Discrimination against Catholics still took place. Where the 3rd ERV had started, Rangers had continued. The Glasgow club had embodied an anti-Catholic tradition, and had refused to employ Catholic players (Finn, 1993). The policy seems to have been based on a traditional allegiance to a conspiracy ideology that saw Catholics as untrustworthy. Catholic players, it was believed, would not and could not be loyal to Rangers. John Lawrence, then the chairman of Rangers, stated in 1969 that 'the policy of not signing Catholics has been with us since the club was formed . . . in the ninety-six years of the club's existence, the policy has always been the same' (*Daily Express*, 2 June 1969). Former player, trainer and chief scout, James Smith, explained why this was the case. It was to do with ensuring that all players in the team were united behind the one cause (*Daily Express*, 3 June 1969) 'To my mind, the solution to having a good team is harmony, and you cannot have harmony if there is the possibility of Catholic players and Protestant players in the same team getting into cliques'.

Clearly the view of contact between Protestants and Catholics within Rangers was that it could only lead to further division. However, a few years later, an incident within the club revealed a belief in another variant of the simple contact hypothesis. Just as John Hope had warned Protestants of the dangers of contact with Catholics, there remained, a century later, staunch Protestants who were suspicious of co-religionists who had associated with Catholics. Indeed, to have had genuine personal contact with Catholics could even lead to another 'staunch Protestant' being discriminated against as a lesser Protestant. To be too close to a Catholic was to be someone close to being a Catholic.

Lawrence was still the chairman of Rangers in 1973 when the club celebrated its centenary year. Almost half way through the centenary year and on the advice of his doctor, Lawrence, then aged 79, decided to stand down as chairman but to remain a director. In addition, he wanted Lawrence Marlborough, his grandson, and Willie Waddell, the club's general manager and a former player and manager to join the board and become the managing director. Lawrence very strongly and publicly advocated that the new chairman be his fellow director, David Hope. Hope had responsibility for the Rangers Social club and for the very successful Rangers Pools, the source of a substantial income that enabled the club to undertake a rolling programme of improvements to Ibrox Park. As a result of Lawrence's comments after a board meeting, the Glasgow based Daily Record stated that Lawrence's resignation was 'confirmed' and, 'It looks certain that David Hope – named yesterday by Lawrence as his successor – will be the new chairman'. The paper also reported that only Lawrence would talk after the meeting. Elsewhere in the paper it also noted: 'As one prominent shareholder told me yesterday, "That new stand might not have been built but for David Hope and his pools. No one outside the club knows just how hard he has worked . . ."' (*Daily Record*, 30 May 1973).

Despite this 'confirmation' of Hope as the next chairman, the next day the Record commented on the 'Ibrox somersault'. An official club statement had relayed 'the unanimous decision of the board' that 'Mr Lawrence, despite doctor's orders to the contrary, will remain chairman to the end of our centenary year'. The newspaper concluded that there was 'clearly a board room wrangle' (*Daily Record*, 31 May 1973). On the next day, the Record had a sensational, front-page account of what Lawrence described as 'the most tragic board meeting I've attended in twenty years' (*Daily Record*, 1 June 1973). Lawrence had given to the newspaper an emotional interview in which, despite efforts to keep private the matters discussed at the meeting, his own anger and irritation ensured that he gave much away. He was 'staying on because of crisis'. He continued:

> The board is split. I have no idea if David Hope will resign. I made it perfectly clear I wanted him as my successor. I'm sorry it didn't come off. Davie Hope is a good man, and a good Ranger. No one has done more for the club. It's a shame that David, who has done more for this club than any other director, should be pilloried like this.

Lawrence then went on to discuss Hope's marriage. Hope had, some 43 years before, in 1930, married a Catholic in a Catholic Church, a Catholic who had died many years before this crucial board meeting. Lawrence refused to confirm that this was the issue that had let other directors to deem Hope an unacceptable choice for chairman: 'It was a private meeting and I cannot discuss what was said there'. Yet Lawrence tellingly added: 'I'm against bigots', before he went on to repeat his earlier sentiments: 'It's a shame that Davie, who has done more for the club than any other director, should be pilloried in this way'. Expanding on his theme, while angrily thumping his hands together, Lawrence went still further:

> It has never been a secret that Davie Hope fell in love with a young Catholic girl and married her. All the directors were aware of this. I had never heard any object to it before. We are supposed to be Christians. So what if he married a Catholic in a Catholic Church? What's wrong with that? She was a Christian. I'm sure your Catholic readers will be pleased to read how a person in that position came up through the club all the way to become a director.

Once more Lawrence refused to confirm that it was Hope's marriage to a Catholic that had so diminished him in the eyes of his other fellow directors. He then talked briefly about himself and how he daily prayed that he would hurt no-one, 'Yet, Davie can be hurt in this way'. Again he returned to the matter of Hope's marriage, but this time he made the reason for the split within the board crystal-clear:

> Nine persons out of ten will agree it's a shame that because Davie married a Catholic girl years ago he can't become chairman. It's beyond me. I don't ask a man whether he is Catholic or Protestant. As it happens, Davie is a staunch Protestant, and one of nature's gentlemen.

Other directors were more tight-lipped, if also split, on exactly what had taken place at the meeting. George Brown, a retired school headmaster and former Rangers player, was a friend of Hope's. He admitted that Hope's marriage to a Catholic had been raised but denied that it had any influence upon the proceedings, arguing that if Hope was fit to be a director then he was fit to be club chairman. However, the vice-chairman, Matt Taylor, denied that the matter had been raised at all: 'This has never, ever been raised in the boardroom, and certainly not at last night's meeting'. The remaining director, Rae Simpson, a surgeon, declined to discuss the meeting. And Hope also refused to discuss what had been said at a private meeting but denied that his marriage had contributed to the outcome.

The story rumbled on (*Daily Record*, 2 June 1973). The next day Hope declared that he still wished to be chairman and he 'would fight hard' to achieve the position. In an interview he stated that he had never hidden his marriage to a Catholic: 'Why should I? Although I'm not a regular church-goer, I am a staunch Protestant'. He expanded on his earlier denial that his marriage had anything to do with his failure to become chairman. A number of directors had visited him at home and knew his wife and, 'When she died suddenly eleven years ago, the Ibrox board attended her funeral – a Catholic ceremony'. He continued: 'I am a Rangers man. That has been my life. And I emphatically deny that the question of my marriage to a Catholic had any bearing on the so-called split in the board'. He did admit that he regretted turning down Lawrence's offer that he become chairman some eighteen months earlier, a refusal he had given because he did not want to be seen moving in on the club's centenary glory. He did not explain if, or why, he would have been any more acceptable to the board at that earlier date. However, with the appointment of a new chairman still unresolved, Hope had good reason to play down any possibility that he was an unacceptable candidate. Hope's hopes probably ensured, understandably, that he publicly presented, perhaps not altogether in good faith, a charitable account of the actions of other directors.

Yet Hope's interview was not the big story in that edition. On the same day as he had been interviewed, there had been another board meeting in the evening. Lawrence had been confirmed as the club chairman for the remaining seven months of the year. The official statement from the club was that 'the matter is now closed' (*Daily Record*, 2 June 1973). When the meeting had concluded, Taylor had said: 'Everyone's happy. There's no question of trouble on the board'. Hope himself said, 'I'm happy with the outcome. I don't want to say any more'. The Record observed that, despite the protestations of peace, the split in the board had led to a special unscheduled board meeting and it provided some background to the decision taken. There had been concern that the boardroom battle would be taken to an extraordinary general meeting where the internal dispute would become 'very public indeed'.

Details about shareholdings were given. Taylor owned 40,000 shares. Lawrence personally only had 150 shares but his company controlled around 50,000. Simpson had nearly 11,000 shares. The other directors, Brown and Hope owned 684 and 387 respectively. The directors controlled around 100,000 shares. Ownership of double that amount lay outside of the boardroom. However, the small shareholder had very little power. There were substantial private shareholdings. One 'prominent shareholder' had claimed to be in control of a consortium 'close to 100,000 shares'. And a 'mystery purchaser' had bought 1,000 shares at five pounds each. The largest shareholder outside of the board was John F. Wilson, son of the chairman before Lawrence, and a former vice-chairman who had left the board after a disagreement in 1967, around the time that Hope was invited to join.[2] The story of substantial purchases of shares was confirmed elsewhere. There was a 'steady demand' for Rangers shares which were now to be found in the range of 510 to 515p a share (*Glasgow Herald*, 2 June 1973).

After this meeting it did seem as if peace had been declared. In the newspapers the story had gone cold. Very few additional comments were printed in the media. The Rangers Supporters' Association claimed not to have discussed the matter at its own meeting. One official dismissed the differences as 'power politics' and claimed that the 'real reason for the boardroom dispute had not been made public by the directors'. The Supporters' Association had, of course, not been involved in any way with the actions of the board, but those few comments that were made by any of the Association's office-bearers indicated clear support for Taylor. The argument put forward by one spokesman was that: 'It's normally accepted that when a chairman steps down the vice-chairman steps up. We have a lot of shareholders in the Association and I'm sure that they would back Mr Taylor'. The same spokesman also argued that it was a decision of the board of directors alone to choose the new chairman (*Daily Record*, 4 June 1973). Over the next week or so, the press seemed to have lost interest in the story. Elsewhere heightened interest was apparent. Just under a fortnight later

Rangers shares were wanted at 560p each, and it was commented that, 'continued demand for Rangers shares provided the feature of the Scottish floor of the Stock Exchange yesterday' (*Glasgow Herald*, 13 June 1973).

LOST HOPE

By then the board dispute seemed over, or at least postponed for another seven months, until the end of the club's centenary year. But, seven months appears to be a much shorter time than promised in the world of footballing politics. The first board meeting had taken place on 1 June and peace had been declared by Taylor after the emergency board meeting of 2 June. Yet, Lawrence's supposed reign until the end of the year actually ended little more than a fortnight later when, at another unscheduled board meeting on 19 June, Lawrence now finally stepped down. The story was headlined, 'Secret deal ends Ibrox battle' (*Daily Record*, 20 June 1973). Yet the new chairman was not Hope. Instead, Lawrence himself had now nominated Taylor as the new club chairman. Rae Simpson, who had 'supported Taylor during the boardroom struggles', became the new vice-chairman. John Wilson, former vice-chairman of the club, whose father had been a staunch Protestant, Orangeman, Unionist, and chairman of Rangers, now returned to the board that he had left after a dispute some years before.[3] In addition, those directors that Lawrence had intended bringing onto the board at the first meeting were now accepted. Willie Waddell and Lawrence Marlborough, his grandson, now became directors of Rangers. Hope had no comment to make, Hope expressed no hopes for the future.

Hope never did fulfill his hopes of becoming chairman of Rangers. After a sufficiently decent interval, he retired from the board two years later because of 'ill-health'. Ironically, his main rival, Matt Taylor died very shortly after Hope's resignation. Taylor was succeeded by his loyal supporter, Rae Simpson, who had become vice-chairman after only six months on the board, and who was himself the grandson of the very first Rangers chairman (*Glasgow Herald*, 27 August 1975; 11 September 1975; 17 September 1975). After the meeting that decided on Taylor as the new chairman, Lawrence had stated that Hope would remain as a director. But it was the next day before it became clear that the outspoken Lawrence, now titled club president, would no longer be expected to attend board meetings. 'He has done his share of work for the club and I think he fully deserves a happy retirement', said Matt Taylor. And, thus, Taylor, who had been described as the 'new Master of Ibrox' demonstrated the power he now wielded (*Daily Record*, 20 June 1973; 21 June 1973).

Retrospective analyses of the boardroom battle by journalists who followed events make it clear that Hope's marriage to a Catholic was indeed a very contentious and decisive matter within the boardroom. On Hope's death, one journalist, Jack Webster wrote about Hope's failure to become chairman:

> At the heart of the matter was the fact that he had married a Roman Catholic lady in 1930, a situation regarded as untenable by a section of those who follow the long blue trail to Ibrox Park. Though the matter was all hushed up in a well worn

tradition of the Rangers boardroom, the fact of Hope's marriage to a Catholic became an issue. There are people who might try to deny this now but, as a journalist who stayed close to the story at the time, I can assure you it did.

Webster confirms Lawrence's version of the Hope affair. Despite the clear participation of club directors in this example of anti-Catholic prejudice, he somehow persists in making the usual attribution of responsibility to the club's supporters. Webster's account is that Hope won a majority vote of the directors but that Taylor then sent a note to Lawrence pointing out that he had the majority share-holding and that he would make the appointment of Hope, a matter to be decided at a share-holders general meeting. At the final board meeting to resolve the crisis, 'Lawrence proposed Taylor as chairman and Hope stood down to avoid further damage to the club.' (For retrospective accounts, see both *Glasgow Herald*, 21 July 1987 and the *Sunday Standard*, 5 July 1981).

Accounts of the distribution of the club's voting power vary, but the real power lay in the hands of those who owned, or held the proxies for, large blocs of shares. Although the directors apparently held only 100,000 of the 300,000 shares, it appears that Taylor had the support outside the boardroom of a handful of large shareholders. All of this does show that there was indeed a power struggle going on, but it also strongly reveals that the issue of Hope's marriage to a Catholic was important, not to fans, but to all sorts of share-holders. It was not only to those with a small share-holding, those fans who might be represented by the Supporters' Association, that Hope's marriage was an important matter. Those with substantial shares in the club were the only ones able to influence the decision. Nor was it the ordinary fan that was purchasing substantial blocks of shares at inflated prices. Many of the details of this boardroom battle still remain unknown and will remain so.[4] The main protagonists are now dead. Any new accounts are now more likely to attempt to present the events in a less damaging light than that of a seeming battle for a pure Protestant ascendancy on the Rangers board.

Indeed, it may even be the case that Hope's Catholic wedding to a Catholic woman was opportunistically used against him in a boardroom struggle that also involved the more usual concerns of pride, prestige, power and money. Even if the religious dimension was only one of the considerations, its appearance as a factor in discussions at boardroom level should not be minimised, the question of a director's wife's religious affiliation was still an appropriate weapon with which to damage an opponent in a Rangers board-room battle. Nor should Hope's need to proclaim that he was a 'staunch Protestant' in juxtaposition to his marriage to a Catholic be ignored. It is the nature of the discourse in the Hope affair that demonstrates in a most revealing way the considerable emotional significance that Catholics and Catholicism had for very important Rangers shareholders and directors. The antagonism against Catholicism and Catholics was not only directed against adherents of that religion but extended to those who associated with Catholics. To be married to a Catholic, even to a Catholic who had died more than ten years previously, was a weapon to halt Hope's hopes of becoming chairman of Rangers.

ANTI-CATHOLICISM AND SCOTTISH SOCIETY

Analysis of accounts of events uncovers much of the psychological structure of everyday beliefs (Billig, 1991; Fraser and Gaskell, 1900). Detailed analysis of the accounts given in the Hope affair would display much about the potency and acceptance of anti-Catholicism in everyday thinking in Scotland of the early 1970s. Hope's marriage to a Catholic was inappropriate behaviour for a Rangers director. His only recourse to this challenge was to assert his own Protestant orthodoxy, that he really was a 'staunch Protestant', and to proclaim that, regardless of his marriage to a Catholic, 'I am a Rangers man. That has been my life'. Hope's disclaimers betrayed much but other Rangers directors divulged more. Lawrence revealed all, and his other comments stripped his own prejudices bare. Hope was 'a person in that position', simply because he had married a Catholic who died before he became a Rangers director. So Lawrence assumed that, 'as a person in that position', Hope's rise to the boardroom would have 'pleased' many Catholics. Lawrence's own prejudices were self-evident: successful Protestant Scots who had overcome the handicap of marriage to Catholic Scots were, literally, in a remarkable position.

Yet, unlike others with power at Ibrox, Lawrence clearly tolerated close associations with Catholics, though even he still felt it necessary to assert Hope's credentials as 'a staunch Protestant', not of course that he enquired about these matters, or so he claimed. Of course, Catholic Scots had known that Rangers did not accept Catholics on the playing staff; a policy that both Lawrence and Taylor had defended only a few years previously on two separate occasions. (For Lawrence's comments, see the *Daily Express* and *Daily Record* of 2 June 1969; for Taylor's, see *Daily Express*, 10 May 1967). Lawrence had employed the classic defence (Billig, 1985) against an accusation of personal prejudice when he upheld the right of Rangers to discriminate against Catholics: he boasted of his own close associations with Catholics. 'Two of my greatest friends in football, Jimmy McGrory of Celtic and Sir Matt Busby of Manchester United, are Catholics', he said, 'But in the 96 years of the club's existence, the policy has remained the same'.

The only surprise in the Hope case was the demonstration of the extent of the anti-Catholic prejudice at Ibrox. Occurring shortly after both Lawrence and Taylor had publicly confirmed and defended the club's policy of discriminating against Catholic players, and when it was not uncommon to hear stories that Rangers' Protestant players' careers had ended because they had married a Catholic (Murray, 1984), Hope's own blighted career could please few Catholics. Now Catholic Scots had confirmation that the dominant 'Christian' power bloc was uncertain of 'staunch Protestants' who had married Catholics some 43 years ago and who had been widowers for more than a decade.

At least Lawrence did appear to recognise that there was something shameful about these boardroom events. Perhaps the silence and disinformation provided by other directors reveals a similar recognition but it could just as easily be seen as evidence of their belief that it was an internal matter. This latter position received some explicit and implicit support from the media coverage of the board's actions. The *Glasgow Herald* proved to be strangely reticent in its coverage of this story. Scotland's biggest circulation broadsheet had very little to say when Scotland's best supported club, well known for its staunch Protestantism, demonstrated the extent to which anti-Catholic prejudice could be found at the centre of the club. The refusal of the paper to say much about the issue of religious discrimination and Rangers may have been linked to its own editorial stance. The Herald was historically pro-Conservative and Unionist (an allegiance which is no longer true), and that political bloc had relied significantly upon an anti-Irish, anti-Catholic, working-class Tory vote for its electoral strength in Glasgow and its environs (Miller, 1985). Rangers matches were venues for the expression of this Protestant populism (Walker, 1990). Perhaps these influences meant that the paper, like the football club, had taken this peculiar version of a politicised Scottish Protestant commonsense too much for granted and saw little wrong inside Rangers. Certainly the paper found little to comment upon and displayed considerable reserve in reporting the story.[5]

For example, after the first stormy meeting of the board, the Glasgow Herald merely relayed the official club statement and then, the next day, spoke of a 'possible tussle' over the successor to Lawrence and revealed that there was a background of changing ownership of club shares. 'Rangers board settles differences' was how the paper described the subsequent meeting. This article did refer to the religious element in the decision-making, but quoted an unnamed director (presumably George Brown on the basis of the attribution in the *Daily Record* story), who dismissed the significance of the matter: 'During the meeting the question of Mr Hope's marriage to a Roman Catholic woman was raised, although, according to one director, this had no bearing on the decision that Mr Lawrence should remain in the chair until the end of the year, the club's centenary'. No other comment was made about this aspect of the story.

However, in the paper's letters column a couple of days later, a reader judged that the controversy surrounding the failure of the first board meeting to appoint a new chairman was:

> . . . proof positive of the drift in recent years of the reputation and performance of a club whose name and fame had been a credit to Scottish football. To infer that the proposed successor to the chair was unfit because he had married a Catholic some 43 years ago and now deceased some twenty years ago is again indicative of the rot which exists at the kernel of Ibrox.

It is revealing that even this writer still retained a belief in a glorious Rangers past which 'had been a credit to Scottish football'. Yet the revealed 'rot' was the result of some light being shone on one facet of the club's traditional anti-Catholic policy. This policy was synonymous with the club's name and had already led some to see the club in terms of infamy rather than fame. Nonetheless, even in this highly unusual situation, the Scottish press hardly departed from its traditional response, which was, as Murray (1984) has shown, to pass little or no comment on Rangers' anti-Catholic policy.

When, in late June, Taylor was announced as the new chairman, the Herald still spoke of the sequence of events in terms that would have been acceptable for any other boardroom battle: it commented on the changes in share-ownership and on what it described as a 'power struggle between Mr Hope and Mr Taylor', and explained that Lawrence's retention of the chairmanship had been 'to avert possible resignations'. The only departure from any usual boardroom report was the almost word-for-word repetition (the reference to the supposed duration of Lawrence's extended chairmanship was well and truly deleted) of the unidentified director's denial that Hope's marriage had been influential. Now, even if that denial was accepted as being accurate, a judgement which other evidence contradicts, the statement that Hope's Catholic marriage had merited boardroom discussion should have been sufficient cause for some critical journalistic comment. Yet there was none. Presumably such examples of anti-Catholic prejudice were so commonplace as to be both unremarkable and acceptable within much of Scottish society. Certainly genteel Glasgow society does not seem to have been much offended by the actions and discussion within the Rangers boardroom: to be associated with Rangers was still positively prized. A few days later a polite rebuke about the content of the reporting of Rangers' decisions was delivered at the prize-giving ceremony of the locally prestigious, selective and fee-paying, High School of Glasgow by its Rector: 'Listing some of the school's distinguished former pupils, Dr Lees said that reports last week about change in the board of Rangers Football Club did not mention that the new chairman, vice-chairman, and one of the new directors were all "old boys" ' (*Glasgow Herald*, 26 June 1973).

The tabloid *Daily Record* was, unlike the Herald, an open supporter of the cause of Labour in Scotland and had the largest circulation figures in Scotland. Nor was its readership drawn heavily from that section of society represented by the Rangers boardroom or the distinguished former pupils of Glasgow High School. But Scotland's Catholics have demonstrated a disproportionate level of support for the Labour movement. And, although the massive Rangers support could not, and increasingly cannot, simply be categorised as Conservative (Walker, 1990), the West of Scotland Unionist-leaning working class did traditionally support that party, as did substantial sections of those Rangers supporters drawn from the middle, business and professional classes (Miller, 1985). The actual influence of these socio-political factors on the paper's approach is conjecture. However, the Record did treat the story differently from the Glasgow Herald. The Record made much more of the turmoil within the board of Rangers and particular attention was paid to the religious dimension. Critical comments about Rangers and religious prejudice were made but, even here, the criticisms were initially confused before eventually disappearing altogether (*Daily Record*, 30 May 1973; 1 June 1973; 2 June 1973; 4 June 1973; 20 June 1973).

Following the first fateful meeting of the directors, columnist Alec Cameron commented on the 'exclusive' nature of the Rangers board and that some directors of the Bank of England would be deemed unacceptable. However, Cameron's discussion of the Hope affair was less than pointed: there was no mention of anti-Catholicism. Cameron simply stated that 'Hope has passed every test so far and it would be shameful if his marriage 43 years ago were now to be used – as Mr Lawrence says – to "pillory him". It was a happy marriage and Hope is rightly proud of the fact'. Nonetheless, under the headline, 'Faith, Hope and Charity', there was a back-page editorial comment that was much stronger and to the point:

> Was the question of the religion of a Rangers' director's late wife raised at this week's stormy Ibrox board meeting? The directors are split about this. The *Daily Record* says: Religious bigotry can't be stamped out on the terracings if it is still voiced in the boardroom.

Nonetheless, the final sentence of the comment was disappointing: 'A club must surely have more charity in its centenary year'. Presumably the Record did not really wish to imply that in any other year there would be less cause for concern.

Yet it did seem as if the *Daily Record* might be going to take Rangers to task for its anti-Catholicism, even if, surprisingly, there was no mention of the bigotry displayed on the playing field by the club's selection policies. Following the emergency meeting that ensured that Lawrence continued as chairman, the paper continued to ask questions about the reality of the supposed settlement and, in very general terms, about the nature of the internal debate:

> But 24 hours earlier Chairman John Lawrence had talked openly of a boardroom split, a possible resignation and bigotry. The Ibrox affair may have been shelved. It cannot be closed. For the sake of Scotland's soccer image: What goes on in the Rangers boardroom?

Two days later, John Calder, another *Daily Record* columnist, made some telling comments and provided some examples in which majority group prejudice had been overcome. He drew the attention of the Rangers directors to the election of the first black mayor of Los Angeles, despite the four to one white majority in that city. However, an example from closer to home metaphorically struck much closer home. Calder pointed out to the Rangers directors 'that the 95 per cent Roman Catholic Republic of Ireland has just elected a Protestant as its fourth President'. Calder's piece on anti-Catholic Rangers was liberally sprinkled with disapproval: words like 'disturbing', 'tatty', 'nasty' and 'scandalous' were used to reveal his own disgust. Thus, it was to be Calder who revealed the true extent and depth of the problem of anti-Catholicism in Scotland, when he ultimately expressed his acceptance of Rangers' right to be anti-Catholic: 'Their choice of office bearers is their own affair just as their implacable opposition to signing a Catholic player – however deplorable, that is – is also their own business'. The 'rot' was not only at the 'kernel of Ibrox', there was substantial 'rot' at the 'kernel' of Scottish society.

Anti-Catholicism was such a strong force in Scottish society that those opposed to it believed themselves unable to act against it; they were overcome by a sense of apathy, even those, like Calder, clearly disgusted by this prejudice. In the face of such widespread and profound anti-Catholic beliefs, little could be done, or so it was believed. Voices could be raised against it, but not too loudly, and no actions were proposed at all. Soon the Record had fallen silent, and when Taylor finally came out on top, the paper went quietly. The club was now congratulated on the satisfactory outcome and this new, 'good board of directors' was welcomed by a number of the Record's journalist. Beneath an editorial entitled 'Rangers belongs to . . .', in a statement open to a variety of interpretations, the newspaper said to the new Rangers board of directors: 'We welcome you with this thought: Rangers belongs as much to the fans as to the shareholder. *Play it cool at the top*' (Original emphasis).

At the end of the boardroom intrigue, Davie Hope was being described in the Record as a 'lonely figure' after his 'night of disappointment'. Hope, despite having been married to a Catholic who had died before he became a director, remained a director of anti-Catholic Rangers for another two years without becoming chairman of the club, before leaving the board and then remarrying, sometime later, yet another Catholic. (And in that complicated sentence, the complex, complicated and contradictory nature of personal, social contact is partially revealed.) Hope made no comment when Taylor was appointed chairman. The matter of his treatment had already disappeared as an issue from the Record and not appeared at all in journalistic comment in the Herald. The issue of anti-Catholicism had also disappeared from the story. This disappearance is less surprising than that of Hope's treatment, as anti-Catholicism had never fully appeared as a topic. And Hope never publicly commented on this aspect of his club's policy either, but then he was, as he proclaimed, 'a Rangers man' and 'staunch Protestant', even if he had once married a Catholic, as he did again when he remarried a few years later. Ironically, following an appreciation written immediately after his death, his silence was applauded and it was suggested that Hope was 'possibly the greatest Ranger of them all'. He was 'a true Christian' who had behaved with 'supreme dignity and selflessness on behalf of his beloved Rangers (*Glasgow Herald*, 21 July 1987; 28 July 1987). As a director, Hope must have agreed with the more overt Rangers' policy of anti-Catholicism, the refusal to employ Catholic players. So his collusion with Rangers' anti-Catholicism in this, his own case, is understandable, even if Hope's prejudice must be puzzling to faithful followers of the contact hypothesis, who see him as husband to two Catholic wives.

CONCLUSION

In Scotland, more often than not the Catholic Irish-Scots have been portrayed as the instigators of that intergroup conflict described as 'sectarianism' (Finn, 1990a, 1991a, 1991b, 1992, 1993). Yet, John Hope and his 3rd ERV reveal once and for all that the Catholic Irish-Scots football clubs did not introduce bigotry, either religious or political, into Scottish football. The character of the 3rd ERV was not simply Protestant, it was an anti-Catholic club. Sport invariably reflects the socio-political nature of the wider society (Jarvie, 1991) and Scottish football clubs inevitably reflected the various social and political currents found within Scottish society. The proud Protestantism of Scotland meant that exclusively Protestant clubs were inevitable. Historically, Protestantism, which was a protest against Catholicism, has spawned many variants of a vibrant anti-Catholicism (Bruce, 1985) and Scotland, as a result, has had a strong anti-Catholic culture. Soccer clubs with an anti-Catholic orientation were also to be expected with Scotland and all this meant that Catholic soccer clubs were essential if Catholics were to be able to participate in the sport. The maintenance of anti-Catholicism as such a strong and potent force in Scottish football was much less predictable, and its specific retention in the form of Rangers' anti-Catholic selection policy is really surprising: the common belief that this was an inevitable outcome (Murray, 1984, 1988) is mistaken. None of the clubs in Northern Ireland that is associated with Loyalism or Unionism has continuously followed such a policy (see Finn, in press).

Nonetheless, anti-Catholicism and Unionism was, and may even still remain, the dominant characteristic of Rangers. As Walker (1990) has observed, it remains to be seen whether the signing in 1989 of Maurice Johnston, brought up as a Catholic, genuinely ends or merely interrupts that tradition.[6] The case of Davie Hope reveals how anti-Catholic tradition remained strong, not only at Ibrox, but in Scottish society. Anti-Catholicism was upheld, and legitimised, by the popular and populist Protestantism of Rangers (Walker, 1990) and until relatively recently press criticism was silent or muted (Murray, 1984). This detailed account of Hope and Rangers is advanced to support the interpretation that the conspiracy tradition was the 'rot' at the 'kernel of Ibrox' (Finn, 1993). Even more important is the issue of the 'rot' at the 'kernel' of Scottish thinking about the Catholic Irish-Scots, and the contemporary potency of a range of more subtle anti-Catholic beliefs. That is what these case studies can be said to reveal.

NOTES

1. Hope believed the various missions to Catholic Irish-Scots to be relatively ineffective and gave the Edinburgh Irish Mission only faint praise (Jamie, 1900, p.273). Yet this organisation was so vigorous – its missionaries insisted on entering Catholic homes and forcing the occupants to pray – that Edinburgh Catholics petitioned the police to stop this missionary tactic (Handley, 1947, p.103).
2. The estimates of the actual share holdings do vary from one report to another. The present estimates are based on reports at that time, plus later reports of shareholdings and boardroom struggles: see note four.
3. Reports of the year of Wilson's resignation from the board vary. Sometimes it is given as 1966, but more often it is given as 1967, the same year that Hope is reported to have become a director. Is it possible that the events were not totally unconnected?
4. The extent to which the directors could command more than fifty per cent of the shares in the club is demonstrated in the battles for control in late 1975 and in 1976. See *Glasgow Herald*, 14, 15, 21, 22 April 1976 for various share-holding details. In the *Glasgow Herald* 12 December 1975, Simpson claimed that the board held voting rights for fifty-two per cent of shareholding. See *Glasgow Herald*, 9 and 10 December 1976 for an actual vote at the club's AGM, when the board obtained fifty-nine per cent of the votes cast (56 per cent of the total vote available). Note that, unlike in the Hope/Taylor affair, on this occasion Taylor's old allies had the Lawrence company votes but the deceased Taylor's shares had been purchased by

those challenging the directors. Eventually both challengers, Tom Dawson and Jack Gillespie, were allowed to join the board.
5. See *Glasgow Herald* 30 May 1973, 1, 2 and 20 June 1973. The reader's letter was published on 4 June 1973. Cyril Horne, who wrote for the paper in the 1950s and 1960s, did strongly criticise Rangers, but he was an exception among all the journalists of those days. Moreover, his criticisms were not overtly related to Rangers' anti-Catholicism, but to a range of other features of the club: see Murray, 1984.
6. I am preparing this case-study: for a brief account, see Finn, in press. It certainly seems to be the case that the religious affiliation of the spouse no longer seems to be of much concern at Ibrox.

Sincere thanks are due to the Training and Employment Research Unit, University of Glasgow, and especially to Professor Alan McGregor, for the considerable help and facilities made available to me during my sabbatical there. I am also very grateful to those members of the Board of Governors of Jordanhill College who supported my application for sabbatical leave to do research into this general area.

BIBLIOGRAPHY

Billig, M., 1985, Prejudice, categorisation and particularization: from a perceptual to a rhetorical approach, *European journal of social psychology*, 15, pp.79–103

Billig, M., 1991, *Ideology and opinions. Studies in rhetorical psychology*, Sage, London

Bruce, S., 1985, *No Pope of Rome. Militant Protestantism in modern Scotland*, Mainstream, Edinburgh

Canning, B. J., 1979, *Irish-born secular priests in Scotland, 1829–1979*, Bookmag, Inverness

Docherty, G. and Thomson, P., 1975, *100 years of Hibs, 1875–1975*, John Donald, Edinburgh

Dovidio, J. F. and Gaertner, S. L., 1986, *Prejudice, discrimination and racism*, Academic Press, Orlando

Finn, G. P. T., 1987, Multicultural antiracism and Scottish education, *Scottish education review*, 19, pp.39–40

Finn, G. P. T., 1990a, Prejudice in the history of Irish Catholics in Scotland, *Paper to the conference of the history workshop journal*, Glasgow, November 1990

Finn, G. P. T., 1990b, In the grip? A psychological and historical exploration of the social significance of freemasonry in Scotland, in Walker, G. and Gallagher, T., (eds) *Sermons and battle hymns. Protestant culture in modern Scotland*, Edinburgh University Press, Edinburgh

Finn, G. P. T., 1991a, Racism, religion and social prejudice: Irish Catholic clubs, soccer and Scottish society – I The historical roots of prejudice, *International journal of the history of sport*, 8 (1), pp.70–93

Finn, G. P. T., 1991b, Racism, religion and social prejudice: Irish Catholic clubs, soccer and Scottish society – II Social identities and conspiracy theories, *International journal of the history of sport*, 8 (3), pp.370–97

Finn, G. P. T., 1992, Inter-ethnic prejudice and the dialectics of past and present, *Paper to the 1st international ethnic studies conference: Conflict and change*, Portrush, June

Finn, G. P. T., in press, Racism, religion and social prejudice: Irish Catholic clubs, soccer and Scottish society – III Rangers and the conspiracy tradition, *International journal of the history of sport*

Finn, G. P. T., forthcoming, Sporting symbols: prejudice and football in Scotland and Northern Ireland, in Wood, I. S., (ed.) *Scotland and Ulster*, Mercat Press, Edinburgh University Press, Edinburgh

Fraser, C. and Gaskell, G., 1990, *The social psychological study of widespread beliefs*, Clarendon Press, Oxford

Glaser, R., 1986, *Growing up in the Gorbals*, Chatto Windus, London

Glaser, R., 1988, *Gorbals boy at Oxford*, Chatto Windus, London

Glaser, R., 1990, *Gorbal voices, siren songs*, Chatto Windus, London

Handley, J., 1947, *The Irish in modern Scotland*, Cork University Press, Cork

Hewstone, M. and Brown, R., 1986, *Contact and conflict in intergroup encounters*, Basil Blackwell, Oxford

Jamie, D., 1900, *John Hope. Philanthropist and reformer*, Andrew Elliot, Edinburgh

Jarvie, G., 1991, *Sport, racism and ethnicity*, Falmer Press, London

Maan, B., 1992, *The new Scots. The story of Asians in Scotland*, John Donald, Edinburgh

Mackay, J. R., 1986, *The Hibees. The story of Hibernian football club*, John Donald, Edinburgh

Mackie, A., 1959, *The Hearts. The story of Heart of Midlothian football club*, Stanley Paul, London

Miles, R., 1982, *Racism, and migrant labour*, Routledge, Kegan Paul, London

Miller, W. L., 1985, Politics in the Scottish city, 1832–1982, in Gordon, G., (ed.), *Perspectives of the Scottish city*, Aberdeen University Press, Aberdeen

Moorhouse, H. G., 1984, Professional football and working class culture: English theories and Scottish evidence, *Sociological review*, 32, pp.285–315

Murray, B., 1984, *The old firm. Sectarianism, sport and society*, Mainstream, Edinburgh

Murray, B., 1988, *Glasgow's giants. 100 years of the old firm*, John Donald, Edinburgh

Rafferty, J., 1973, *One hundred years of Scottish football*, Pan Books, London

Van Dijk, T. A., 1986, When majorities talk about minorities, in McLaughlin, M. L., (eds), *Communication year book 9*, Sage, Beverly Hills

Walker, G., 1990, There's not a team like the Glasgow Rangers': football and religious identity in Scotland, in Walker, G. and Gallagher, T., (eds), *Sermons and battle hymns. Protestant culture in modern Scotland*, Edinburgh University Press, Edinburgh

Watson, M., 1985, *Rags to riches. The official history of Dundee United*, David Winter and Son, Dundee

Wilkie, J., 1984, *Across the great divide. A history of professional football in Dundee*, Mainstream, Edinburgh

8

PLAY, CUSTOMS AND POPULAR CULTURE OF WEST COAST COMMUNITIES 1840–1900

Hamish Telfer

A recent newspaper article on the North Uist Highland Gathering of 1989 went to some length to explain the distinctiveness of this sporting custom which it dated back to the early 1900s (*The Guardian*, 26 July 1989). A special emphasis was placed on the words 'Gathering' and 'community' with the day's events being seen as a joyous celebration of community loyalty and friendly rivalry among people who knew each other well. The North Uist Highland Gathering was described as informal, and local, and while the event was recorded as part of the official Highland Games circuit, the connection was tenuous in the sense that mass commercialization, tartanry, and many of the traditional Highland Games events were noticeable only by their absence from the programme. There was no caber tossing at this Gathering since North Uist had no trees to cut down while hill running was made improbable since the island hardly rises above sea level. The timing of the Gathering took due cognisance of the pattern of working peoples lives since the events always coincided with the Glasgow Fair in July, when many of the islands' exiles came home for a fortnight.

The terms used by the newspaper correspondent to describe this modern event have often been used by many writers to describe an ideal set of characteristics associated with pre-industrial or traditional forms of sport and recreation. Local, informal, reflecting of sharp class and gender divisions, spontaneous, with the timing of events often dictated by tradition and formal seasons are but a few of the ways which have been used to differentiate the traditional from the modern or the industrial from pre-industrial and in some cases, rural from urban (Bailey, 1987; Cunningham, 1978; Davidoff and Hall, 1987; Malcolmson, 1984). Yet the problem with such labels is that they often tend to obscure rather than clarify the process of change *and* continuity: a process which is invariably more complex and uneven than a single transition from one historical phase or period to another. For example, cities clearly existed prior to industrialisation and villages clearly survived and developed after the industrial revolution. The task at hand then is to be sensitive to the process of continuity and change in looking at some of the sporting customs of the West Coast communities (mainly Argyllshire) between about 1840 and 1900.

Perhaps one of the most important points to establish about recreation in the 1800s is that as a category of experience it would have been less easily recognisable. People knew when they were working and when they were not, and yet the boundaries between play, recreation and work were often negotiable and blurred. The conventional dichotomy of work and free-time for leisure did not always accord with the experience of working people's daily lives in many nineteenth century West Coast communities. The Ten Hours Act of 1847 may have created new opportunities for pleasure in many urban communities but it is doubtful if such opportunities were experienced as evenly amongst the remote rural communities of Argyllshire.

Clearly, it is not possible to draw examples from all forms of play, pleasure and sport but at a concrete level I should like to consider several forms of sporting custom and practice found in many typical West Coast communities between 1840 and 1900. What is common amongst all these illustrations is that they are connected by different paths to a theme of custom, particularly within the culture of working people during the nineteenth century (for a more detailed discussion of sport in nineteenth century Scotland see Neil Tranter's chapter in this book.) Various social and economic pressures meant disruption to many valued patterns of custom, pleasure and work. As early as 1841 the parish minister of the Diurinish, on Skye, noted in the statistical account that all public gatherings whether for shinty playing, or throwing the putting stone, for drinking and dancing, for marriages or funerals have been discontinued (Macdonald, 1992, p.3). Such customs and social practices did not simply disappear, indeed many survived in different forms, but they were actively marginalised by a process of rationalization. There are many reasons why shinty in Skye fell into hard times during the 1850s but one of the reasons is pinpointed by Mairi Mhor (Macdonald, 1992, p.3):

> Bho'n chaill sinn am fearann
> Gun chaill sinn an iomain
> S cha mhor gu bheil duin' ann tha eolach oirr'.
> (Since we lost our land
> We lost shinty as well
> And there are few men left who are skilful now.)

During the latter half of the nineteenth century shinty games between villages in Argyll were a regular occurrence. The fact that the custom has strong roots is partly evident from the nature and size of some of the villages taking part. Adnistanig and Anaheilt clashed at Strontian in 1876, Ockle and Kilmory played at Branault Farm in 1883, while Onich were entertained at North Ballachulish in 1890. Although a shinty association was inaugurated on 10 October 1893, not many West Coast clubs were represented (*Celtic Monthly*, vol. II (2), October 1893). Good crowds were common, even for small games, since the games themselves provided an occasion for meeting and exchanging news. In 1876 between 300 and 400 spectators watched a shinty match involving 70 players played out on the beach on the Ross of Mull. Large numbers of men from Tynribbie, Ardnaclach, Rhugaive and Inverfolla came to watch a game at Achnacone, in Appin, in 1890 (Hutchinson, 1989; Macdonald, 1992; Whitson, 1983).

Apart from the fact that there were great numbers taking part in each game, as many as 100, the revelry and drunkenness associated with the traditional customs meant that attempts to codify the games and give patronage to the custom, could only take place with patience (*Oban Times*, 9 January 1869). The life of an estate worker was hard with long hours and little pay although a tied house and a degree of security for the worker and his sons and daughters was reasonably assured. The children were often employed, when of age, in the work of the estate and while other means of employment could often be found, men and women invariably looked to the estate, or to the big cities for a living. Whatever attempts were made to make leisure time more respectable, either by codification or by socially engineering the circumstances, the response and resistance to such attempts was often ingenious.

Impromptu games occasionally took place, such as the occasion on the Calgary sands on Mull when the MacLeans played the Campbells (Cameron, 1967). Rituals of team selection endured outside of the officially codified versions of rules. Recollections of such customs on the Isle of Eigg at the turn of the century are recounted by Hugh MacKinnon a resident of Cleadale on the island (MacDonald, 1978, pp.51–52):

> Two young men would be approved from the group to choose sides. One would throw a caman to the other who would catch it half way up the shaft, whereupon the one with the last hand hold would say 'Buail am port' (Strike up the tune) and the reply would be 'Ligidh mi leat' (I'll allow you). The person with the last hand picked the first man. Camans would then be thrown into the air to land on the beach and depending on whether it landed 'a'bheulag' (forehand) pointing north or south that would be the direction of play for that team. Stones were used as goals, hazel root fashioned by knife for a ball and oak for a stick.

With or without hogs-heads of whisky as prizes or the application of 'mountain dew' during competition, the games were keenly contested affairs (*Oban Times*, 1 January 1870; 15 January 1876). Games between estate workers under the patronage of landowners were common. The famous Winterton, on the Duke of Argyll's Estate at Inverary, was to become home to the Inverary Shinty Club. On these occasions it was not uncommon for the patron to join in. During the match on New Year's Day in 1888 between the opposite sides of Upper Loch Fyne, playing on a pitch some 500 yards long with 50 men to each side, Lord Walter Campbell was hit in the mouth by the hardwood ball (*Oban Times*, 11 January 1988) – 'The doctor, summoned from a distant part of the field, follows with all speed. And so the wound is dressed – simply suture – the young hero winching not the while'.

This show of paternalism with the workers was very much in keeping with the assumed responsibilities of the landowner of the nineteenth century. While clubs tended to replace these festivities of patronage, the need to preserve the rights of patronage was crucial to the power and influence of the landowners. It is tempting to suggest that the issues of class expression and social control were closely connected to this process of paternalism. Leisure should not be *over*-politicised as an arena of struggle; it is not simply a matter of class expression on the one hand and social control on the other. Sometimes social institutions and popular customs are simply rendered anachronistic; but it is equally dangerous to interpret the disappearance or marginalisation of certain popular customs as a huge defeat. Certainly, more structured display of games followed the rather less structured village version where rather less socially acceptable events occasionally occurred.

There are numerous precognitions contained in the Scottish Records Office of the Procurator Fiscal relating to disturbances and violence during festivities and games. Once such precognition of Daniel Mactaggart the Procurator Fiscal of Kintyre in Argyll, states that (*Procurator Fiscal*, 13 January 1818):

> . . . at a Shinney play which yesterday took place upon the estate of Largie, Archibald W. Murchy son of Thomas W. Murchy, Farmer at Lenauboyach without any justifiable cause or provocation whatsoever, struck John Galbreath, Tacksman of Tayinloan several violent blows to the head with a Shinney or club, or some other weapon which he had in his hand at the time whereby the jaw bone of the said John Galbreath was broke and several of his teeth knocked out, and he was otherwise so severely cut and wounded upon the head that his life is just now in danger.

The precognition goes on to give warrant for the arrest and imprisonment of Archibald Murchy, a resident of Kintyre, in the Tollbooth of Campbeltown to await trial. The game was played on the twelfth and mention is made of the game being on New Years Day in the 'Old Style' as was the usual custom.

The process of rationalising numerous public holidays meant that customary shinty matches at New Year had to vie between the date of the 'Old' New Years day, on 12 January and the 'New' New Years day on 1 January. The celebration of the Old New Year in the Highlands carried on well into the latter half of the nineteenth century. Christmas was a relatively new celebration for West Coast Highlanders in the nineteenth century. The Free church's attitude towards festival and popular custom during this period, especially after the disruption of 1843, meant that very few communities observed the occasion. Sporadic and spontaneous celebrations often broke out in such diverse places as the Castle lawn at Inverary in 1867 (*Oban Times*, 28 December 1867) and on the Plain of Kilbarr on the Isle of Barra in 1866 (*Oban Times*, 26 January 1866). Christmas remained for many a relatively anonymous celebration, a point that is substantiated by the *Coleraine Chronicle* of 29 January 1877:

> The great yearly festival is taken very little notice of here – at least among the natives. About the only parties who carve geese and swallow plum pudding, etc, on this occasion are the strangers who were reared in the more modern climes across the border.

As the dates of Michaelmas, Epiphany, Hallowe'en, All Saints Day, St Andrew's Day, Handsel Monday and Fastern's E'en all disappeared from the traditional calendar of sporting occasions, so too did the dates of the traditional local festivals. Occasions such as Am Margadh na L-Caglais at Kingarth and St Brioch's Fair at Rothesay, Isle of Bute, all disappeared (Scott, 1923). One writer argued that many games and customs had gone out of fashion as early as 1833 in Lochs and Uig due to emigrations which 'took the most active younger men and frequently left older men who had no heart to continue . . .' (Cameron, 1967, p.24).

Certainly the pattern in Argyll as the traditional dates disappeared from the calendar, was for new forms of festival to appear. These were often organised around the dates when the Commissioners of Supply came together for their business in the spring and autumn of each year. The arrival home of the Marquis and Marchioness of Lorne in 1842 was one such occasion when the Commissioners organised activities such as dancing, rifle shooting, archery, footraces and riding at the ring (*Commissioners of Supply*, 1823). These activities, organised exclusively by the gentlemen of the Burgh, differed in organisation, content and ceremony from many earlier cultural practices organised by people of the Western Isles. Games and customs often took on a new meaning and credence because events such as Highland Gatherings were often subject to the patronage and control of the local landlord or landlady. The timing of events, for example, often suited the social calendar of the patron more than the working pattern of estate workers and other fractions of the working class. Thus, it might be argued that leisure and recreational forms themselves were subject to a process of negotiation and struggle. What was often at stake was the power to define what leisure was and what leisure should be. Efforts to repress and exclude undesirable customs and uses of free time and replace them with more constructive leisure patterns has been an age old issue in the development of leisure and recreation in Britain.

Original recreational customs did not simply disappear but were subject to increasing pressure and competition from new forms of play, games and sport. One writer, referring to the late 1880s, talks of the ceilidhs of Lewis in which story telling, singing, music, proverbial sayings and riddle solving during the winter were marginalised by the emergence of quoits, putting the shot, jumping and vaulting with oars during the summer (Macdonald, 1978). The tradition of the ceilidh was an important aspect of family life in many remote areas. Some have argued that its folk origins are derived from the gathering of village people at times when itinerants such as packmen or tinkers brought news or stories to the community (Martin, 1984; Thompson, 1984). Other forms of popular gatherings often took place on the village green; popular pastimes were often governed by local rules, and practised in an informal unstructured way. One local newspaper carried an article demurring the fact that:

> . . . hulking big fellows who might well be better employed were meeting daily to play cards and pitch and toss surrounded by young children who must surely suffer from the pollution which the witnessing of such conduct, and listening to the impure language of the many engaged must necessary entail. (*Campbeltown Courier*, 19 June 1875)

There remains a vivid account of the meetings on the village green at Lochgilphead recounted some seventy years later in the *Argyllshire Advertiser*. While the article is specific to the Lochgilphead of the 1860s and 1870s, it is worth quoting at length because of the insights into aspects of village life at the time (quoted in Carswell, 1938, p.5):

It was a common Saturday evening sight in summer after the weekly 'divide' by the fishermen, and at the conclusion of their general chat at 'Fraser's Corner' (now Post Office corner), to find forty to sixty men, with many senior supporters, repair to the 'Wee Green' across the street and strip, to throw the stone, engage in the long jump, the hop step (or hop hop) and jump or shift the three stones. The best exponents of stone-putting were Archie Gillies ('Garra'), Sandy MacEwan ('Neeger'), Duncan MacNaughton ('Kilmichael'), Johnnie MacVicar ('Jenkins'), Archie MacKellar, teacher. Finally in these many friendly contests supremacy of prowess fell to 'Neeger' and 'Big Carswell'. The latter, being the younger and having acquired 'the happy knack', plus a modicum of strength, went to the top and other strong contemporaries had in the end to 'spectate' approvingly. Parenthetically, Carswell was an apt pupil of 'Big Sandy MacKay', an Asylum attendant of magnificent physique and muscular power who competed annually with Donald Dinnie, George Johnstone, Kenneth MacRae, Owen Duffy etc, who were professional leaders of the period. In the jumps the best 'boys' were 'Jenkins' already named, Archie Crawford ('Whittle'), Dunkie Sinclair ('Croft'), Donald Crawford ('Crean'), Neil James Gillies ('The Mell'), his brother Archie MacKellar, Dunkie MacVicar, Big MacKellar ('The Dummie'), Duncan MacVean, chemist, and again Carswell. Of laterdate Hughie MacVean and Johnnie (Duncan's brothers) maintained the family reputation with Dunkie Johnson, shoemaker, also very prominent. Of outstanding merit, however, were the jumps of Alick McNair ('Bodach Fisher') tailor and latterly of the 94th–2nd Batt. Connaught Rangers. 'Bodach' as an apprentice tailor with MacTaggart (a brother of the well know Scottish painter – RSA) in Argyll Street, never required to place his hands on the railings enclosing the Greens. He 'took' the fence in his stride and leapt straight over . . . Many a good football match was played on the 'Wee Green' before the days of standardised pitches and goal posts. Outstanding players who delighted spectators with tricky dribbling were Duncan MacBrayne, clerk; Dunkie Johnson, Alick MacVean, Distillery; Neil MacMillan ('Stab'); Archie MacKellar; Lachie Sinclair (latterly Manchester); 'Jenkins'; Donald Crawford ('Swan'); Sandy Campbell ('Spang').

At one level this account is invaluable because of its attention to detail, and its insights into popular culture; the nicknames of the men, their trade on occasions and the fact that the timing and location of such games were often played after the weekly divide of the fish. Work having been completed, men would indulge in recreation and talk. Yet at another level such accounts also provide an insight into notions of community and place. In a simple sense many of the games and pastimes of the West Coast communities were not simply voluntary activities but actively engaged in the process of keeping communities and ways of life alive. Such play and customs often contributed to and were constitutive of community time, and nation. It might be argued that such forms of recreation contributed to a form of identity for small communities in opposition to external forces, such as the land issue, or to more conservative, patronising forms of recreation, such as the formal Highland Gatherings and the popular games of mainland Scotland. Along with other customs and traditions what such experiences meant for certain people was a sense of a relatively stable community, a sense of neighbourhood, a sense of class and a sense of gender and identity; identities which were often marginalised when one moved out into other regions or localities which made up the Scottish nation of the nineteenth century.

A Scottish community or nation that did not depend upon the same sense of custom, collective community or neighbourhood as that described above was in the process of forging out what it meant to be a nineteenth century Scot. It was not a Scot but a Welshman who, perhaps, has articulated most strongly the abstract association between a specific understanding of community and the broader sense of a community or nation under stress and under attack (Williams, 1973, Williams, 1992). In short, the point that needs to be made here is that it is not necessary to see recreational customs or sporting traditions at the local level as not contributing to any sense of community or nation. In terms of a distinct sense of community, a distinct sense of custom and popular culture, sport and recreational practices in Argyllshire during the nineteenth century contributed to Scottish sport in the making of the nation. Yet as the introduction to this book clearly illustrates all such contributions to such a cause have been timebound, selective and expressive of certain images of Scotland and certain ideas about Scotland. The differences between such expressions of community and nation have in many cases been as great as the similarities. The process of continuity and change between rural and urban, Highland and lowland, West Coast and East Coast, and conservative and transformative forms of sport have been complex and far from uniform.

The sense of community and place around the village green in Lochgilphead is similar and yet different from the sense of community and place that is expressed in something as grand and conservative as the Argyllshire Gathering and the Oban Ball. The first Argyllshire Gathering was recorded in 1871 with the Games being added to the Gathering in 1873. The nineteenth century Gatherings would invariably end with the Grand Oban Ball. By 1885 it appeared to be the done 'thing to attend the Royal Highland Yacht Club Regatta on the Thursday when no Games were held' (Malcolm, 1971, p.15). By 1893 the Gathering and Games had become so prestigious and imperial that the first Battalion of the Argyll and Sutherland Highlanders offered to contribute to the pipes and drums, but also to a display of physical drill, to music, and to an attack on an outpost (Malcolm, 1971, p.18). The Argyllshire Gathering and Oban Ball was invariably the occasion for the 'coming out' of the young ladies of certain noble standing. Protocol had to be strictly followed, as in the case of Olive Inverneil of which one account relates: 'She looked very well and was moderately well got up but she had a coloured dress on the second night instead of being in white both times which would have been much better' (Malcolm, 1971, p.22).

It is tempting to compare the Argyllshire Gathering and Oban Ball of the nineteenth century with similar events of the 1990s. An account of the events of August 1992 explains that this tradition remains inextricably linked to high society (*The Guardian*, 22 August 1992). The day's events are described as formal, regimented, and being part of a rather grand affair on the social circuit. The Ball itself was restricted to about 400 invited people. The Duke of Argyll, suggests the writer, jealously guards his active presidency of the Gathering which incorporates two nights of solid reeling in an Oban hall. The same article argues that, ordinary folks would not expect to attend the ball, which like the games, is often sponsored by one of the Duke's companies. The conventions of ritual, custom and social hierarchy are established, interwoven features of the more conservative Argyllshire Gathering. If one compares this vision of the Argyllshire Gathering with the events of the North Uist Highland Gathering, described at the beginning of this paper, one gets two different images of Highland Gatherings in different West Coast communities and yet both images and sets of practices are equally modern, equally patriarchal, and equally rooted in Highland and Island West Coast communities. Such expressions reproduce a different sense of class, a different sense of regional identity and a different, yet similar, sense of Scotland. In the same way, many points of continuity exist between the Argyllshire Gathering of the nineteenth century and the Argyllshire Gathering of the late twentieth century; and yet the people in attendance at such events would have lived through a similar, yet different, sense of Scotland and Argyllshire.

Just as the Duke of Argyll carefully guards his current Presidency of the Argyllshire Gathering so did many of the local dignitaries and landowners of the nineteenth century. Many vied with each other as to who would be the principal patrons and benefactors at certain Gatherings and Games. The associated costs and the frequent deficits did not seem to deter volunteers from bidding for the title of principal patron. Most of the Games of the time could expect substantial patronage from the likes of Colonel Gardyne (Glenforsa Games) and Maclaine of Mull (Lochbuy Games), while the Games of Bonawe and Tobermory relied upon more than one benefactor. Crowds were sometimes as large as 5000. This was the case in 1876 when such a number turned out to see the great Dinnie appear at the Argyllshire Gathering where he won prize money of eight pounds plus another pound for favouring the spectators with a trial of strength. Large crowds that often helped to enhance the reputation of the patron, since the bigger the occasion, the more successful the Games.

Perhaps it is slightly misleading to compare the aristocracy of nineteenth century Argyllshire with Veblen's accounts in the *Theory of the Leisure Class* (1953) since the writer was primarily trying to explain the conspicuous consumption of leisure and the misuse of wealth by the *nouveau riche* of late nineteenth and early twentieth century America. Veblen passed harsh judgements on the frivolity and wasteful consumption of wealth. Leisure became the medium for wasting time and money – it was the time for patronage and the opportunity to put one's wealth on display. Involvement in leisure became a question of prestige, or mark of distinction in Bourdieu's terms (Bourdieu, 1991). It was not enough simply to put your wealth on display; to gain real status you had to be seen to be actively wasting your wealth on leisure pursuits – hunting in particular. What emerged was a 'leisure class which, given due honour and prestige, was able to avoid useful work, undertake warfare, government, sport and organised religion. None of this according to Veblen, contributed to the well being of community. Perhaps Veblen's 'leisure class' describes more than the *nouveau riche* of the Victorian period and those who moved into the Highlands with the development of sporting estates. Leisure certainly contributed to the privatization of sociability.

While many of the occasions for games and recreation show similarity in the nature of their activities, the smaller meetings and village occasions provided the greatest variety of events. While the 'heavy events' of the

Games such as putting the stone, caber throwing and hammer throwing were common, so too were short races of 100 yards, quarter mile races, three legged races and a long race of either a mile or half a mile. However, many events were unique to each occasion. The Kilmartin Games at Ri Cruin included sack races, plus races for boys under ten years of age and a wheelbarrow race. The Games at Castleacres, Kintyre featured the seemingly impossible hurdle sack race, vaulting with a pole, a race for ploughmen over half a mile and a fisherman's donkey race (*Argyllshire Herald*, 6 January 1883). A blindfold wheelbarrow race took place at the Kintyre Athletic Sports of 1878 (*Argyllshire Herald*, 5 January 1878).

Novelty events were popular at most Games. There were consolation races, married men's races, old men's races and old wives' races. Catching a greased pig and throwing it over the shoulder, climbing poles for legs of lamb and pig racing (which if caught within a given distance or time, the pig was the victor's), were just as popular. Prizes were usually cash or some useful commodity such as tea. Winners of the youngsters races additionally received 'sweeties' (*Oban Times*, 10 July 1869).

The fact that children took part is in no small way due to the nature of the schooling found in many West Coast communities. Schooling was inextricably bound, in many cases, to the production of food from land and sea. Survival for many families meant that each member had to contribute to ensuring that enough food was available for all. Communities would often seek collective ways of relieving hardship. The school log of Acha on the Island of Coll recorded that 'Children of the poorer class received a share of the clothes left by the "ladies of Coll" for the poor on the Island' (*Acha School Log Book*, 4 November 1878). Other school logs of the day testify to school attendance being disrupted by the need for children to attend to the more basic elements of existence. At Tobermory on Mull the school log records, 'Fine day, of which advantage was taken to carry home peats for fuel, which most of the poorer villagers accomplished by bearing them on their back in creels and in which even the children are engaged' (*Tobermory School Log*, 30 December 1863)

Notwithstanding the everyday pressures of living, a degree of physical exercise was undertaken, both legally and otherwise. The Tobermory School dismissed at 3.00 pm on 1 January 1864 'to allow the boys a game at shinty' (*Tobermory School Log*, 1 January 1864). At Islay, absences for caddying at the golf courses were common (*Port Ellen School Log*, 1896). The schools recorded holidays for Regattas and Sports Days, evidence of the growing status these events held in the community compared to even a few years earlier. It seems that while little formal exercise or games were encouraged in the schools, there was tacit encouragement for participation in the games of the community. The process of education was generally seen to be far too serious to accommodate regular bodily exercise.

School treats were recorded as special days, possibly the forerunners of school sports days when the children were allowed to indulge in games and sport. There is record of the children of Barcaldine on at least two occasions being treated to tea by a local benefactor after which 'the boys indulged in football' (*Oban Times*, 29 April 1876). At Tayinloan, in a public field adjoining the school house, the children of the school indulged themselves after their annual treat with 'races, leaping, jumping and other games. The most amusing being the sack race.' (*Oban Times*, 12 January 1878).

The fact that children found little outlet within school for activity of a sporting nature was symbolic of the times. The state school system and the schools of church influence, of which there were many in west coast Scotland, tended to merely reflect the nature of thought regarding those activities not directly related to God and labour. The Disruption of 1843, with its differing versions of protestantism, served at one and the same time to both liberate and suppress the popular growth of sporting pastimes during the latter part of the nineteenth century. A strong Highland tradition of affiliation to the Free Church and its rather less than liberal orthodoxy ensured that games and pastimes were undertaken in stolen moments outside of the stern gaze of the Church. The system of education prior to the Disruption was sufficiently diverse as to ensure that no relatively coherent picture emerges with respect to tolerance or otherwise of the games of the community. There were Parish Schools, Endowed Schools and the infamous adventure schools run for profit and taught by decaying gentlewomen. Added to these were the 'Ragged' children's schools all of which presented various threads of provision throughout the community.

Nevertheless, it is in relation to the church that we gain some of our more insightful glimpses of the way in which popular culture struggled for opportunities to indulge in games, sports and pastimes. One of the primary objectives of the church was to ensure that the community kept the Sabbath. Some success would appear to have been gained since 'the village corner where, on the Sabbath mornings, the football matches of the preceding day had been discussed, and the plans were made for the poaching raids of the day, was now deserted, the lads being at the church in town' (MacRae, 1923, p.49).

The stern paternalism of the Free Church was occasionally at odds with its ideology and the opportunity for amusement through games and other forms of recreational activity were seldom missed. The pauper funerals of the west coast were particularly singled out by Ross who tells of the distribution of free drink to attract crowds of mourners and the ritual of body watching where concurrently, 'all sorts of tricks were practised, games of leaping and wrestling were indulged in . . .' (Ross, 1976, p.108). The efforts of the church to control popular amusements often related to a great extent to what it saw as the abuse of alcohol.

While this chapter has not attempted to provide an abstract explanation of the relationship between custom, culture and community, I should like to finish by highlighting two simple points which have been central to my thinking on play, custom and popular culture of the West Coast communities between 1840–1900. Firstly, the issue of custom and culture. It is undeniable that popular customs during this period were subject to pressures to reform. But these pressures were in some cases stubbornly resisted. Many popular pastimes, such as shinty on Skye, were marginalised and suppressed for a while but they were not completely destroyed by either the rational recreation or Free Church movement. Custom, including recreational customs were conveyed and displayed. The negotiation and conflict between laird and worker, urban and rural, pre-industrial and industrial, celtic and lowland were often symbolised through popular and conservative forms of recreation. Conservative culture appealed to, and sought to reinforce, traditional usages of recreation, community and even nation. Class relations may have defined the overarching limits within which popular pastimes were played out, but in many cases it did little to change the overall content or character of recreational patterns within West Coast communities. Many of the folk origins of past recreational customs can be found in modern sport and leisure forms. Thus it has been necessary to address issues of continuity and change.

Secondly, during the nineteenth century the immediacy or locality of community related to a sense of direct, common, concern for a way of life for different groups of people. The notion of community was often contrasted with more formal forms of social organization such as state, society or nation. Forms of sport contributed to a sense of community and identity in Argyllshire and other West Coast communities during the Victorian period. The passion which the socialist and nationalist land reformer John Murdoch had for shinty in the mid 1880s resulted from Murdoch's belief that shinty contributed to a sense of Highland identity and celtic culture. On the one hand, it has to be argued that forms of sport, play and recreation in many West Coast communities actively contributed to a sense of community and nation. On the other hand it is more difficult to explain which nation or which expression or image of the nation games such as shinty were talking to; Scottish, British, Highland or Celtic? People identify with community as they do nation but the irony is of course that nationalism in the late twentieth century is probably the gravedigger of many nation-states and communities.

BIBLIOGRAPHY

Acha school log (Isle of Coll) County Archivist, Argyllshire (No 5/100/1)
Argyllshire Herald (various dates)
Bailey, P., 1987, *Leisure and class in Victorian England: rational recreation and the contest for control 1830–1885*, Methuen, London
Bourdieu, P., 1991, *In other words: essays towards a reflexive sociology*, Basil Blackwell, Oxford
Cameron, W. P., 1967, *Cowal journal*, Forestry Commission, Edinburgh
Cambeltown Courier (various dates)
Carswell, A., Annals of Lochgoilhead and Mid Argyll, in *Argyllshire Advertiser*, 23 March 1938, pp.5–6
Coleraine Chronicle, Museum of Islay Life, Port Charlotte, Islay
Colquhoun, I. and Machell, H., 1927, *Highland gatherings*, Heath Cranton, London
Commissioners of Supply, papers, vouchers, subscription lists, minutes, Country Archivist, Argyllshire (C06/1;C06/1/10)
Crawford, S. A. G., 1987, Some comments on the nineteenth century pattern of British sporting and recreational life in *Physical Education Review*, 10 (1): pp.21–29
Cregeen, E. R. 1968, the role of the Ducal House of Argyll in the Highlands, *ASA Monograph*, no. 7
Cunningham, H., 1978, *Leisure and the industrial revolution*, Methuen, London
Davidoff, L. and Hall, C., 1987, *Family fortunes*, Hutchinson, London
Grigor, I. F., 1979, *Mightier than a lord: the highland crofters struggle for land*, Agair, Stornoway

Hatfield, J., 1991, Proud possessors of homeland to call our own in *Scotland on Sunday*, 18 August 1991, pp.10–12

Hobsbawm, E. and Ranger, T. (eds), 1983, *The invention of tradition*, Cambridge University Press, Cambridge

Holt, R. (ed.), 1990, *Sport and the working class in modern Britain*, Manchester University Press, Manchester

Hutchinson, R., 1989, *Camanachd, the story of shinty*, Mainstream Publishing, Edinburgh

Jarvie, G. 1991, *Highland games: the making of the myth*, Edinburgh University Press, Edinburgh

MacDonald, D., 1978, *Lewis, a history of the island*, Wright, Edinburgh

Macdonald, M., 1992, *Skye camanachd, a century remembered*, Skye camanachd, Portree

MacDougall, D., 1876, Inspector of the poor, *Journal*, Easdale Museum, Argyllshire

MacKenzie, J., 1992, How the Scots put ethnic into empire *Newsview*, University of Lancaster, no. 12. pp.1–5

Macphail, I. M., 1989, *The crofters war*, Acair, Stornoway

MacRae, Al, 1923, *Revivals in the highlands and islands in the nineteenth century*, Mackay, Stirling

Malcolm, G., 1971, *Argyllshire gathering 1871–1971*, Oban Times, Oban

Malcolmson, R., 1984, 'Sport and society: a historical perspective' in *British journal of history of sport*, May, vol. 1, no. 1, pp.63–74

Martin, A., 1984, *Kintyre: the hidden past*, John Donald, Edinburgh

Oban Times (various dates)

Port Ellen school log book (Islay), Museum of Islay Life, Port Charlotte, Islay

Precognition of the procurator fiscal, Scottish records office, Edinburgh, (No AD/14/18/113)

Redmond, G., 1971, *The caledonian games in the nineteenth century America*, Associated University Press, New Jersey

Reid, W. S., (ed.), 1979, *The Scottish tradition in Canada*, McClelland and Stewart, Toronto

Ross, A., 1976, *The folklore of the Scottish Highlands*, Batsford, London

Scott, H., 1923, *Fasti ecclesiae scotticanae vol. iv synods of Argyll and of Perth and Stirling*, Oliver and Boyd, Edinburgh

Smout, T. C., 1986, *A century of the Scottish people 1830–1950*, Collins, London

Thompson, E. P., 1991, *Customs in common*, Merlin Press, London

Thompson, F., 1984, *Crofting years*, Luath Press, Ayrshire

Tobermory school log book (Isle of Mull), County Archivist, Argyllshire

Veblen, T., 1953, *Theory of the leisure class*, Mentor books, New York

Whitson, D., 1983, Pressures on regional games in a dominant metropolitan culture in *Leisure studies*, vol. 2, no. 2, pp.139–155

Williams, R., 1973, *The country and city*, Flamingo, London

Williams, R., 1992, Homespun philosophy in *Borderlands*, Channel Four, London

9

BATTLING ALONG THE BOUNDARIES: THE MARKING OF SCOTTISH IDENTITY IN SPORTS JOURNALISM

Neil Blain and Raymond Boyle

'Much could be written about Scottish symbols, ritual and mythology . . . but ideology? A Scottish theory of nationality in general, of Scottish nationality in particular?' (W. J. M. Mackenzie, *Political Identity*, p.172).

'Scots beaten but march on' (back page headline, *Scotland on Sunday*, 18 October 1992).

INTRODUCTION

Noting the deficiencies in much thinking about the various phenomena of identity, particularly the tendency to see identities as 'given' and 'fixed', Philip Schlesinger rightly argues the need for a social action perspective in which identity is seen 'as a continually constituted and reconstructed category' (Schlesinger, 1991, p.173).

We take it for granted in this chapter that the national dimension of collective identity is not only centrally important in human experience but also rendered visible in particularly revealing ways by the discourses of the mediation of sports events.[1]

In this chapter we are interested, therefore, both in media sports discourse in itself, and also as a component of political discourse: and hence as a constituent of political identity.

As we have noted elsewhere, the media discourse of the 'national dimension' – of national identity, character, feeling, difference – is, as such language often tends to be in culture generally, locked into ahistorical conceptions of national cultures which are remarkably resistant both to material change and local specificity.[2]

That these discourses of the national dimension may be said to construct and reconstruct national identities implies a theoretical tension (after a period of ascendancy of postmodernism theory), namely a tension between a traditional conception of the media 'representing' real-world activities, and later,

Lyotardian, more recently Baudrillardian, conceptions of 'invention' wherein no assumptions are made beyond the domain of discourse itself. We will not dwell overmuch on this distinction as a difficulty.[3]

It seems unavoidable, in writing about 'representation', that we should all now carry this conceptual tension along with us. Our use in this chapter of terms like 'invention' and 'construction' refers to our perception that media discourses are best approached as fabrications whose relation to their correlatives in the political world is problematic: as well, that is, as referring to the belief that the phenomena of identity are best seen as continually reconstituted within culture generally.

SPORT, THE MEDIA AND COLLECTIVE IDENTITY

Media consumers negotiate meanings with media texts from a number of collective identity formations. In sport, constructions of class, gender and age emerge both from the general position of sport within culture and, very potently, from the coverage of sport in the mass media.[4] We are required to be as specific about our readerships as about our media encodings.

The feeling of 'national identity' is intermittent: Scots, like other putative 'nationalities' mostly live in a world in which they are addressed through other aspects of their identity. We look below at sports whose zones of inclusion and exclusion nominate readers principally in aggregations of class and gender (and always of age) and which have their own inflections.

Those Scottish sports which are especially 'celtic' (like shinty) have little mainstream visibility. Soccer, rugby football, athletics, probably three of the four main vehicles for the expression of Scottishness in sport, are in no way especially Scottish: golf is a slightly different matter, as we shall see. (Boxing is a sport which we consider below.) There may also be something characteristic in a rapid Scottish adoption (a sub-behaviour of the necessary Scottish attribute of adaptability) of novel and often foreign sports, which we treat collectively.

Soccer (hereafter 'football') and rugby union football (hereafter 'rugby') by themselves suggest differences in the kind of Scottish identity symbolized by different sports. Rugby is associated both with regional and class characteristics which differentiate it strongly from football: despite overlaps (there is plenty of West of Scotland interest in, and some working class, especially rural, following for rugby, and also considerable middle class interest in football) in general rugby has a middle class following and is associated with the East of Scotland (and the private school system), and the Borders, while football is a regionally widespread game with a mainly working class following and an identity which is essentially urban.

The mediation of these games is not in the passive sense merely a 'reflection' of their demographics. The (overall) Glasgow-centric nature of the Scottish media, for example, is apt to place the particular urban experience of Glasgow at the heart of football in Scotland. This is arguably more true of television and radio than of the press however (and especially the English media), because despite the *Herald's* and *Daily Record's* Glasgow base, newspapers such as the *Aberdeen Press and Journal*, the *Dundee Courier*, and the Edinburgh-based *Scotsman* offer alternative locations in the editorial topography of Scottish sport, as do a variety of local radio stations and newspapers, as well as Grampian and Borders television. (We consider questions of the political economy of Scottish media sport separately below.)

Scotland may be only a third the size (say) of Oregon but is about a third of the area of the United Kingdom too, and with relatively non-interacting regional populations, and divisions such as those between Highlands and Lowlands, and those based on religion and ethnic minorities. In fact, she replicates the profusion of sub-national identities found in every other country.

Of additional relevance here are the gendered nature of accounts from football and rugby. Athletics in Scotland brings this into focus. In the early 1990s, the two premier Scottish athletes (Liz McColgan and Yvonne Murray) are female, producing, in distinct contrast to the especially masculine discourses of football and rugby, an alternative view of what might constitute a sporting Scottish identity.

Underlying what we have to say below, therefore, about the specifically national aspect of identity, is the awareness of the national component as one among several.

SPORT WITHIN THE TRADITION OF REPRESENTATIONS OF SCOTLAND

While much has been written about Scottish literature over a long period of time, it is mainly within the last ten years or so that there has been a development of work on the representation of Scotland within the mass media. Initial work on the cinema focused (some have argued too much) on the so-called 'tartan' and 'Kailyard' traditions. Probably it is another, younger, industrial-urban, masculine discourse which has been identified in Scottish film and television which is closer to aspects of the language of some sports journalism. But it would be unproductive to try to fit this latter style into the categories currently available from studies of other aspects of Scottish culture, given their limitations even when applied to their own domains. The whole study of discourses of Scottishness is still relatively underdeveloped.[5]

In the media in general, the problem for Scots is that control of their own production is very significantly limited, given patterns of centralization in broadcasting and external control in the press, and (more complicatedly) the ideological ramifications of Scotland's unusual stateless-nation's existence.

But sport is an interesting part-exception: while it is true that questions of broadcasting centralization and external press ownership must impact on the shape of the indigenous production of sports journalism, this is nonetheless an area in which journalists and editors may expect a relatively free reign in both media. What we get must bear at least some relation to what we would get if its production were, in fact, autonomous. We use this qualification because, of course, Scotland's ill-defined socio-economic and politico-cultural status can be argued to artificially depress certain aspects of the production of sports journalism (we will not pursue the point here). But it is a field in which Scottish media producers do enjoy relative practical freedom (though psychological freedom is another matter altogether).

This relative freedom in the field of sport is worth pursuing a little further in another connection. We have explored elsewhere the role of constructions of collective identity in media sport in sustaining relations of dominance in British society (Blain et al, 1993, Chapters 1 and 2). Evidence of this role is not wholly lacking in Scottish sports journalism. But the national dimension permeates most of Scottish sport, complicating its discourses and dislocating them from their potential role as bulwarks of dominant ideologies within structures of Britishness.

FOOTBALL IN THE SCOTTISH MEDIA

'Our penchant for making inglorious exits never ceases to amaze and if our football had behind it such creativity we would probably be on the verge of a World Cup triumph rather than yet another depressing departure. One wonders how much longer the charade will continue: how many more times will the national football team make us all suffer?' (James Traynor, *Glasgow Herald*, 13 June 1990). 'Don't call Scots louts: the English are, Mr Mellor' (front page headline, *Daily Record*, 15 June 1992).

'The scoreline read like the first set of a titanic tennis struggle; the two managers looked like men who had been strung upside down on a big dipper; the referee declared himself OK after having been flattened by a coin. This is Downtown Brockville of a Saturday afternoon. We all had to have a lie-down afterwards (Ian Paul, *Herald*, 21 September 1992).

It is football whose coverage in the media makes it carry the national-symbolic weight. At Italia 90, the Scots bounce back from defeat from Costa Rica, and the *Glasgow Herald* (as it then was) correspondent sees it as the 'Calvinist demand for humiliation first, salvation second' (*Glasgow Herald*, 18 June 1990). The Scots are prone, like many other nationalities, to see Scottish history and character writ large in events on the football field. It is frequently small countries, especially those with psychologically problematic relationships with large neighbours, who invest sport with added symbolic (strictly speaking often indexical) significance (see Blain et al, 1993, Chapter 7 for discussion of Portuguese and Catalan reactions in this respect in coverage of the 1992 Barcelona Olympics). Scotland is not even a semi-autonomous region. Yet her political aspirations involve, at their extreme, the most ambitious dreams of independence while in the waking world the reality is of near-utter impotence.

If the Scots, therefore, are especially prone to sensitivity over symbolic events it is hardly surprising.

When a Scottish nationalist politician referred after the 1992 election campaign to 'ninety-minute patriots' (those who, limiting their partisanship to sport, would not vote for the Scottish National Party) he was exemplifying the way in which the complex and painful daily politics of Scottishness are refigured in the frustrations of football.

The arc between ambition and failure in Scottish football is drawn on a political template. 'Free by 93' said the Nationalists before the fiasco of the 1992 election. 'BRING ON BRAZIL', roared the *Sunday Post* (17 June 1990) after a victory over Sweden and before Scotland's exit from the tournament.

There is a perpetual movement in Scottish culture between outrageous confidence and ironic bitterness.

This characteristic trajectory is inscribed within the culture by a hard political history which has nonetheless seen great achievements: the problem is that they have so often seemed a triumph of will over infrastructure. This sense is strong in sport. It is hard to look back at Celtic's European Cup triumph in Lisbon in 1967 and then at Celtic in 1992.[6]

This sense of Scotland operating against large odds is the core of most sports commentary. The surges of triumphalism are grounded in memories of exceptional performance, but the irony and bitterness are born of weary familiarity with defeat. In football, the media explanation for Scottish success usually lies in attributions of personality characteristics other than sporting talent. Talent is given to Italians and Spaniards, Germans and Swedes, Cameroonians and Ukrainians.

By late November 1992, Rangers striker Ally McCoist, having won the 'Golden Boot' award as Europe's highest goalscorer the previous season, had scored 30 goals, an improbably high figure, yet a *Herald* correspondent (6 November 1992) cannot resist a qualification: 'McCoist . . . has proved himself just about the deadliest finisher in Britain'. 'Just about' seems strangely hesitant.

Of course, the argument beyond discourse is that the Scottish Premier League is less competitive than comparative leagues, and that Scottish talent requires to be proved elsewhere. As Scottish military history has its past glories, there is also a footballing Golden Age – the age of Jim Baxter, Denis Law and others – against which present shortcomings are measured (see Richard Holt's chapter in this book).

Scotsman sports writer Hugh Keevins comments (of Rangers' then imminent 'Battle of Britain' clash with Leeds United) that the Rangers' manager thinks the match will be 'a test of how good the best in Scotland really is when exposed to what might be called the real world' (4 November 1992).

When Scotland beats Sweden unexpectedly at Italia 90, the *Sunday Post* is clear enough about how Scottish character brings it about: 'All it took to change failure to success was a bit more gas in the tank and a whole lot more fire in the belly . . . Up went the sleeves, in went the tackles, off at the toot went the runners, their legs going like drumsticks, and the hard-earned win was achieved' (17 June 1990).[7]

This is a very pervasive account. In the 1990s there is growing embarrassment by Scottish journalists at what is seen to be the manic pace, brutality and lack of sophistication of the Scottish game. To what extent this is an accurate account of real-world relative divergence and to what extent it is a by-product of a growing European conspicuousness in British culture, and Scottish political embarrassment, is hard to judge. 'There is no use denying that playing in the sort of league where the artist has given way to the labourer is a positive handicap to success on the Continent' (Archie Macpherson, *Sunday Mail*, 8 March 1992). 'Rangers are happy to face six of the best'/'Ibrox men against cream of the crop' are two nervous back-page headlines in the *Herald* (6 November 1992), after Rangers' victory in the 'Battle of Britain'.

Superficially it seems that hetero-typification from expert sources matches this self-judgement. Under a back-page headline 'HERR TODAY, GONE TOMORROW! Mein Gott . . . Berti takes no prisoners: Germans savage Scotland', the *Daily Record* (15 June 1992) carries a story about German team manager Vogts' warning that the Germans can be as physical as the Scots. 'We're fully aware that it will be a physical game . . . we'll have to show commitment, aggression, and will power', Vogts is quoted as saying. Strong attacks are made by Borussia Dortmund staff on Celtic's supposed over-physicality after Dortmund's victories over Celtic in the autumn of 1992; Standard Liege of Belgium make similar complaints about Hearts during the same period. Marseille owner Bernard Tapie promises, before the European Cup match between his side and Rangers (according to a *Herald* headline, 25 November 1992) that 'his men will fight fire with fire': 'he mumbled something to the effect that the Italians last week and the Germans in the European Championships last summer know how physical Scottish sides could be'.

Curiously, after such matches, Scottish journalists are then forever being impressed by how 'physical' European sides can be. This physicality can sometimes be deduced from the numbers of fouls recorded dispassionately : 'Schulz was lucky not to be booked when he brought down Nicholas, but his team-mate Schmidt was not so fortunate a minute later when he was booked for a foul on Creaney' (*Scottish Daily Express*, 4 November 1992, on the Celtic-Borussia Dortmund second-leg). At other times, foreign aggression needs stronger language: 'there were times when it seemed as though Mike Tyson was not in prison in America, but playing at the back for Marseille wearing the number four jersey, and calling himself Basile Boli' (*Herald*, 26 November 1992, on Rangers-Marseille).

This leads naturally to questions about the extent to which identifying features of the Scottish game emerge from the football field or from the domains of myth and ideology.

Apparent bolstering of these myths by European observers may be little more than the uncritical reproduction of symbolic categories. These may in turn arise from Scotland's psycho-political state as much as from the nature of her football.

We have commented very extensively elsewhere on the durability of ahistorical judgements on national character in European media sport. Categories within which nations establish mutual identification are remarkably resistant to alteration by any form of contra-indication. It is far from unlikely, theoretically, that various kinds of misreading of the differences between Scottish football and its rivals are reproduced through ideological operations whose sources lie in Scotland's exasperating political entanglements.

Specifically, Scotland must be constructed as a nation, society and culture whose ability to secure difficult objectives is invariably a matter of superhuman effort. This, in turn, reconstitutes Scotland as a constantly embattled state. No metaphor is so familiar in descriptions of Scottish sport as the military metaphor. It is used frequently by other nations' journalists to describe their teams' performances. But in Scotland it is at the core of the nation's perception of itself. In this way, the impossible difficulties which always face them justify to the Scots their own political inaction.[8]

As in most European countries, it is only football fans who take on sufficient significance in Scotland to be considered in any sense typical of the culture. Yet European fans in a number of other countries carry no significant role of this kind.

As previously, we face a question here about the relationship between real-world changes in fan behaviour and the construction of fan behaviour characteristic of media accounts. Unease existed in certain quarters during Italia 90 over accounts of English fan behaviour which were felt to be unduly influenced by media requirements. Perhaps Scottish club fan misbehaviour in the 1990s has received less attention than previously, in part because it can no longer be rendered comprehensible within the dominant narrative of Scottishness?

Just as Scotland's 'embattledness' has seemed more acute as her political inactivity has seemed ever more embarrassing, the contra-myths of English brutality and Scottish amiability also developed and strengthened in the Thatcher and immediate post-Thatcher years. If Scotland's national side seems unable to compete at the highest levels, her fans are the nicest in the world. Their amiable clowning might, indeed, seem the apt response of such a politically comical nation. In fact, there are few cities in Europe which will really look forward to an invasion by Rangers or Celtic or Hibernian or Hearts fans in 1993 any more than in the heyday of Scottish hooliganism in the early 1970s. Yet the press is full of welcoming quotes from enriched German publicans and affable Scandinavian police chiefs.

This cannot be merely a question of journalists' rhetoric. The good behaviour of the national side's fans has begun to dismay Scottish journalists. The *Herald*'s consistently nonconformist James Traynor comments, after being provoked by the fans' apparent celebration of Scotland's defeat by Switzerland in Berne, that 'the Scottish fan is becoming an almost pathetic caricature of himself, someone who has come to believe all the hype and publicity': and later advises that the Scotland manager should 'discourage the fans from celebrating second best, indulging in ludicrous laps of defeat' (*Herald*, 11 September 1992).

The notion of the English fan performing his role of hooligan, and the Scot his of amiable clown, each made pathologically self-conscious by his different forms of exclusion from the modern world of Europe, is a persuasive one (perhaps it is all rhetoric).

Tabloid language

The role of the tabloid press in the reconstitution of the British football fan is of considerable importance, closely connected as it is with an overall construction of its readership and an account of the nature of foreignness.

It is instructive to note differences in the degree of degradation of language employed by the *Daily Record* and the *Sun*. A characteristic *Sun* headline – 'KRAUT OF THIS WORLD: Blitz kids storm through on a Euro glory night' (about a Scotland U-21 victory over Germany) – is probably a degree or so more xenophobic than the *Record* would tend to be (more so for example than the 'HERR TODAY, GONE TOMORROW' headline cited above). While the *Record* does occasionally use the term 'Krauts', the *Sun* does so unhesitatingly, as it will frequently refer to the French as the 'frogs'. 'FROGS WON'T CATCH US ON THE HOP AGAIN!' says the *Scottish Sun*, 7 November 1992, referring to Rangers' European opponents Marseille, while the *Daily Record* (7 November 1992) has the relatively literate 'C'est magnifique says Rangers boss: I'M READY FOR YOU'. Any significant difference might be explained either in terms of a lower degree of ethnocentricity in Scottish culture and/or a less certain ideological role for the *Record* in relation to its working class and underclass readership.

There are other intriguing differences, between the Scottish and English editions of the *Sun*. The contrast between their reporting of the second leg of the Rangers-Leeds tie highlights the importance of specific readership markets, and their presumed ideological requirements. (Interestingly, in the week we examined both editions of the *Sun* the only real difference between the papers was in its sports coverage.) English readers were informed how 'ATTILA THE KILLER' (Mark Hateley) had helped dump the English champions:

> The man nicknamed Attila in his Milan days, left England's champions bruised and battered and surely with a growing respect for the style and class of football north of the border . . . Leeds will be gutted by this failure as they were twenty-two years ago when Celtic the other half of the Old Firm defeated them just as dramatically in the semi-final of the European Cup. (*Sun*, 5 November 1992).

Words such as 'style' and 'class' are not often used in Scotland to describe Scottish football, as we have seen. While the *Scottish Sun* was hailing Rangers as 'KINGS OF BRITAIN', and enthusing about how they had 'struck a stunning blow for Scotland' and silenced their English critics, the *Daily Record* was placing the Scottish performance within that frame of reference noted above: 'DIDN'T WE DO WELL, . . . It was great to be a Scot in the tense Elland Road cauldron as battling Rangers shot the champions of England down ruthlessly in the Battle of Britain' (*Daily Record*, 5 November 1992).

ASPECTS OF THE POLITICAL ECONOMY OF THE SCOTTISH SPORTS MEDIA

The press

In his examination of sports writing Rowe (1991) criticises sports journalism for: 'being embedded in, rather than illuminating, its subject and, in a broader sense, for being complicit with rather than obstructive to the mobilisation of ideologies of dominance in and through sport' (Rowe, 1991, pp.88–89). While this may or may not be the case, it acts as a useful starting point when discussing some of the economic and institutional factors impinging on the production of sports journalism.

More newspapers are read per head of population within Scotland than elsewhere in Britain (Linklater, 1992). The Scottish national press is dominated by the tabloid *Daily Record*, part of Mirror Group Newspapers, which outsells its nearest tabloid rival the *Scottish Sun* (part of the News International stable) by over two to one (750,000 to 290,000, January to June 1992). The broadsheet press in Scotland consists of the Glasgow based *Herald* (120,000: January to June 1992), and the Edinburgh-based *Scotsman* (86,000: January to June 1992), the *Dundee Courier* (115,000: January to June 1992), and Scotland's biggest selling evening paper Glasgow's *Evening Times* has a circulation of 156,000 (January to June 1992).

At the popular end of the market both the *Daily Record* and the *Scottish Sun* are engaged in an intense circulation battle, in which a newspaper's sports coverage (particularly in the lucrative west of Scotland advertising market), and football coverage specifically, play an important part in its attempts to attract and build an urban readership.

In particular, stories relating to Glasgow's two major clubs Celtic and Rangers sell newspapers. Part of the *Sun's* strategy in competition against the *Record* has been to devote more attention to its sports coverage and forge closer links with particular clubs. During Graeme Souness's reign at Rangers, for example, relations between the manager and the *Sun* newspaper resulted in a number of exclusives for the paper, the most notable being the signing of Catholic Maurice Johnston for the club in 1989.

The 'Old Firm' links with sports journalism in Scotland is interesting, and highlights some of the geographical problems faced by journalists working within a relatively small sporting environment. The degree of attention devoted in the press and broadcasting to the 'Old Firm' is a source of constant irritation to football supporters outside the west of Scotland.

This is related to the importance of sources in aiding journalists. In such a relatively small pond, it sometimes appears that journalists are not keen to upset some of the bigger fish. Indeed it could be argued that there appears at times to be a cosy consensus among various sections of the Scottish media on sporting issues. There have been notable exceptions. The *Herald's* James Traynor incurred the wrath of (then Rangers manager) Souness with his criticism of their poor European record, and was banned from the ground. Much of the sports writing in *Scotland on Sunday* has also been willing to dissent from some of the more settled relationships existing within Scottish sport, the latter typified, for example, by inattention to the issue of sectarianism and racism in Scottish sport (again with exceptions such as Ian Archer, who writes currently for the *Scottish Daily Express*, and the *Evening Times*).

Moorhouse (1991), has argued that the media portrayal of Glasgow as a tribal city, with two 'warring' communities (Catholic and Protestant) is popular in Scotland:

> . . . and possibly more so in England where it exudes that enticing whiff of primitive savagery which it is one of the cultural roles of the fringe 'nations' of the UK to provide . . . it is often not realised outside how proud the Scottish football culture is of the clash of Rangers versus Celtic – 'the greatest club game in the world' as it is routinely referred to – as something the English have not got and cannot match. (Moorhouse, 1991, pp.204–05)

While agreeing that the media play a key role in constructing a particular version of the 'Old Firm', which helps not only to sustain interest in the clubs and the fixture, but has the important economic element of selling news-papers and attracting viewers to television, we should not, however underesti-mate the power of alternative discourses: there are others surrounding the clubs, which circulate among supporters through a variety of networks used to challenge some of the dominant media assumptions, a point we return to briefly below (Boyle, 1991, 1993).

Most sports journalists working in the country are Scottish, a fact which can tend to add to the claustrophobic atmosphere within the field of domestic sports writing. Within a British national context many Scots are to be found in media industries and sports journalism is no exception. Among Scottish journalists based in England are Hugh McIlvanney and Patrick Barclay at the *Observer* and the Chief Football Correspondent of the *Sun*, Alex Montgomery. There is a similar Scottish penetration of network sport on television, with notable Scottish commentating and summarizing presences in football, rugby, golf and boxing. Potential narrowness in the account of Scottish sport is not countered by the fact that within the print media there are in Scotland no mainstream women sports journalists.

It is in fact worth speculating about the representativeness of Scottish sports journalism, about its relationships to views held in Scottish society as a whole.

Newspapers such as the *Daily Record* and the Scottish *Sun* have large readerships, partly based on the quantity and nature of their sports coverage. But it is important to note that this does not necessarily mean that they offer universally popular views on sport or that sports fans think they are well served by the press on offer. The growth in recent years of the fanzine movement suggests a less than happy readership, the feeling being that too many journalists no longer articulate the feelings and frustrations of various supporters (if indeed they ever did). (Also see the chapter by Moorhouse in this volume.) Among certain groups of football supporters there is even a strong perception of bias existing against certain clubs in particular news-papers, and among certain journalists (Boyle, 1993). Newspapers' purchasers may be actively critical of their content.

It is important to emphasise the close links which exist across the various media covering sport in Scotland. There is a clearly defined media culture within the Scottish sporting environment. For example, Chick Young will write for Glasgow's *Evening Times*, regularly appear on BBC television's *Sportscene* and Radio Clyde's (ILR) *Super Scoreboard*, Gerry McNee will write for the *Scottish Daily Express* and also be Scottish Television's main football commentator on *Scotsport*. In one sense, because of the small size of the country (and the market) this is not surprising. However there remains a question over how healthy it is to have such close ties within the sports media. It tends to increase the probability of aberrant accounts of Scottish sport, to increase the likelihood that dominant symbolic structures continue to pre-dominate even when lacking sufficient flexibility and appropriateness.

Broadcasting

Sports coverage is important to broadcasters in Scotland. BBC Scotland, with its remit to reflect the cultural life of the country, has suffered from an identity problem among viewers, and sport is an important positive component in its search to improve recognition of its separate output.

Its main sports programme *Sportscene* is broadcast on a Friday evening and Saturday night. On BBC Radio Scotland, *Sportsound* is broadcast on a Saturday afternoon on direct competition in the west and central belt of Scotland with ILR's Radio Clyde's hugely popular *Super Scoreboard*.

Within the Channel Three sector in Scotland there are three companies: Border, Grampian, and the dominant company, Scottish Television, which serves the central belt where most of the population live and which is the most lucrative in terms of advertising revenue. It retained its franchise to broadcast as part of the Channel Three network with a bid of £2,000 (being aware that it had no opposition). Scottish Television has devoted a lot of energy in marketing itself as a distinctive regional broadcaster, with a distinctive Scottish programming remit (under the new franchise it committed itself to increasing the hours of domestically produced programming by 340 hours). Within this programming, coverage of Scottish sport is viewed as vital, in particular the coverage of domestic football. *Scotsport* (sponsored by Tennants Lager) is broadcast on a Sunday evening with a sports preview programme (sponsored by Tartan Special export beer) broadcast on a Friday night.

In addition STV runs a discussion programme, *Sport in Question*, which regularly has guests from south of the border and is chaired by Archie MacPherson, formerly of the BBC, columnist with Scotland's best selling Sunday newspaper the *Sunday Mail* (sister paper of the *Daily Record*) and radio commentator on Radio Clyde's *Super Scoreboard*. The family atmosphere of sports coverage in Scotland, with its recurrent figures such as MacPherson, Dougie Donnelly and Chick Young, is a phenomenon of the media world in general, not just of the press. Shortcomings in the mediation of Scottish sport are almost certainly connected with the limitedness of fresh, alternative comment.

BEYOND FOOTBALL

The symbolic operation of sport has characteristics particular to individual sports. Considerations of whether the games are played by teams or by individuals are important, as are questions of location – a site such as Wimbledon carries its own mythic load, as do Parkhead or Hampden. Questions of the relative visibility of fans are likewise important (Blain and O'Donnell, 1993).

Golf, for example, is seen round the world as a game quintessentially of Scotland, but its discourses are cosmopolitan (see John Lowerson's chapter in this book). Highly visible players such as Sandy Lyle and Colin Montgomerie are frequently signalled as Scottish by both the Scottish and English press, but this is no more than a recording of nationality and it is not uncommon to find copy on both players which does not mention their Scottishness at all (though the reasons for this may be different in the Scottish and English presses).

The idea that there is a Scottish style of golf – that, for example, Lyle's inconsistencies are a Scottish trait – does not in fact emerge. There is obvious pleasure in the Scottish press when Scots golfers succeed: when two or three golfers from the country are enjoying success in one tournament, the fact is recorded in terms of 'Scottish presence' but that tends to be all.

If there is a discourse within golf journalism which is nationally significant, it is an account of tradition, a Royal and Ancient bolstering of the construction of Scotland's densely-textured historical past. This is coupled in a complex manner with another cosmopolitan discourse of Scotland as servitor-nation to the world's rich; Scotland-as-Gleneagles.

There is probably a structural connection with this view of Scotland and an older psycho-cultural use made of the country by the European imagination in its responses to the work of Sir Walter Scott and others (Chapman, 1978).

At an extreme from golf's symbolic indications, or the restricted symbolic reach of the traditional celtic sports, is quite another account of Scotland, the sporting Scotland whose work is American football, baseball, basketball; or tae kwon do, synchronized swimming, indoor beach volleyball and the complex textures of the rapidly expanding symbolic world of personal fitness (the international community of step-aerobics). The worlds of these pursuits are those of late modernity and postmodernity (in distinction to that of most of Scottish football, though the latter is being increasingly reconstituted under the leadership of David Murray's Rangers). The spatio-temporal refigurations within Scottish culture implied by strong enthusiasms for these newer and foreign sports have their parallels elsewhere in Scottish culture, such as in continuingly heavy American influences in Scottish popular music.

And just as Scottish popular music also produces, alongside its American reformulations, some reworkings of indigenous musical tendencies (Runrig, The Proclaimers), likewise in sport we find a rich mixture of historical and geographical elements in a highly complex sports culture. As yet, the mediation of these alternative sporting pursuits is limited, yet they figure, like world music on pop radio, as an intriguing cosmopolitanizing of the media picture.

It is in this context – perhaps surprisingly – that the sport of boxing is best placed, certainly boxing 'as a signifying practice'. Despite the sport's affinities with an urban, industrial, masculinized account of Scottishness, the interest of boxing in the 1990s lies more within the domain of 'postmodern' Glasgow.

Boxing has never been as central to accounts of Scottishness as it might have been had Scotland produced one or two significant heavyweight fighters, but she has produced and continues to produce world champions such as Jim Watt and Pat Clinton, and there is a rich vein of Scottish fight mythology.

But it is in the context of the rejuvenation of the postindustrial city that boxing is now arguably most significant in Scotland. Glasgow is actively marketing itself as a 'fight city', an interesting deployment of one corner of its heritage potential. It is a reputation consonant with certain aspects of its mythic identity which in general the city's publicists have not sought to emphasize, but such contradictions are inherent in the assemblage of identities typical of the recent reconstitution of postindustrial cities and regions.

We have discussed elsewhere (in the context of the 1992 Barcelona Olympics) the complex constructions of 'Britishness' and 'Scottishness' and 'Englishness' which emerge from Scottish and English coverage of that event. We noted that during Barcelona 1992, English commentators referred to English athletes uniquely as British, and to Scottish athletes as both British and Scottish. Scottish commentators, on the other hand, also referred to English athletes uniquely as British, but to Scottish athletes uniquely as Scottish.

Scottish identity at Barcelona was therefore maintained by both sides whereas English nationality had seemingly disappeared. By way of explanation, we speculated that for English commentators, Britishness and Englishness are presumably identical. In athletics, unlike the instances of football, or rugby, there is a 'British' team, which raises some interesting forms of linguistic behaviour from journalists and commentators (Blain et al, 1993).

These practices are not confined to Olympics coverage, but appear to be an athletics subdiscourse of national identity, for example: '*Britain's* Olympic 100 metres champion Linford Christie and *Scotland's* Tom McKean both tasted defeat at last night's Grand Prix athletics meeting in Cologne' (*Herald*, 17 August 1992, our emphasis).

Athletes' performances, like those of footballers, carry a heavy burden of representativeness. The nature of both McColgan and Murray is constructed within the paradigm of infrastructural incapacity identified as the conceptual framework for football journalism, above. No wonder that the 'flair' of Tom McKean is so suspect: Scottish success is built on 'slog' and 'guts' and 'character'. McKean's performances have about them a 'Latin' inconsistency which the available symbolic framework has difficulty in accommodating ('Bellshill star Tom McKean flopped again', as the *Record*, 3 August 1992, puts it, unfeelingly, after his failure to qualify for the Barcelona 800 metres final).

Infrastructural incapacity is usually combined in the account of the Scottish athlete with moral excellence, a Scottish reformulation of a widespread discourse of Olympianism: 'A heartbroken Yvonne said: 'When I tried to go, there was nothing there' . . . Back home, the Honest Toun of Musselburgh, Midlothian, shared in Yvonne's agony'. From the editorial perspective of Glasgow, being from small towns like Liz McColgan's Arbroath and Yvonne Murray's Musselburgh in itself constitutes a moral advantage, derived merely by not being from Glasgow. These towns, whose whereabouts Glaswegians can only guess at, are perceived as pre-modern, and therefore innocent and wholesome.

McColgan is in fact an athlete hard to handle within the available discourses either of Olympianism or of Scottishness. She is relentlessly modern and professional, and her outlook is entirely cosmopolitan, her Arbroathness probably neither here nor there: this may explain her not entirely widespread popularity in Scottish journalism circles.

We end this section with a consideration of rugby, a sport which has offered the main ritual conflict between Scotland and England since football's Home International series was abandoned.

The natural disadvantages of Scottishness take on an especially persuasive form in rugby. Scotland's status as one of the world's top four or five rugby nations in the 1990s does indeed seem extraordinary given the lack of actual participation in the game compared to rugby in New Zealand, Wales or England. In rugby above all, auto- and hetero-typification produce concurrent accounts of a country of scavengers living off rare pickings. This is a reformulation of a more central (English) metaphor of Scottishness dating from the post-Union period. 'Spirited Scots live on starvation diet' (*Herald*, 18 June 1990) neatly encapsulates this especially concentrated view of inherent Scottish disadvantage which rugby journalism reproduces. Scotland are touring New Zealand, whose cupboard is rich (though the metaphor displays a rapid change): 'whatever else was proved by New Zealand's Test victory over Scotland on Saturday at Carisbrook, Dunedin, the tourists were reminded of how much of a handicap it is to have to soldier on with restricted ammunition'.

There is room for a recognition that Scotland are often really quite good at the game: 'there was a time when Scottish teams awaiting the arrival of the French would pray for rain to soak the edges off Gallic flair. Nowadays, thankfully, wind and rain are no longer essential . . .' (*Scotland on Sunday*, 8 March 1992).[9]

But the woe expressed at the retirement of a pillar of the game like a John Jeffrey or a David Sole is testimony to the sense of insecurity surrounding the construction of media rugby.

The gentle (but not always) cross-Border provocations which daily help to reconstitute Scottish-English identities produce parallels between football and rugby. Just as English journalists were wont to see England's Mark Hately as Rangers' key to success over Leeds in the 'Battle of Britain' in the autumn of 1992, whereas Scottish writers were prone to cite Durrant and McCoist as the chief agents, English newspapers are not invariably kind to the Scottish rugby game.

'Edwards stands out on day of mediocrity' is the *Sunday Telegraph* headline (8 March 1992) after the Scotland victory over France: the piece continues, 'Neil Edwards, a cheerful Londoner, popped across the border to do Scotland a favour by scoring the only try of a low quality match at Murrayfield. It might set a few Scottish teeth on edge to know that an Englishman and Harlequin had such a strong influence, but he did secure a victory for Scotland that their mediocre showing hardly deserved'. This kind of English approach to Scotland has its equivalent, of course, in the Scottish media account of the best English soccer teams as, essentially, the products of Scottish playing or managerial skills.

The Scottish rugby Grand Slam of 1990 – victories against England, Ireland, Wales and France – was as explicit as reconstruction of the Wars of Independence as could be imagined in sport. On television and in the press alike the historical framework was explicit. Much as 'Edward's proud army' had (according to the song) been sent thoughtfully southwards by Bruce's men, the overweening English rugby squad was stopped in its tracks by Sole's grim little band. The *Telegraph*'s 'cheerful Londoner' whom we encountered above comes from a land of plenty whose inhabitants can sometimes relax.

David Sole's men featured on the network news broadcasts of that night shouting the remarkably persistent 'Flower of Scotland' discordantly into the cameras, like men with some embarrassing obsession (probably Scotland's embarrassing obsession with its Scottishness).

CONCLUSION

It was a commonplace in Scottish political circles at the end of the 1970s that success, instead of embarrassing failure, as for Scotland in the 1978 Argentina football World Cup, could have transformed the nature and result of the 1979 referendum on devolution: or even that year's General Election. It was not usually intended as a wholly serious comment, but nor did it ever sound entirely absurd.

We have tried to demonstrate how Scotland might indeed be heavily thrown back upon a symbolic mode of political existence and how sport not uniquely but very powerfully becomes an arena of symbolic contestation in the absence of real Scottish political power. We have attempted to indicate the conservatism of much of Scottish sports journalism's account of Scottishness, and to suggest psychological, economic and institutional reasons for these possible inadequacies in dominant Scottish media accounts of Scottish sport.

We have, likewise, noted that the complex nature of collective identity formations associated with Scottish sport parallels the complexity of Scotland as a political entity.

'Scots must strike for independence in Europe' is the headline in a *Scotland on Sunday* piece by Kevin McCarra on European football club competition (18 October 1992), a recycling of the SNP slogan 'Independence in Europe'. A month or so later, unfortunately, only Rangers remained. The existence of such an ambition in Scottish football seems as much a guarantee of disappointment as the parallel aspiration in politics.

But perhaps not so. We have noted several instances in Scottish sport where the message seems to be one of serious Scottish engagement with the outside world. Better, in the instance of Rangers Football Club's ambitions, is the sense of not being 'outside' at all, but of being, or seriously aspiring to be, a European club in the league of Marseille or Milan.

If that level of ambition were sustainable in Scottish sport, even if only in one or two instances, and rewarded by consolidated success, then such achievements would force a large breach in the symbolic language of inherent incapacity (of which sports discourse is only a component) than has yet been possible. That would therefore be, primarily, an ideological and, potentially, political development.

The odds (as we are bound to say) are against it.

NOTES

1. See Gellner (1983). For contrasting views on the operation of the national dimension in contemporary life, see Hobsbawm (1990) and Nairn (1990).

2. Blain, Boyle, O'Donnell (1993) Sport and National Identity in the European Media, Leicester, especially Chapters 1, 4, 6 and General Conclusion.
3. See inter alia Raymond Williams (1977), especially part II, 'Cultural Theory', Jean-Francois Lyotard (1988), Mark Poster (1988), Dick Hebdige (1988), and Christopher Norris (1990): more polemically Christopher Norris (1992). For further discussion in this field specifically in relation to sport, politics and the media, see Blain, Boyle, O'Donnell (1993), Chapter 1, and General Conclusion.
4. See Goldlust (1987), Hargreaves (1986) and Whannel (1992).
5. Colin McArthur's (ed.) (1982) book is a significant landmark in the discussion of the mediation of Scotland, despite a probable over-emphasis on 'Tartan' and 'Kailyard' traditions. See also E. Dick (ed.) (1990). Chapters 4 and 7 of David McCrone (1992), provide some intriguing syntheses of economic, culturalist and sociological perspectives on Scottishness, despite not mentioning football.
6. Celtic were the first British (and non-Latin) team to win the European Cup, in 1967, defeating Inter Milan in the final.
7. No other newspaper would say 'off at the toot': this is a singular discourse stemming from the *Post*'s persona of Dundonian couthiness, an example of the linguistic element in its hugely impressively niche-marketing success.
8. See Blain, Boyle, O'Donnel (1993). The military metaphor in European football, and the media construction of Scottish fans – and English fan behaviour – are discussed in Chapter 4.
9. Ron Atkinson interviewed before the start of the Rangers-Marseille European Cup game in November 1992 (he was commentating), opined that the worse the wind and rain became, the better Rangers would do. Marseille players in fact ran Rangers off the park for eighty minutes, looking supremely comfortable in the dreadful conditions, but the myth of foreign inability to tough it out in Scotland's harsh conditions survives across sports. The converse myth is of Scottish incapacity in hot and humid foreign conditions (a kind of climatic equivalent of unfair foreign referees). This despite Liz McColgan's 10,000 metre world title triumph in the heat and humidity of the Tokyo World Championships. When Yvonne Murray endured defeat at Barcelona 1992, more than one commentator imagined how much better she would have run on a cool wet night in Edinburgh.

BIBLIOGRAPHY

Blain, N. and O'Donnell, H., 1993, The stars and the flags: individuality, collective identities and the national dimension in Italia 90 and Wimbledon 91 and 92 in Giulianotti, R. and Williams, J. (eds). *Modernity and identity in global football culture*, Leicester University Press, Leicester
Blain, N., Boyle, R. and O'Donnell, H., 1993, *Sport and national identity in the European media*, Leicester University Press, Leicester
Boyle, R., 1991, *Faithful through and through: a survey of Celtic football club's most committed supporters*, National Identity Research Unit, Glasgow Polytechnic
Boyle, R., 1993, 'We are Celtic supporters': Celtic, Celtic supporters and questions of identity in modern Scotland', in Giulianotti, R. and Williams, J. (eds) *Modernity and identity in global football culture*, Leicester University Press, Leicester
Chapman, M., 1978, *The Gaelic vision of Scottish culture*, Croom Helm, London
Dick, E., (ed.), 1990, *From limelight to satellite*, BFI/SFC, London
Forsyth, R., 1992, Sport, in Linklater, M. and Denniston, R. (eds) *Anatomy of Scotland*, Chambers, Edinburgh
Gellner, E., 1983, *Nations and Nationalism*, Basil Blackwell, Oxford

Goldlust, J., 1987, *Playing for keeps: sport, the media and society*, Longman Cheshire, Melbourne
Hargreaves, L., 1986, *Sport, power and culture*, Polity Press, Cambridge
Hebdige, D., 1988, *Hiding in the light*, Comedia, London
Hobsbawm, E. J., 1990, *Nations and nationalism since 1780*, Cambridge University Press, Cambridge
Linklater, M., 1992, The media, in Linklater, M. and Denniston (eds), *The anatomy of Scotland*, Chambers, Edinburgh
Lyotard, J. F., 1988, *The difference: phrases in dispute*, Manchester University Press, Manchester
Mackenzie, W. J. M., 1978, *Political Identity*, Manchester University Press, Manchester
McArthur, C., (ed.), 1982, *Scotch reels*, BFI/SFC, London
McCrone, D., 1992, *Understanding Scotland: the sociology of a stateless nation*, Routledge, London
Moorhouse, H. F., 1991, On the periphery: Scotland, Scottish football and the new Europe, in Williams, J. and Wagg, S. (eds), *British football and social change: getting into Europe*, Leicester University Press, Leicester
Nairn, T., 1990, *The modern Janus – the new age of nations*, Radius, London
Norris, C., 1990, *What's wrong with postmodernism*, Harvester Wheatsheaf, Hemel Hempstead
Norris, C., 1992, *Uncritical theory: postmodernism, intellectuals and the Gulf war*, Lawrence and Wishart, London
Poster, M., 1988, *Jean Baudrillard: selected writings*, Polity, Cambridge
Rowe, D., 1991, That misery of Stringer's cliches: sports writing, *Cultural studies*, vol. 5, January
Schlesinger, P., 1991, *Media, state and nation*, Sage, London
Whannel, G., 1992, *Fields in vision: television sport and cultural transformation*, Routledge, London
Williams, R., 1977, *Marxism and literature*, Oxford University Press, Oxford

10

NANCY RIACH AND
THE MOTHERWELL SWIMMING PHENOMENON

Graham Walker

Sport and nationalist feeling in relation to Scotland have been linked
promiscuously by commentators both lay and scholarly. The links are undeniable, but it is seldom made clear precisely what the nature of the
nationalism expressed through the medium of sport is? 'Nationalism' is a
term which has most political analysts and commentators on the trail of
separatist or exclusivist designs and objectives; it is often forgotten that in
the Scottish context at least it functioned for a time largely as a means of
emphasising Scotland's identity within the wider British nation state. The
way such nationalism was expressed through sport has largely been lost sight
of. This chapter discusses a sporting phenomenon which helps to recall it as
well as raising other questions about gender, religious sectarianism, class
loyalties, and local identity.

MOTHERWELL AND LANARKSHIRE

Of those parts of Scotland renowned for breeding national sporting heroes,
industrial Lanarkshire has pride of place. From this soil has sprung not only
the trio of outstanding football managers – Matt Busby, Bill Shankly and Jock
Stein – but also contemporary stars such as Tom McKean (athletics) and Ally
McCoist (football). The steel town of Motherwell – today an industrial ghost
town – reared its share of famous footballers, such as Ian St John, but its
sporting folklore also includes the less likely phenomenon of a local swimming club.

In 1935 the Orcadian poet, Edwin Muir, wrote in his 'Scottish Journey':
'Aridrie and Motherwell are the most improbable places imaginable in
which to be left with nothing to do; for only rough work could reconcile
anyone to living in them' (Muir, 1985, p.2). Muir's bleak commentary related
to a serious point about the effects of industrialisation on Scotland and his
'Scottish Journey' was written at a time of continuing economic depression
(Harvie, 1977, pp.166–67); his was also an intellectual's perspective in which
sport's mass appeal and romance did not intrude. However, the mood and

atmosphere of Motherwell a few years later during wartime defied such a picture of social alienation, and the contribution of the town's swimming club to a sense of local pride was considerable; even Muir might have been impressed.

On the face of it, Motherwell's transformation into a focus of local and national sporting enthusiasm during the war and for a short time afterwards was improbable, first, because of the sport which was in many ways still a middle class one in Britain in general (Mason, 1988, pp.78–79), and second, because it was mostly women, and one woman in particular, who were the national idols. Nancy Riach's impact, from the time, aged fifteen or so, that she was at her record-breaking best was profound; her tragic death from polio in 1947, aged twenty, genuinely stunned not just Motherwell, but the nation.

The phenomenon that was the Motherwell Amateur Swimming and Water Polo Club (ASWPC) becomes easier to appreciate when it is remembered that the war adversely affected the competitive quality of mass spectator sports such as football and resulted in the call-up of so many young males. There was thus an opportunity for traditionally less glamorous sports to emerge more prominently, and for women performers to attract attention. In the case of Motherwell, there was also the astuteness of the town's Council in seizing the chance to promote the already high-achieving swimming club and grasping the civic possibilities the situation offered. In the event, the town was able to bask in the club's triumphs and war-time morale was given a signal boost.

DAVID CRABB AND A SPORTS PHILOSOPHY

Swimming, as Richard Holt points out, became, during the twentieth century, 'the single most popular physical recreation after walking' (Holt, 1989, p.347). However, its popularity was as a recreation, rather than as a competitive sport. Women's swimming won official Olympic recognition before track events (Mason, 1988, p.11) and national swimming events for women were held in Scotland from 1892 (Holt, 1989, p.130), but the notion that swimming was more 'appropriate' for women on account of being less competitive died hard in male-dominated sporting opinion (Mason, 1988, p.71).

One male sportsman who did not hold such an opinion was David Crabb, the architect of the Motherwell success story. Crabb, in his youth a champion diver and gymnast, became a swimming coach on his appointment to the job of superintendent of Motherwell Corporation Baths in the 1930s. To Crabb must go the credit for the discovery and the cultivation of so much talent: he was the coach of the female swimmers who were to achieve national and international renown – Nancy Riach, Cathie Gibson, Margaret Bolton – and also the male water polo team which, effortlessly supreme in Scotland, entered and won in the post-war years, the English water polo cup.

Crabb's philosophy was to 'catch them young'; indeed, he spent a lot of time training his 'water babies' aged around seven, as well as his older celebrities. He had great faith in his own ability to rear champions provided he was able to exert his influence early enough. By all accounts he was a powerful and compelling personality who got the best out of a large number of swimmers, none more so than Nancy Riach who 'set the standard' in terms of national and international prestige for the rest (*Motherwell Times*, 19 September 1947). She was undoubtedly his greatest protégé.

But Crabb's sporting philosophy and dedication were conditioned by more than a sense of personal fulfilment. He had deeply held political convictions. He claimed to be a Communist although it is not certain if he was a member of the party. The Communist Party was relatively strong in Motherwell, particularly in the steel workers' trade unions; in fact in 1922 the area returned the first Communist MP to Westminster, J. Walton Newbold. As an industrial centre the town possessed a disputatious political temper; intense political arguments took place between working men at the town's turkish baths every Saturday night (oral evidence: David Jarvie). Popular Conservatism, drawing on religious loyalties, was as notable a political phenomenon as socialism. Crabb was a left-wing crusader rather than a party political animal. He was a man with missionary intent: to encourage working class people to express themselves through the medium of sport and to rise out of the social and economic misery in which many were immersed. Former members of the club recall how he constantly reminded them that they could 'change the world'; they remember him leading the singing of 'the Red Flag' on coach trips and lending out to club members books such as Robert Tressell's *The Ragged Trousered Philanthropists* (oral evidence: Margaret and David Jarvie).

Crabb always stressed human potential: 'there's a champion up every street' was one of his favourite sayings. But inseparable from this was an attitude very typical of the Left in Scotland from the Independent Labour Party (ILP) through to the Communist Party: that of working people 'improving' themselves through education, sport, political work or some such avenue. The role of the organised Left in using sport as a kind of political weapon has been much neglected, but as Stephen Jones has shown, there were a 'myriad' of left-wing organisations in Britain in the inter-war period which vied for influence and control over different areas of sporting activity; the working class, it has also been argued, did not allow itself simply to be used as turnstile or playing fodder by an exploitative bourgeoisie (Holt, 1989, pp.357–67; Jones, 1988). The Communist Party made its most concerted attempt to influence sport in the 1930s through the British Workers' Sports Federation (BWSF) (Jones, 1988, Chapter 4). The Left, as well as the Establishment, were capable of viewing sport in terms of social control and of 'rational recreation': a healthy mind in a healthy body'. In fact, former club members' recollections of Crabb are of someone with pronounced puritanical and autocratic streaks (oral evidence: Margaret and David Jarvie) which, although they conflicted with other more subversive traits, fashioned a similar message – 'work hard, play hard, discipline yourselves, improve yourselves' – to that of the political right, the educational establishment, the churches and their ancillary influential social organisations such as the Young Men and Young Women's Christian Associations, and the Boys Brigade and Girl Guides. The difference was that Crabb believed that successful participation in sport could be liberating for an oppressed working class; the right saw it as complementary to a healthy 'naturally' competitive social order.

Crabb certainly stressed the importance of collective values and of team spirit and effort. However, his personality was a mixture of collectivist and individualist impulses; he may have thrived on the tension between them (oral evidence: Margaret and David Jarvie). He was fiercely competitive and encouraged his 'charges' to be; it is doubtful if such swimmers as Nancy Riach would have achieved so much without this element of individual competition within the team framework. As Ross McKibbin has argued, it is a serious mistake to assume that all manifestations of working class life were, or should be, collective, and that collectivist values always eclipsed individualist ones (McKibbin, 1990, p.163).

Crabb was instrumental in giving working people access to swimming and other water sports. He persuaded the Motherwell and Wishaw Council to keep the public pond open in wartime, and, indeed, to open it on Sundays for practice sessions for the club. He successfully lobbied the Council to reduce the price of a season ticket to benefit those of limited means. Crabb shrewdly cultivated local councillors and won an important ally in Bailie George Barr who was a key figure in local government finance. Crabb appealed to notions of civic pride, and his ability to bring to Motherwell big names in the aquatic sporting world, some of international repute, convinced the Council of the value of the sport to the community, particularly in wartime. During the war, and after it, the sport was central to a vibrant social life in Motherwell.

As the club's reputation grew so did invitations to galas and events throughout Britain and on the continent. In 1946 the club participated in 120 galas, and its role call of success in this year comprised 21 new records, 38 championships, three water polo leagues and one polo cup; the local paper was moved to claim, with some justification, that 'the steel town has no equal at the aquatic sport in Great Britain today' (*Motherwell Times*, 27 December 1946). This burst of success came on top of similar feats during each wartime year. Central to it was the figure of Crabb consciously and skilfully tapping local, civic, and national pride and loyalties, and in the case of some, class consciousness and a determination to overcome the social odds.

THE MAKING OF NANCY RIACH

Nancy Riach was somewhat different from the run of Crabb's protégés, and not just on account of her exceptional swimming ability. Her social background was more favoured; her father, originally from Inverness, rose through the ranks of the Motherwell police to become an Inspector, and was Conservative in his politics; her mother was a primary school teacher. The Riach family – she had a younger brother, Fraser, who was also in the Motherwell Club – lived in a two room flat with kitchen and an inside toilet; most of the other club members came from poorer backgrounds and lived in tenements with outside lavatories (oral evidence: Margaret Jarvie). The family was sufficiently financially secure to enable Nancy to stay on at Dalziel High School and qualify to become a teacher.

The Riachs must also be viewed in the context of the social influence of religion in Motherwell and in the west of Scotland in general. The family were church-goers, and Nancy, from her early teens, sang in the church choir and gave addresses to the congregations (*Glasgow Weekly News*, 20 September 1947). Moreover, she refused to swim on a Sunday, and this does not seem to have been solely the result of parental pressure.[1] The family's Protestant- ism also extended to connections with the Orange Order; it appears that Nancy's parents, and perhaps Nancy herself, were members. A recent Scottish Orange Order publication has certainly claimed her as a member (McCracken, 1990, p.42), and the Ladies Section of the Order was involved in fund-raising for a memorial to her (*Daily Record*, 18 December, 1947). Orange flute bands paid tribute to her memory by playing her favourite hymn, 'By Cool Siloam's Shady Rill', at the 12th of July parade the year following her death (oral evidence: Alex Walker). The Orange Order's politics, at least at leadership level, were Conservative, and the Order's role in local politics was a significant one until the Second World War. It was, for example, the means by which a populist Conservative (and Orangeman), Hugh Ferguson, was returned as MP for such a working class constituency in 1923.

Motherwell, and industrial Lanarkshire generally, had witnessed waves of immigration from Ireland in the nineteenth and early twentieth centuries. This migration was both Catholic and Protestant, and the Orange-Green bitternesses were simply reproduced on Scottish soil as the panoply of secret sectarian societies – Orange Order, Ancient Order of Hibernians, Knights of St Columba – was erected anew (Devine, 1991; McFarland, 1991). Religious barriers were still formidable in the Motherwell and Lanarkshire of the 1930s and 1940s, and they could impinge directly on sport as biographies of the area's famous sons testify (Crampsey, 1986, pp.29–30; Dunphy, 1991, chapter 1). Employment was also, to some extent, channelled through religious affiliation; the Chairman of Colville's steelworks in this period, Sir John Craig, was also Chairman of the YMCA and it is said that attaining employ- ment in Colville's was contingent on YMCA membership (oral evidence: David Jarvie). The YMCA in Motherwell had been associated with organised sport for several decades. Certainly, in the late nineteenth century, the range of religious-based social activity in Motherwell could be said to have outweighed the secular (Harvie and Walker, 1990, p.350), and easy assump- tions about religion's decline as a social force in the twentieth century should be resisted (Brown, 1987).

Crabb, befitting his politics, set his face against religious sectarianism, and it does seem that the club played a significant role in helping to dismantle barriers and promote friendships between Protestants and Catholics. However, parental suspiciousness sometimes lay in the background, and fears of a son or daughter getting romantically involved with one of the 'other sort' were probably conveyed quite clearly. Nancy Riach seems not to have expressed sectarian sentiments of any kind, and she was undoubtedly sincere and positive about her faith. It should also be said the wider reputation of the large and active ladies section of the Orange Order was, by dint of much visible charity work, far better than that of their male counterparts (Walker, 1992).

The balance of influences between her father's Conservatism and Crabb's radicalism seems to have proved productive rather than unsettling for Nancy. Crabb also encouraged the breakdown of barriers between the sexes; for example he introduced mixed bathing at Motherwell. In addition, Nancy's mother might be said to have been quasi-feminist in her outlook; she instilled in Nancy the determination not to be overawed by men. Nancy was, in fact, quite independently-minded, and her religious and socially 'respectable' background did not, for example, prevent her modelling new lines in swim-wear which, for the time, were somewhat risky (oral evidence: Margaret Jarvie). Souvenir brochures of the time reveal a clear sexual suggestiveness, something deliberately contrived by those who, in a modest way by today's standards, were realising the marketing potentialities of Nancy and the advantages of creating a cult around her personality and achievements.[2]

A rift between Crabb and the Riachs eventually occurred after the war by which time Cathie Gibson was rivalling Nancy as the club's outstanding achiever. In 1946, aged just fifteen, Cathie set twelve new British records (*Motherwell Times*, 27 December 1946). The Riachs at this time moved to Airdrie and Nancy did her training there. Her father, former members remember, took the view that Crabb was now concentrating on the up and coming Cathie – she was eventually to win a bronze medal at the London Olympics in 1948. This, rather than matters political or religious, seems to have been what the falling-out was about (oral evidence: Margaret and David Jarvie). Certainly, the core values Crabb held, regardless of how they might be interpreted, were shared by Nancy and her family to the end: the celeb-ration of sport as a central part of healthy living, and the honour which dedicated participation brought to the individual, his or her family, town and country. After Nancy died, Crabb struck a traditionalist note in his tribute: '. . . in everything she was honest, generous and radiated those noble quali-ties of womanhood which are the ideal of every man. Yes, we shall not forget our Nancy' (*Motherwell Times*, 19 September 1947).

'FOR SCOTLAND, REX!'

Swimming and water polo were popular sports in certain parts of Scotland – Paisley, for example, boasted a lively set-up not dissimilar to Motherwell's. In this period Glasgow had three water polo leagues, each with sixteen teams. However, Motherwell's dominance of water sports in Scotland was so con-summate that the club made frequent trips to England to find keener competition.

There was a profound nationalistic edge to these affairs. The club, for example, would travel to England attired in kilts, and the prospect of defeat-ing the 'auld enemy' on their own soil fired the members (oral evidence: Margaret and David Jarvie). It was a sporting adventure akin in miniature to the Scottish football trip to Wembley; Scottish patriotic fervour was given free rein (Moorhouse, 1989). Mixed with national pride would also be a sense of class consciousness when the club visited well-heeled towns such as Cheltenham where the opposition was drawn from prosperous locals (oral evidence: Margaret and David Jarvie). Crabb seems to have demonstrated psychological skills in so priming club members during such trips, although many may have been in no need of external motivation.

However, the most accomplished cultivator of national sentiment around the Motherwell swimmers, and Nancy Riach especially, was the *Sunday Mail* sports columnist 'Rex' Kingsley. 'Rex' took a keen interest in Nancy's career from the time she was winning school championships as a twelve year old. By 1943, when she was sixteen, he was largely responsible for generating interest in her throughout Scotland, and in turning her into a 'forces' sweetheart' for the Scottish servicemen in action abroad. 'Rex's stock-in-trade was couthy, unabashed chauvinism. Reporting Nancy's record-breaking 880 yards free-style swim at Blackpool in 1945 he described his own part in it as follows:

> Then near the end as the strength-sapping drag of this long pond began to tell its tale, she was slipping. With one and a half to go, consternation – she was about four seconds outside the record.
>
> At a signal from her dad and David Crabb I, being at that end, I rushed to meet her, on the turn for her last length and in the welter of spray she set up in the swing round, I cupped my hands and bawled – 'Scotland'.
>
> Galvanised into life, she went to the winning post like a real champion to the thunder of yellings and programme-waving by the 2000 excited spectators.

The record broken, Nancy, according to 'Rex', took the microphone and proclaimed she was proud not for herself but for Scotland, proceeding to pull on her kilt. 'Rex' continued: 'Blackpool loved it. I loved it more for pre-gala talk with English folk indicated they did not expect a new record. But they got it and how!'.

'And the happiest, jauntiest folk . . . were a dozen or so Scots (some of them in the kilt and some now permanently resident here) as they beamed around with a "Wha's Like Us" look in their eye' (*Sunday Mail*, 3 June 1945).

In his column following her funeral, written on 20 September 1947, 'Rex' wrote: 'She was a fighter. In the blur of that sea of faces she emerged . . . pulling off her bathing cap, shaking out her hair, laughing merrily that she'd made another record . . . not for Nancy Riach . . . "but for Scotland, Rex!" '

'Oh, Rex, remember that time we all went down to the Derby baths, Blackpool, for my attempt on the 880 yards? And all of us paraded along the promenade wearing the kilt. And remember that other night in the Marshall Street Baths in London, when I won the 100 yards All-Nations Challenge – and the Scots RAF boys in the gallery had the time of their lives?' (*Sunday Mail*, 21 September 1947).

'Rex's' promotion of Nancy as a focus of Scottish national pride brought an especially enthusiastic response from servicemen. In this there was a potent blend of nationalism and eroticism, epitomised in the 'Nancy Riach Swim Souvenir' which was produced by 'Rex's' newspaper at the end of 1944 'in response to the many appeals' from servicemen. The souvenir contained a photo of Nancy in her Scotland costume (complete with thistle motif) and a list of her swimming records; 'Carry this with you and you'll always be able to keep your head above water!', enjoined 'Rex'. Indeed, the servicemen were more than happy to boast of Nancy's feats to 'get one over' on the English. As a correspondent from the India Command – the fan mail from the forces was said to have reached 'alarming' proportions (*Evening Times*, 15 September 1947) – informed 'Rex' in a letter published in the *Sunday Mail*: 'A tribute to Nancy Riach. Some of the English boys here scoffed when Nancy's name began to be mentioned. A common remark was "wait till she travels to England and swims in a big pond against the best opposition" '.

'Nancy certainly made them swallow their words . . . some time ago one or two of "us Scots yins" agreed that every time Nancy broke a record we would put something in the "kitty" and when we got home make a small presentation in token of our gratitude for keeping "Auld Scotia" in high esteem' (*Sunday Mail*, 15 October 1944).

In July 1944 'Rex' was delighted to announce that Sir Harry Lauder would preside at a forthcoming Motherwell swimming event when 'this wee Scots lassie Nancy pits another gem in Scotland's sporting crown' (*Sunday Mail*, 2 July 1944).

On a scale of political nationalism the kind of sentiments aroused by such as 'Rex' and expressed by Nancy Riach and her admirers ranks fairly low. It can be placed in the context of what might be called 'Empire-oriented nationalism': Scottishness passionately expressed within an accepted wider context defined by the British state and empire. Even by the time of the Second World War an imperial cultural framework had great significance for most Scots, and a Scottish-English rivalry operated within it, with particular seriousness for Scots. If English sporting passion was harder to rouse and complacent attitudes about being 'fit to rule' still abounded, the Scots always wanted to prove themselves; to prove on a bigger stage the talents and the virtues on which they were encouraged to pride themselves. Bettering the English was the ultimate joy, and the most appropriate response to English aloofness or pejorative interpretations of the Scots' 'Junior Partner' status. The Scots, in this cultural context, were easily riled to nationalistic passion, but this would have lost its edge outwith the structures which threw Scots and English together and stimulated such rivalry. Hence the rivalry between Scots and English servicemen, a phenomenon which, if anything, was, and is, regarded as a source of productive tension within the British armed forces overall.[3]

It would be invidious to infer too pointedly any political corollaries to such nationalistic expressions, but it is safe to say that they did not reflect fundamentalist nationalist political positions of the kind taken up by cultural figures in the 1920s like the poet Hugh MacDiarmid.[4] The very cultural context on which they fed precluded separatism, although not necessarily the belief in some kind of Home Rule. It was the kind of 'keep our end up' nationalism which, for example, the Scottish Convention movement in favour of self-government espoused during the war. At a meeting of this group in 1944 a resolution was passed instructing a committee to 'watch the misuse of the terms "English" and "England" instead of "British" and "Britain" ' (*Sunday Mail*, 25 June 1944). Patriotism rather than nationalism was the keynote. It reflected a tendency on the part of Scots compulsively to define themselves against their English neighbours and rivals. It is also highly likely that Nancy Riach herself, given her family's allegiances and connections, was happy to be patriotically Scottish within a British loyalist context. She was particularly supportive of campaigns in aid of the war effort.

In the case of the Motherwell club in general there was an overwhelming desire to compete with the English to raise standards, to push abilities to new limits, and to express what were believed to be quintessential Scottish qualities: fighting spirit, tenacity, shrewdness, resourcefulness, self-reliance. The club was undoubtedly used in a nationalistic sense, even exploited; yet, the proud Scottish national legend they came to represent was created from below as much as it was hyped from above.[5] It was forged through real, tangible achievement and it stood in contrast to other sporting endeavours in the nation's history in which the nationalist factor served to distort the nature of the achievement or even disguise the lack of it. The Motherwell club, and its star performers, did not play on nationalist sentiment artificially to inflate their reputation.

'BY COOL SILOAM'S SHADY RILL'

Nancy Riach died on 15 September 1947 while in Monte Carlo for the European Championships with the British swimming team. She was a victim of the polio epidemic which was then sweeping Britain. In the week before Nancy's death there were 159 cases of polio in Glasgow alone, and the Ministry of Health announced that there were 662 notifications of cases in England and Wales during the week ended 6 September (*Glasgow Herald*, 15 September 1947). Although very ill, Nancy insisted on swimming her heat of the 100 metres free style event; in doing so she probably hastened her death, but it was indicative of her extraordinary courage and commitment (*Motherwell Times*, 19 September 1947).

The reaction to her death was one of profound grief throughout Scotland and, of course, especially in her home town. Crowds packed the surrounding streets of her family home for a moving funeral service at which a friend sang Nancy's favourite hymn, 'By Cool Siloam's Shady Rill'. Afterwards, 'Rex' wrote of the 'wonderful heart-catching melody' hanging over the crowd (*Sunday Mail*, 21 September 1947). Tributes flooded in from all quarters; she was hailed by Sydney Hirst, Chairman of the United Nations Swimming Committee, as 'the finest swimmer that the British Empire has ever produced, and the finest ambassador of sport that Scotland or any other country within the British Empire has ever turned out' (*Hamilton Advertiser*, 20 September 1947). David Crabb spoke of his 'great sorrow' that she would not reach the goal of Olympic glory which he was sure awaited her (*Hamilton Advertiser*, 20 September 1947). The *Glasgow Weekly News* mourned for 'the lass who won all hearts' (*Glasgow Weekly News*, 20 September 1947).

Yet, amidst the welter of tributes and heartfelt messages, Nancy Riach was not saluted, as arguably she should have been, as a woman who had scored a triumph for her gender as well as her country; nor did Scotland allow such a triumph to alter the deeply masculine nature of the nation's sporting imagery. In a way, Nancy Riach had allowed her identity to be appropriated during her peak years and was pleased to bear aloft traditional values and ideals of Scottish nationality; after her death the process of appropriation continued and different groups and interests vied to be associated with her name and to associate her with different causes.

One example of how she was used is provided by the local paper, the *Motherwell Times*, whose editor commented after her death as follows: 'To the youth of this country and especially to those of the joint burgh of Motherwell and Wishaw, she was not only an example of a "good sport" with an instinct of fair play and its complementary attributes, but also a truly noble creature, clean living, unassuming in manner, and full of that exquisite womanly kindness and sympathy which are so remarkably absent among many of our youngsters today' (*Motherwell Times*, 26 September 1947).

Nancy Riach's name and fame were thus less than subtly hitched to a campaign against juvenile delinquency, about which there was something of 'moral panic' at this time. The subject had also preoccupied the wartime Secretary of State for Scotland, Tom Johnston, who sought to combat it with the teaching of citizenship in schools (Walker, 1988, pp.159–60). Nancy provided a convenient role model, especially when it could be recalled that she had exalted sport as a means to spiritual well-being (*Glasgow Weekly News*, 20 September 1947).

A nation-wide appeal was made to raise £20,000 to provide a fitting memorial to Nancy Riach. However, although substantial sums of money were thought to have come in, effective action was thwarted by the wrangling which took place between the many parties who made it their business to be involved in the project. A suitable memorial never materialised.

CONCLUSION

Nancy Riach was, decidedly, a local hero, as well as a national one. Her achievements belonged most of all to Motherwell and to the outstanding aquatic phenomenon fashioned by David Crabb. She owed her celebrity status and wider popularity to the peculiar circumstances of wartime: she hit the high spots just when people needed most to be cheered, at home and in war zones overseas. Thanks to Crabb and the Motherwell Council she had a strong local base from which to metamorphose into stardom, and thanks to her highly talented club colleagues she had constant inspiration and motivation. She was 'a light that continued to shine' in wartime,[6] but many others made that possible. She was also an early example of the making by the media of a sporting idol; but Crabb as well as 'Rex' employed some formidable public relations skills on her behalf. She was never the personification of the working class hero Crabb wanted to emerge to inspire others in downtrodden circumstances; but, in any case, sport was as likely to function as a means of upward social mobility and social dislocation as to provide a fillip to class solidarity. However, sport was, unequivocally, a valued source of a range of identities – personal, club, community, national – and all of these were played out vividly in the Motherwell context, and in the short sporting life of Nancy Riach.

NOTES

1. The parallel here with an earlier Scottish sporting hero, the runner Eric Liddell, is too obvious to miss, although Nancy Riach was never put in the position of sacrificing Olympic or other honours by refusing to compete on the Sabbath.
2. Note the pose in the *Sunday Mail* Nancy Riach souvenir, produced in 1944 and probably the idea of journalist 'Rex' Kingsley whose patronage of Nancy is discussed in the text.
3. This topic is interestingly explored in James Kennaway's novel, *Tunes of Glory* (Edinburgh: Mainstream, 1980); for a critical commentary see Trevor Royle, *James and Jim: A Biography of James Kennaway* (Edinburgh: Mainstream, 1983, pp.115–24). See also Ian S. Wood, 'Protestantism and Scottish Military Tradition' in G. Walker and T. Gallagher (eds), *Sermons and Battle Hymns: Protestant Popular Culture in Modern Scotland* (Edinburgh: Edinburgh University Press, 1990).
4. In the 1930s the Scottish National Party (SNP) stood for a policy of Home Rule within the Empire, and repudiated the Gaelic fundamentalism associated with nationalists like Erskine of Marr and Hugh MacDiarmid. For an enlightening discussion of the different meanings of Scottish Nationalism in the inter-war period see Richard J. Finlay, 'Nationalism, Race, Religion, and the Irish Question in Inter-war Scotland' *The Innes Review*, vol. XLII, no 1, Spring 1991, pp.46–67.
5. 'Rex' campaigned in typical style, for example, for a National Swimming Centre – a swimmers' 'Hampden' – which would be more worthy of the Motherwell (and other) swimmers. This was 'Rex' in his element but it was a fair indication of how much more important Motherwell had made swimming to Scotland's overall sporting image. See *Sunday Mail*, 10 June 1945.
6. The phrase is David Jarvie's. I am deeply indebted to both Margaret and David Jarvie for their recollections and for access to source material in their possession.

BIBLIOGRAPHY

Brown, C., 1987, *A social history of religion in Scotland since 1700*, Methuen, London
Crampsey, B., 1986, *Mr Stein: a biography of Jock Stein*, Mainstream, Edinburgh
Daily Record (Glasgow), 18 December 1947
Devine, T., (ed.), 1991, *Irish immigrants and Scottish society in the nineteenth and twentieth centuries*, John Donald, Edinburgh
Dunphy, E., 1991, *A strange kind of glory*, Heinemann, London
Evening Times (Glasgow), 15 September 1947
Glasgow Herald, 15 September 1947
Glasgow Weekly News, 20 September 1947
Hamilton Advertiser, 20 September 1947
Harvie, C., 1977, *Scotland and nationalism*, Allen and Unwin, London
Harvie, C. and Walker, G., 1990, Community and culture in Fraser, W. H. and Morris, R. J., (eds), *People and society in Scotland*, vol. 2, John Donald, Edinburgh, pp.336–57
Holt, R., 1989, *Sport and the British*, Oxford University Press, Oxford
Jones, S. G., 1988, *Sport, politics and the working class*, Manchester University Press, Manchester
McCracken, G. A., 1990, *Bygone days of yore*, County Grand Orange Lodge of Glasgow, Glasgow
McFarland, E., 1991, *Protestants first! Orangeism in nineteenth century Scotland*, Edinburgh University Press, Edinburgh

McKibbin, R., 1990, *Ideologies of class*, Oxford University Press, Oxford
Mason, T., 1988, *Sport in Britain*, Faber and Faber, London
Moorhouse, H. F., 1989, 'We're off to Wembley': the history of a Scottish event and the sociology of football hooliganism in McCrone, D., Kendrick, S., and Straw, P. (eds), *The making of Scotland: nation, culture and social change*, Edinburgh University Press, Edinburgh
Motherwell Times, various dates
Muir, E., 1985, *Scottish journey*, Fontana, London
Sunday Mail, various dates
Walker, G., 1988, *Thomas Johnston*, Manchester University Press, Manchester
Walker, G., 1992, The orange order in Scotland between the wars in *International Review of Social History*, vol. 37, no. 2

11

ROYAL GAMES, SPORT AND THE POLITICS OF THE ENVIRONMENT

Grant Jarvie

INTRODUCTION

If game was not separated from the ordinary produce of the soil, for their use, the land would be worth more to the farmer, who would consequently pay a larger rent for it, and be liable for a larger assessment for the poor. Why, therefore, should the poor be deprived of this larger assessment, or the poor-rate increased upon all other classes, for the special convenience of sportspeople? Game preserving, by injuring crops, and retaining large tracts of land in a state of waste, is one of the principal sources of pauperism; and instead of exempting sportspeople from the burden of the poor, it would be more reasonable and politic to assess them double. (Somers, 1985, p.38)

The above remarks are the observations of one correspondent as he toured through the Highlands of Scotland in 1847. Like many social and historical narratives on the Victorian period (1837–1901), Robert Somers' piece was critical of the landowners and large tenant farmers whom he described as 'having been raised to a position of wealth and indolence over the necks of the people (Somers, 1985, p.ii). While his *Letters from the Highlands* provided an insight into the attitudes and behaviour of a certain social elite, Somers' letters also add substantive weight to the establishment of sporting estates during the middle of the nineteenth century. By 1846 the writer had already warned that if sporting estates in the North continued to develop at the same rate as they had over the last quarter of a century, then the Gaels would 'surely' perish from their native soil (Somers, 1985, p.i).

During the 1990s the liquid asset of a sporting estate, or a salmon river or a brown trout loch, has been losing its attraction for many modern sporting landlords. The new rich of the Lawson years, the top earners whose tax burden was cut from 60 to 40 per cent in 1988, have been trying to off-load many of the sporting estates in which they invested during the property boom of the late 1980s. The following are but a few of the many estates put on the market during the early 1990s: the 23,000 acre Ben Alder estate in the old country of Inverness-shire; the Garynahine estate on the Island of Lewis, which offers game shooting as well as salmon fishing; the 77,000 acre Mar

Lodge estate next to Royal Balmoral and the 17,000 acre Knoydart estate which was put on the market during August 1991 by its owner, a Surrey millionaire property dealer (*The Glasgow Herald*, 28 August 1991, p.2). From Ben Alder in the North West, to the Hebrides in the West and the Grampians in the East almost thirty prime sporting estates, covering over 300,000 acres, were officially put on the market, during late 1991 and early 1992, with a collective price tag of almost £30 million (*The Guardian*, 1 February 1992, p.24).

Despite the occasional idealist claims that sport and leisure often transcend the conflicts and problems of modernity, changing social and economic patterns of development apply to everyone. Discussions on sport and leisure in the Highlands have tended to rely upon a number of common arguments:

(i)   that the systematic development of sporting estates has led to an exploitation of natural resources and subsequent profit for some;

(ii) that involvement in certain sports has served to reproduce both symbolic power and social space;

(iii) that the whole notion of private sport or a leisured class is contradictory to residual ideologies which assert that the land and its contents belong to all the community and not just landowners;

(iv) that struggles over sport and leisure forms have contributed to broader popular struggles over land use;

(v)   that royal involvement in sport in the Highlands has helped to strengthen not just the popularity of the monarchy but also reproduce the very substance of Anglo-British nationalism; and

(vi) that all the main rural resources, including those for agriculture, forestry, sport, recreation, nature conservation and quarrying remain controlled within the same pattern of landownership.

What is common to all these considerations is that they vividly dramatise sport and leisure as important arenas through which various groups actively re-work their relationships and respond to changing social conditions as a whole.

The importance of sport within a changing way of life did not escape the attention of Neil Gunn who, during the 1930s, continually questioned the commercialisation of the Scottish Highland Games and the spectacle of the professional athlete travelling from village to village collecting any money that local labour and patronage could gather (Gunn, 1931, pp.412–16). Commenting upon one particular incident, Gunn recalls an occasion when the dancers were called together and the prize piper, who had carried off all the money that day, appeared not in traditional Highland dress but in a blue suit and bowler hat. The judge, obviously astonished, called the piper over and asked him to explain what the rig-out meant. Not recognising the importance of the blue ribbon tradition of the best piper having the honour of playing for the dancers at the last event, the piper explained that he had wanted to catch an early train and therefore had jettisoned his borrowed kilt so that he could 'beat it' at the earliest moment (Gunn, 1931, p.413). At one level, the humorous dismissal of the incident may seem insignificant and yet at another level, the writer's point is intrinsically a serious one since what Gunn was in fact commenting upon was the decline of a Highland way of life in the 1930s and the in-roads being made by a more urban, commercialised culture which took little cognisance of tradition, local people and local customs. What seems clear about Gunn's writings on sport and society is the view that sport both contributed to and was constitutive of Highland tradition and culture. Sport was symbolic, it occupied a certain social space and was involved in the making of the nation (Gunn and Murray, 1991; McCulloch, 1987).

The central theme of this chapter, while it touches upon many of the afore-mentioned themes, is not to explain the development of sport and leisure in the Highlands in all its different forms and contexts. Nor does this chapter attempt to re-evaluate, yet again, the sociological and historical literature on the Highland clearances or de-construct more of Scotland's Highland tra-ditions. At a substantive level, this specific contribution starts by asking the question to what extent was the recent controversy over the sale of Mar Lodge estate symptomatic of a much longer historical relationship between sport, landowners and the monarchy since about 1840? While such a theme is worthy of attention in its own right it is capable of providing insights into a number of secondary areas of concern such as the contemporary politics of the environment, the symbolic power of sport and leisure, and changing patterns of landownership and social development both in the Highlands in particular and in Scotland in general.

In order to address these themes, I have divided this chapter into three parts. The first part considers the relationship between sport and the monarchy in the Highlands. The Royal Family are, of course, among the nation's principal landowners and yet playing the royal game has meant much more than just promoting a love of sport and recreation on Royal Deeside. The second part of this chapter briefly considers the extent to which the development of sporting estates in the Highlands was implicated in the politics of land reform and popular protest during the Victorian period. A passing comparison is made between the politics of sport and nationalism in both the Highlands and Ireland during this period. The final part of this chapter is more contemporary in that it considers patterns of landownership during the twentieth century and the extent to which the power behind the pattern has controlled the main rural resources in the Highlands including those for sport, recreation and conservation.

PLAYING THE ROYAL GAME

Through the work of a number of historians and political theorists, we are beginning to understand how the pageantry, royal pomp and ceremony of the twentieth century was hastily contrived towards the end of Queen Victoria's reign (Arblaster, 1989; Billig, 1992; Cannadine, 1983; Nairn, 1988; Thompson, 1990). One of the strengths of Cannadine's work is that while there is a substantive concern with the symbolism and rituals of royal events he does not lose sight of the social context of historical narrative and thus his work avoids the ceremonial antiquarianism which characterises so much of the commentary produced by the media's royal watchers (Cannadine, 1983; Cannadine, 1990). The relationship between Braemar, the Monarchy and sport provides a useful example of the way in which something as seemingly innocent as the Braemar Royal Highland Society Gathering is in fact inextricably linked to the practices by which a fraction of a powerful social group actively strives to legitimate and hold on to its power and, to use Bernard Crick's terms, 'the fading magic of majesty' (*The Guardian*, 6 February 1992, p.6).

The connection between 'Royal Deeside' sport and the monarchy is a bonding which preceded the arrival of Prince Albert and Queen Victoria (1837–1901) at Balmoral by several centuries. Malcolm Ceann-Mor (1058–1093) was associated not only with consolidating the values of a more Anglo-Norman culture but also with hunting royal deer in the Forest of Mar and contributing to the folk-origins of what is today referred to as the Gathering of the Braemar Royal Highland Society (Jarvie, 1991). In a simple sense the shooting of royal deer has always been a popular game for both Scottish and British royals. When Charles I visited Scotland in 1633 he gave the following instructions to his foresters (McConnochie, 1923, p.31):

> These are to entreat yow to do all diligence and caus slay and send in to his Majestie's house at Halyrudehouse against the threttene day of Junii instant, suches sortis of venesone and wyldfoullis as are to be found within your boundis, and so from weik to weik dureing his Majestie's aboad within this Kingdome.

In the shooting of deer during visits to the Highlands in 1842 and 1844 the monarchy was merely indulging in a royal game which had long been established in both Deeside and Scotland. By the time Prince Albert had acquired the lease of Balmoral Castle from Sir Robert Gordon on 8 September 1848, the monarchy had already cemented a bonding of affinity with the Highlands – an association which is depicted in the period paintings of Edwin Landseer. On her first visit to Balmoral in 1849, Queen Victoria commissioned Landseer to paint 'Royal Sports on Hill and Loch', a painting which first appeared at the Royal Academy in 1854. The painting reproduced the Highland myth of environmental harmony and the natural image of Queen Victoria and The Royal Family enjoying sport in the tranquil loyal, royal Highlands (Graves, 1876; Lennie, 1976; Stephens, 1874). This is a Highland myth which, Pringle (1988, p.140) asserts, denies the object of which it speaks, namely Highland history. From this myth and its signification in Landseer's 'Royal Sports', historical and social reality is transformed into an image of natural reality. The royal game in this sense is to present the naturalness of the image of sport in the Highlands while at the same time to deny the existence of popular struggles over land, nationhood and identity.

Her majesty certainly made her wishes clear to the painter (Pringle, 1988, p.144):

> It is to be thus: I, stepping out of the boat at Loch Muich, Albert, in his Highland dress, assisting me out, and I am looking at a stag which he is supposed to have just killed. Bertie is on the deer pony with McDonald (whom Landseer much admires) standing behind, with rifles and plaids on his shoulder. In the water, holding the boat, are several of the men in their kilts – salmon are also lying on the ground. The picture is intended to represent me meeting Albert, who has been stalking, whilst I

have been fishing, and the whole is quite consonant with the truth. The solitude, the sport, the Highlanders in the water, and it will be, as Landseer says, a beautiful exemplification of peaceful times, and of the independent life we lead in the dear Highlands. It is quite a new conception, and I think the manner in which he has composed it, will be singularly dignified, poetical and totally novel, for no other Queen has ever enjoyed what I am fortunate enough to enjoy in our peaceful happy life here. It will tell a great deal, and it is beautiful.

There is no denying the depth of Queen Victoria's emotional attachment to the Highlands, sport and Balmoral. However her understanding of the social and political situation around her has recently been brought into question. Her own diaries reveal a remarkable ignorance of the Kingdom she governed despite having travelled through it (Queen Victoria's Diaries, 1868, vol. I–II). A popular argument is that the actions of the monarch, in particular her close association with the Highlands, helped to create what Nairn (1988, pp.211–312) has recently referred to as the glamour of backwardness. Nairn's main thesis relates to the process by which state and capital have benefited from ordinary folk's love of crown, nation and empire. Love of monarchy helped to cement an Anglo-British version of the nation and deflect popular opinion away from the actions of the British state as it declined into a long-term condition of backwardness. The fact that the 'divided United Kingdom' has survived this long term decline, implies Nairn (1988, p.214), is in no small way due to a number of symbolic fantasies stage-managed by the supporters of both crown and capital. Angus Calder makes a similar point in his analysis of King George IV's visit to Edinburgh in 1822 (Calder, 1989), an event which helped to cement the loyalty of the Scots to King and Crown and convince government, state and the upper circles of both the Scottish and English social formations that the ghosts of Scottish Jacobitism and radicalism had been well and truly put to rest. Royalism helped to bury the past and to secure the belief that the past could not be used as a basis for social or political mobilisation in the present. Playing the royal game, in the last instance, helped to marginalise the political, emotional and ideological dimensions of Highland popular struggles.

What better symbol could the establishment hope for but Queen Victoria as the respected chief of chiefs at the Gathering of the Braemar Royal Highland Society? A closer fusion between the Braemar Highland Gathering, Balmoral and the monarchy first occurred in 1859. On 22 September Her Majesty invited the Braemar Highland Society to hold its annual Gathering at Balmoral. The invitation to Balmoral was issued again in 1890, 1898 and 1899, by which time the Society had become known as the Braemar Royal Highland Society. Symbolically, the close bonding between Balmoral, Queen Victoria, and the Braemar Gathering stood for loyalism, royalism and a tacit acceptance of a particular definition of state, crown and nation. Playing the royal game during the Victorian period helped to promote the glamour of backwardness and consolidate the belief that future insurrection against the monarchy was improbable.

When C. L. R. James, the West Indian writer, first came to Britain in the 1930s what struck him most was the tenacity of the Victorian balance and compromise (James, 1963). Sport, in the form of cricket, served as a means of the renewal of English ideology and provided a natural meeting place for the moral outlook of the dissenting middle classes and the aristocracy. Playing the game came to be felt as, and was constantly declared as, being essentially British (what this really meant was English). Sport was placed on the same super and sub-political plane as royalty and the constitution. However, like cricket, the actual party-political game also required an umpire in the background. With no written constitutions, president or supreme court, the only possibility was for the monarchy to put on the pads. Playing the royal game essentially meant being the referee of Britishness – a role which was essential to the whole game of life and politics.

As the traditional role of the monarchy declined during the nineteenth and twentieth centuries, such royal games became increasingly important. The Royal Family played a key role in the regulating of a particular definition of Britishness which involved the emergence of certain social codes, social calendars and a degree of social closure amongst not just the hereditary privileged but also those who aspired to belong to the upper circles of society. Sport and leisure helped to define a certain schedule of events around which a myriad of informal events continue to occur. Such events in Scotland include the Braemar Royal Highland Society Gathering, the grouse shooting season, the Argyllshire Gathering and the Oban Ball, the pheasant shooting season and the deer shooting season. This nucleus of symbolic sporting activities also continues to contribute to a British sporting calendar which includes the Derby (Epsom), Ascot racing week (Gold Cup) various polo matches, Henley regatta, Cheltenham National Hunt racing (Gold Cup) and the Grand National (Aintree). Sport and leisure occupy an important symbolic and social space within British social structure, a social space which requires the sponsorship of various powerful interests with introduction to the monarchy being the ultimate sign of acceptance for some. Playing the royal game in this sense involves being the 'referee' over certain social codes, prescriptions and prohibitions concerning not only social class and gender but also the reproduction of a distinct form of Anglo-British nationalism.

In *In His Own Words*, the Prince of Wales (cited in Nairn, 1988, p.197) has suggested that

> There isn't any power. But there can be influence. The influence is in direct proportion to the respect people have for you . . . Monarchy is, I do believe, the system mankind (sic) has so far evolved which comes nearest to ensuring stable government . . .

During the early 1990s, such an influence was brought into play during the negotiations to sell Mar Lodge Estate. During 1991 Mar Lodge was put on the open market by its owner Gerald John Panchaud Kludge. The land which lies close to the Queen's Balmoral estate was bought in 1989 by the American fast food billionaire so that his wife could rub shoulders with royalty at Balmoral (*The Courier and Advertiser*, 13 August 1991, p.7). The estate itself contains 25,000 acres of the Cairngorms National Nature Reserve, three of Britain's five highest mountains, remnants of the 7,000 year old ancient Caledonian Pine forest, a host of rare plants and animals and is home to many rare birds including the capercaillie and golden eagle. After separating from his wife,

Mr Kludge informed interested parties that the estate could be bought by conservationists if a quick deal in the region of £10,000,000 could be arranged (*The Sunday Observer*, 7 July 1991, p.7). Such an offer was immediately made by the government's Crown Estate Commissioner (CEC), led by Lord Mansfield, but it was rejected by the owner.

The estate itself was estimated to be worth £13–15 million on the open market but the knock-down price of £10 million was secured after intervention by the Prince of Wales. Playing the royal game meant not only refereeing over the intense struggle by various interested parties to secure the property, but also defining who should own the land and what it should be used for. The Balmoral pressure group prompted the then Environment Secretary, Michael Heseltine, to raise £5,000,000 from government funds so that a coalition involving the World Wide Fund for Nature could put up the £10 million asking price. This brought the Environment Secretary into direct confrontation with the Scottish Secretary who, initially, consistently refused pleas to rescue the estate for the nation (Scottish nation). The essential conflict was raised by the short-term profit that could be gained from running sporting estates and the long-term value of nature conservancy and the development of the landscape (*The Guardian*, 29 March 1991, p.29). Meanwhile with the Old Man of Lochnagar acting in his hereditary umpiring role, Mar Lodge Estate became a pawn in the game of royal sport in the Highlands. Struggles over sport and leisure in the Highlands, have a long history of 'outsider' influences.

POPULAR PROTEST, LAND REFORM
AND THE POLITICS OF SPORT AND LEISURE

As early as 1833 the Earl of Malmesbury offered sporting rights on the Island of Harris for £25 (*Inverness Courier*, 26 April 1833, p.4). About this time, according to Malmesbury, the Highlands began to develop as one of the main sporting and recreational domains of the southern aristocracy. Large sums of money were invested in the conspicuous consumption of a particular form of sport and leisure. It might be argued that the development of deer forests provided a boost to the local economy and helped to cushion the effects of the declining sheep market and the falling price of wool but, in reality, the beneficial effects to the local economy were minimal. Indeed, in his comprehensive study of the development of deer forests during the Victorian and Edwardian times, Orr concludes that the development of the Highlands as a leisure playground for a certain elite actually contributed to the economic under-development of the Highlands (Orr, 1982, p.147).

Table 1 tends to support the assertion that the development of deer forests for sporting consumption was greatest after about 1870. What marked the Victorian period from earlier periods was the systematic development of deer forests as private sporting estates. Undoubtedly, a major factor involved was the status and prestige sought by the new rich of the south once the royal seal of approval had been bestowed upon both Highland sport and Highland culture (Callander, 1987; Cameron, 1991; Grant, 1989; Gray, 1957; Grigor, 1979; Hunter, 1974; Orr, 1982; Maclean and Carrell, 1986). By the 1880s

Table 1 Sporting deer forests formed, 1839–95

Date	No. by evidence	Date	No. by evidence
1839	28	1870	65
1840–50	14	1870–75	11
1850–55	7	1875–80	5
1855–60	7	1880–85	23
1860–65	4	1885–90	9
1865–70	5	1890–95	4

Source: Compiled from W. Orr (1982) *Deer Forests, Landlords and Crofters*

sporting rents had increased to such a level that social class barriers were reproduced and consolidated through the prohibitive cost of sport alone. For example, the Strathconon sporting estate was rented by Edward Baring in 1875 for £1,500; by 1880 the same estate was rented to Lord Manners for £2,500 while by the mid 1880s Edward Guinness had to pay £2,900 for the privilege of shooting deer at Strathcomon (Orr, 1982, p.38). The point of view of the landowner was expressed by one nineteenth century writer in the following terms (Blackie, 1885, p.63):

Come all ye jolly deer-stalkers, who hold the Highland hills
And count your honours by the heads each stout-legged hero kills,
Who gather gold by digging coal, or else by brewing beer,
And scour with me the Highland glens in the season of the year.

For we bought the hills with English gold
    And what we bought we'll keep –
The hills 'tis clear were meant for deer,
    And not for men or sheep

Then come and scour the bens with me, ye jolly stalkers all,
With lawyers to defend your right, and gillies at your call,
Those crofters may cross the sea but we are masters here,
And say to all both great and small, let none disturb the deer.

By 1884 sporting estates accounted for 1,975,209 acres of Scotland while by 1920 the total acreage under deer had grown to 3,432,385 acres (McConnochie, 1923, p.49). Even lowland newspapers such as The *Edinburgh Evening News* reported that the scandal of the Scottish deer forests needed to be exposed (*Edinburgh Evening News*, 16 December 1905, p.7). Deer not only required large tracts of land but they also attacked crops on productive neighbouring lands. This fact is borne out in many of the nineteenth century crofters songs and poems of the period. The following is an extract from a poem by John MacRae which was recited by him in Lochcarron Schoolhouse on 11 March 1866:[1]

We will drive away every gamekeeper,
and every deer that consumes arable land,
chasing them up again to the deer-forest,

and the Nimrods will be brought low;
the English will be repulsed
from coming near the place at all,
since they ruined us completely
by laying waste (our land) with the deer of the hill.

The sheep itself was just as bad
in nibbling us down to the bone;
it caused many to migrate,
driving them down to the shore;
many a time it pained my guts
to be so frequently a slave,
while sheep and deer were on the pasture
that would have fed many Gaels.

Since the sporting tenant or landowner posed an indirect threat to the livelihood of certain social factions of the Highlands it is not surprising that the destruction of deer forests and sporting estates contributed to popular protests for land-reform. Scarcely a decade went by during the late nineteenth and early twentieth century without various forms of protest against the action of landowners. In many cases, the forms of protest were similar; the destruction of sheep farms, the destruction of deer fences which surrounded the deer forests and the refusal to pay rent to factors of landowners. Following the Pairc Deer Raid on the Island of Lewis in 1887, the crofters point of view was expressed by one nineteenth century writer in the following terms (quoted in Maclean and Carrel, 1986, p.31):

We rose early in the morning – compelled by hardship – to bring down the deer from the heights with accurate aim. We set out on Tuesday with banners and weapons; the day was bright and favourable, as we'll all prove to you. Each man with his gun loaded and ready climbed the high hills, and when a bellowing stag was seen, it was struck down. We killed them in their hundreds, we flayed them splendidly (and) we ate them in an orderly way, with generous portions cunningly.

We are no plunderers, as is stated in lies; we are brave people being ruined by want.

We have waited many days and years without disorder, harrassed by poverty, under (the power of) chamberlains and fools. We got no thanks whatever, we were thralls without profit; they were set upon banishing us completely like foxes.

A vast amount of literature has covered the land question in Highland, Scottish and Irish politics and culture during the forty years between 1880 and 1920 (Cullen and Smout, 1977; Hunter, 1974, 1976; Winstanley, 1984). Undoubtedly there are many inter-connecting strands between Irish and Highland political and cultural movements during this period. Like Ireland, the plight of the Highlands was portrayed as a classical example of the English neglect of Scottish questions. The lessons for organisations such as the Highland Land League, the Irish Land League, the Scottish Home Rule Association and the Irish Nationalist Movement seemed to be that Irish and Highland questions only loomed high on Westminster's political agenda when the respective social formations began to organise and mobilise outwith the

British political framework. Many key figures within the various social and political organisations had strong sporting connections.

Michael Davitt and John Murdoch are but two illustrative examples of the connection between sport and politics. Michael Davitt, during the late 1880s, openly attacked the power of Highland landowners. His founding of the Irish Land League in 1879 was one of many factors which influenced the development of the Highland Land League of 1883. The fact that the staunchly presbyterian crofters of Skye asked this nationalist and Catholic Irishman to become their parliamentary candidate is perhaps an indicator of the non-sectarian nature of both Irish nationalist politics in Scotland and the politics of land-reform in the Highlands during the 1880s. As patron to Glasgow Celtic Football Club, Davitt laid the first patch of soil, specially transported from Donegal, at Celtic Park in 1892. His love of football and identification with Irish-Scots did not prevent Davitt from also being a staunch supporter and patron of the Gaelic Athletic Association which openly attacked Irish involvement in such sports as hockey and association football. Such sports were seen to be symbolic of British (really English) cultural imperialism (Finn, 1991; Hutchinson, 1989; Jarvie, 1993; Mandle, 1987; Sugden and Bairner, 1991, 1993).

The formation of the Highland Land Law Reform Association in 1883 was greatly assisted by the tireless campaigning of John Murdoch. To Murdoch the plight of the Irish peasantry, which he saw as analogous to the problems of the crofting community in the Highlands, was the greatest condemnation of the Anglo-Irish Union of 1800 (*The Highlander*, 25 April 1874, p.5). The columns of *The Highlander*, the paper launched by Murdoch in 1873, regularly reported on the developments within Irish Nationalist politics and the politics of land-reform in the Highlands. The paper provided a forum for debate and co-operation between Gaelic speakers and political and cultural nationalists and socialists in both Scotland and Ireland. It also provided regular reports and views on the subject of shinty and, in the kilt versus knickerbocker debate of 1875, it covered one of the great sporting controversies of the late nineteenth century. On this topic the secretary of the Glasgow 'Ossian' shinty club commented (*The Highlander*, 18 May 1876, p.6):

> There are clubs in Glasgow, Edinburgh and Greenock wearing the kilt, and I have not heard of any one getting his nerves terribly shocked by the indecency of their play, nor have I ever heard of a 'caman' getting entangled in a kilt. Besides, no one can pronounce an opinion on either point without giving the kilt a trial. The clubs at present wearing the kilt have the experience of years, and would not exchange if for any other dress, and members who were not previously accustomed to it now declare it to be the best uniform possible.

The Highlander also reported on the triple alliance of 1879 between Charles Stewart Parnell, Michael Davitt and John Devoy and the resultant rapid rise of Davitt's Irish Land League. Murdoch not only shared Davitt's views on internationalism, demands for land reform and Irish home rule, but his paper actively supported them from the beginning. It is perhaps somewhat ironic that although Highland Land League MPs had the support of Parnellites in parliament, Parnell's own opinion of the Scots is enshrined in his remark that Scotland had long since ceased to be a nation. It was different with Davitt, whose Highland speeches in the late 1880s openly attacked not only the landlord system, but also the systematic development of the Highlands as a leisure playground for the southern aristocracy. Indeed popular forms of protest against such developments continued intermittently from the late 1880s right on into the 1920s. Davitt showed an interest not only in Scottish questions and Scottish home rule, but actively agitated for the development of a Scottish Home Rule Association, which itself was founded in 1886. Murdoch, by this time, was in his seventies and, with the demise of *The Highlander*, he spent more and more time on the advancement of the labour movement and yet he had ensured that the Irish influence on Scottish nationalist politics and Highland political struggles was not an insignificant one.

Much more could be said about the sporting background of many personnel who were at the forefront of Highland, Scottish and Irish politics around this time. If one considers the cross-fertilisation of ideas, people and politics between the Highlands and Ireland during this period one is afforded not only insights into the Gaelic connection, and into the similarities and differences between socialist and nationalist politics but also the social and political background of many sporting forms, organisations and personnel. Despite the intimacies of history, politics and culture, no equivalent organisation to that of the Gaelic Athletic Association ever emerged in the Highlands or Scotland (see Chris Harvie's discussion on this issue). Yet, as I have tried to illustrate, it would be wrong to assume that the struggles over sport and leisure in the Highlands were divorced from either the politics of land reform or socialist and nationalist interventions in either Scotland or Ireland.

There is great danger in over-emphasising the role of sport in the politics of the late nineteenth and early twentieth century. However the following themes are worthy of mention:

(i)   that the struggle over land-reform in the Highlands involved the destruction of sporting estates and the involvement of many sporting landowners;
(ii) that sport itself helped to reproduce and define not only social class, but also gender and national identity;
(iii) that the Gaelic Athletic Association in Ireland was inextricably linked to developments within Irish nationalist politics between about 1884 and 1924;
(iv) that the popularity of the monarch and her association with certain Highland Gatherings and Games tended to strengthen not only the popularity of the monarchy but also the very substance of Anglo-British nationalism; and
(v)   that key personnel within many political organisations were actively involved in the promotion of particular forms of sport and leisure.

While it can generally be argued that since the 1920s the transformation of the economy, status groups and the establishment led to a change in the structure of the capitalist class the same generality does not hold true in the Highlands. While many sporting landowners continue to form a significant upper circle within the overall social structure of the Highlands and Britain it is not on the basis of being active agents of any capitalist class, although the social spaces occupied by many upper circles may intersect. There remains today a residue of old high society families together with some newcomers, who pursue the same round of social calendar activities. The maintenance of a healthy 'summer season' of social activity and leisure in the Highlands is but one indication of the continuing existence of a powerful traditional upper circle of people whose symbolic power and social space within British society is rooted in a system of landownership. Yet, while many traditional hereditary landowners remain they have been joined during the twentieth century by a number of corporate lairds, public agencies and anonymous owners.

CORPORATE LAIRDS, SOCIAL SPACE AND SYMBOLIC POWER

It is useful to consider the notion of social space as being similar to that of a geographical space in which different regions and localities are divided up. Spatial distances often coincide with social distances and by the same logic, those agents who find themselves located within a geographical space may also have a number of common properties which bind them together with other social groups (Bourdieu, 1978, 1990, pp.123–39, 156–167; Robbins, 1991). As modern landowners, the Duke of Argyll, the Countess of Sutherland, the Duke of Buccleuch, the Duke of Atholl and the Farquharsons of Invercauld not only occupy a similar geographical space, namely the Highlands of Scotland, but also a similar social space within British social structure. This is a social space which is defined by a number of common properties such as wealth, social codes, social attitudes, sporting tastes and symbolic power.

The vision of the modern sporting landlord as a blend of go-getting capitalist in London and archaic seigneur at home is in many cases misrepresentative. This is not to deny the existence of such a group but it is important to avoid inaccurate rhetoric such as 'capitalist class', or 'ruling class' in the sense that the social space occupied by modern Highland landowners is far from homogeneous. It is a social space in which the power behind the pattern of control often differs. Certainly, many Highland landowners like those mentioned above and others such as Sir Ian Colquhoun of Luss, the Macleans of Duart, and Lord Huntly remain traditional in outlook. Their reproduction of social space remains dependent upon family connections and background, private schooling, old hereditary forms of wealth and a certain allegiance to royalty and aristocracy. As Table 2 indicates, members of this upper circle of people remain not only sporting landlords/landladies but also form a significant residue of old high society families.

For this group both social space and the consumption of sport and leisure serve, amongst other things, as a form of symbolic power. This in a space of life-styles and status groups characterised by different economic, cultural, and political properties. That is to say the practice of sport does not exist independently of those social agents who for a number of reasons are involved in the consumption of sport and leisure. Consider, for example, the Braemar Highland Gathering or the Aboyne Highland Gathering at which a nominal

Table 2   Britain's top ten highland landowners (1990)

Family	Estimated wealth (£m)	Sporting Estate
1. Royal Family	6,700	Balmoral Estates
2. Duke of Westminster	4,200	Westminster Estates
3. E. H. Vestey	1,420	Vestey Estates
4. Viscount Cowdray	352	Dunecht Estate
5. Duke of Buccleuch	300	Buccleuch Estates
6. Paul van Vissingen	148	Letterewe Estate
7. Duke of Atholl	143	Atholl Estates
8. Duke of Argyll	87	Argyll Estates
9. Captain Alwyne Farquharson	87	Invercauld Estates
10. Countess of Sutherland	87	Sutherland Estates

Source: Compiled from newspapers, *Money Magazine* and J. Scott *'Who Rules Britain?'* (1991, p.83)

unity sometimes conceals the fact that at the same event there co-exists different seating arrangements, different styles of dress, different social codes and prescriptions all of which serve both to unite and segregate different social groups. At Aboyne, the ceremonial display of flags is but one small indicator of the social spaces which different people occupy. At the opening of the Gathering the royal banner or flag is the first to be raised, shortly followed by the flag belonging to the Marquess of Huntly in his roles as both feudal superior and local patron to the Aboyne Gathering. Subsequent banners, raised on either side of these two flags, tend to provide not just a galaxy of different colours but also an insight into the upper circles of power and social structure within both the region, the Highlands and Scotland. As one of the organisers conceded 'the flags are enjoyed by the tourist but they also indicate who is present at the Gathering' (Interview, Aboyne Gathering, 2 August 1986).

Yet while such a small group of hereditary families have remained relatively stable throughout the nineteenth and twentieth century they have witnessed the arrival and departure of various people who might fit more easily within any nominal notion of capitalist class or business elite. These are Highland landowners whose power is supported and reproduced through the worlds of industry, commerce and business. The vision of a go-getting capitalist in Europe and archaic seigneur at home in the Highlands fits more easily the behaviour of Philip Rhodes the property developer, Peter de Saveray, Malcolm Potier, Keith Schellenburg and John Kludge. For this group, ownership of Highland property or sporting estates has not merely been a source of capital investment but also a symbol of life-style, status and social prestige. The consumption of sport and leisure has served as a property of distinction in the sense that involvement has helped to reproduce and cement symbolic power relations with other similar and yet different upper circles of power within the social structure of both Britain and the Highlands.

Malcolm Potier, the English property developer bought the Island of Gigha for £5.4 million at the height of the property boom in 1989. The island, with its sporting estate, golf course, private air strip, and award winning hotel, was viewed by Potier as having enormous potential for sport and leisure development (*The Scotsman*, 20 November 1991, p.17). During March 1992 Gigha was put back on the market by the Landlord's bankers. The jobs, futures and homes of the 160 islanders were placed back in to the hands of an assortment of capitalists, pop stars, and comedians who had been associated with the island as possible purchasers (*The Glasgow Herald*, 24 March 1992, p.19). It was not until mid-September 1992 that Holt Leisure Parks eventually purchased the island from the Interallianz Bank of Switzerland for a reputed £2 million (*The Herald*, 10 September 1992, p.2). Peter de Savaray recently outlined his plans for the £9 million sporting complex on his 7,500 acre Skibo Castle estate. Built 100 years ago by Andrew Carnegie, the Scots-American billionaire, the hope is that Skibo will provide a perfect setting for wealthy American tourists (*The Independent*, 29 March, 1992, p.4)

John Dibben is one of Scotland's newer landlowners, a successful Wiltshire businessman and an absentee landowner who uses his 42,000 acre Highland estate to entertain deer-shooting parties at weekends. As owner of Glen Feshie, he is also custodian of a large chunk of one of Britain's most important National Nature Reserves. Having bought the estate for £1.6 million in 1989, during the early 1990s he was prepared to claim £2 million from the taxpayer as compensation for not opening up part of the estate to large-scale logging. As owner of the successful industrial holding, Bremhill Industries, Mr Dibben wanted to bulldoze tracks to create access for timber lorries across the estate. The former Nature Conservancy Council for Scotland protested and the landowner negotiated with the agency to recoup from the public purse the money lost if he agreed not to harvest the timber plantations. In short, Mr Dibben claimed £2 million for doing nothing to his estate. Similar claims on public monies have been made by other sporting landlords such as Lord Marcus Kimball who owns 62,000 acres of Altnaaharra (*The Glasgow Herald*, 20 February 1992, p.11). One-off payments, of more than £60,000 have been pocketed by over fifteen landlowners in Scotland, while a further eighteen have received lump sums of between £35–50,000, all for doing nothing. During 1991 Perthshire landowner John Cameron was paid more than £500,000 loss of profits compensation by the then Nature Conservancy Council for Scotland which had objected to a conifer tree planting scheme on his land in Glen Lochay (*Scotland on Sunday*, 12 May 1992, p.12). Although the Glen Lochay scheme was halted, the award reduced the funds then available for other protected sites.

It would be far too easy to slip into the rhetoric which has clouded many of the accounts of the Highland clearances during the twentieth century, namely that all landlords were bad and all crofters were good. In much the same way it would be easy to condemn all landowners and land usage by landowners as being profit maximising, elitist and non-sensitive to community needs and the popular demands for wider access to the wilderness. In many cases this is indeed the case and yet there are several examples of landowners who have responded well to popular pressures, environmental concerns and community needs. The argument that landlords, like other social groups, are often caught up in external influences beyond their control can often be made without exonerating those landlords who are responsible for exploitation, poverty, environmental destruction and community hardship.

Yet the private landowner of the twentieth century has also been joined by a number of corporate lairds. As agents of the Crown, the military are often viewed within Scottish popular culture as merely replicating the attributes of the modern landowner. They are seemingly beyond democratic accountability, use large tracts of land in an unproductive way with military operations frequently infringing upon public access to land. Between 1980 and 1990 the Scottish land holding of the Ministry of Defence (MoD) increased by 268 per cent to 91,200 hectares (Spaven, 1991).

The State, through the Forestry Commission, owns about one tenth of Scotland. Prior to the then Chancellor, Nigel Lawson, closing the tax loopholes, money for many private investors has literally grown on trees. A number of high profile absentee landlords from the world of sport used forestry development as a popular method of capital investment. Celebrities such as Terry Wogan, Steve Davies, Alex Higgins and Cliff Richard all invested in Highland forestry. Wogan bought 1,250 acres of Scotland's flow country for £88,000. During 1988 Richard is reported to have sold some of his plantations for over £1 million. Forestry investment was also undertaken by companies such as Scottish and Newcastle Breweries and Boots, the pharmaceutical company. There is no doubt that the right trees in the right places, managed by the right methods, may provide a small boost to sustaining local community employment and rural development, but the use of the Highlands for forestry in many cases does not coincide with the use of the forestry for the Highlands. One particular scheme to plant trees in 5,000 acres of Strath Cuileannach during 1992 while attracting £2 million in grant aid from the Forestry Commission failed to create one permanent job (*The Herald*, 23 June, 1992, p.5). Forestry investment and the use of land for recreational purposes for many high profile absentee landlords from the world of sport or the arts has, in many cases, simply been a method of private investment and tax evasion.

The most recent player to join the game of land usage and the politics of the environment has been the Scottish National Heritage Agency (SNHA). Born out of the ashes of the Countryside Commission for Scotland and the Nature Conservancy Council for Scotland, the SNHA has a number of broad-ranging functions which include:

(i)   to acquire, hold and dispose of land;
(ii) to report to the Secretary of State for Scotland on all matters pertaining to the natural heritage of Scotland;
(iii) to secure the conservation and enhancement of land in Scotland, and
(iv) to foster an understanding of and to facilitate the enjoyment of Scotland's natural heritage.

One view is that the SNHA has been too heavily weighted with landowners, developers and political appointees at the expense of local councillors and ecologists. During May 1992 the Agency was criticised for failing to deliver the resources which would have helped to secure the sale of the Mar Lodge

Estate. On the other hand, in putting up £20,000 towards the Assynt Crofter's Trust, the agency came out in support of the public appeal to secure the 21,000 acre North Lochinver estate (*The Herald*, 4 September 1992, p.13). It is perhaps early days to pass judgement on the SNHA but it is difficult to see how the agency can work other than as an extended arm of the State or of the respective government in power. Whose side will the agency come down on when environmental or conservation concerns clash with crofting aspirations? When it comes to considering the vast hierarchy of tastes which arise from leisure demands and leisure needs, what are the criteria by which this agency will make its decisions? When public interests clash with private commercial exploitation of resources, what interventionist powers does the SNHA have? How will the SNHA reconcile the mass leisure and tourism policy of Highland Regional Council with the more conservative leisure class policy of Grampian Regional council?

As this chapter was being completed the leisure playground on the Island of Eigg has been put on and taken off the market by its owner Mr Schellenberg with an asking price of between £1 and £2 million. Lord Kimball has placed Altnaharra's 47,000 sporting acres on the open market place with an asking price of more than £7 million (*The Herald*, 19 May 1992, p.1). The crofters of Assynt, in Sutherland, have exercised their right to buy the 21,000 acre North Lochinver Estate which was put on the market with an asking price of £473,000. In 1989 the estate was sold by the Vestey Family (still owners of estate land nearby) to the English-registered Scandinavian Property Services Ltd for more than £1 million (*The Herald*, 29 July 1992). The dispute over Mar Lodge remains unresolved, and prospective quarry mining on the Island of Lewis has stimulated an intense discussion over employment, conservation, leisure and the ineffectual role of crofting laws in protecting tenants against commercial exploitation and 'outsider influences'.

In the 1990s it would be foolish to suggest that the rise and fall of an old and new leisured class in the Highlands is imminent. The 'reel' society are still likely to buy into a social circuit of events which began over a century ago. The Argyllshire Highland Ball remains a classic example of the privatisation of sociability. In connection with another exclusive event attached to the sporting season in the Highlands, one local shop-owner replied, 'We would not be invited – it is for the nobility' (*The Guardian*, 22 August 1992, p.21). Yet it would also be foolish not to recognise that some deep rooted changes are also taking place. The opening up of Eastern Europe has provided a whole new market for the continental sportsman and sportswoman who have traditionally subsidised the Highland economy. The conservationists are arguing that the environmental damage caused by deer is more costly than the income returned from the sporting estate. The successful attempt by the Assynt crofters to buy out the North Lochinver estate is a sign, not only of a new self-confidence among local people, but also that new owners have *re-entered* the game of landownership (*The Herald*, 9 December 1992, p.1).

In the 1880s, when impoverished Lewis cottars sent a delegation to see Lady Matheson, widow of the drug baron who had cleared Carnish on the island of Lewis, in order to plead for access to land then given over to sport, she retorted that these lands were hers and that local cottars had nothing to do with them. A poem, composed by D. Mackinnon and first published in 1885, made the following observations:

> There are still plenty of antlered stags,
> the salmon is still found live and steep-turning in the river,
> in order to provide sport for the 'Englishmen' who come thick in their pursuit,
> but if we ourselves touch them, we are thrown into prison.

> It is a law, it is not justice, this ordinance that they themselves have made;
> the One who created everything under the sun
> did not ordain for them that they should have everything for themselves,
> every salmon and deer and the birds of the skies.

Whether it be the last decade of the nineteenth century or the last decade of the twentieth century, it would appear that sporting forms and leisure practices are capable of yielding important insights not only into the making of the nation, but also into Highland and Scottish social development.

NOTE

1. I am indebted to Donald Meek not only for commenting upon parts of this essay but also for sending me the translated versions of the gaelic poems by John MacRae and D. Mackinnon. I also benefited from the comments made on an earlier draft of this chapter by Jim Hunter.

BIBLIOGRAPHY

Arblaster, A., 1989, Taking monarchy seriously in *New Left Review*, 174, pp.97–120
Blackie, J. S., 1885, *The Scottish highlander and the land laws*, Heath Cranton, London
Billig, M., 1992, *Talking of the royal family*, Routledge, London
Bourdieu, P., 1978, Sport and social class, *Social science information*, xvii, (6), pp.819–40
Bourdieu, P., 1990, *In other words: Essays towards a reflexive sociology*, Polity Press, Cambridge
Calder, A., 1989, Tartanry and frolics, *Cencrastus*, 32, (1), pp.9–14
Callander, R. F., 1987, *A pattern of landownership in Scotland*, Haughend Publications, Finzean
Cameron, A., 1991, *Bare feet and tackety books: A boyhood on Rhum*, Luath Press, Barr
Cannadine, D., 1983, The British monarchy and the invention of tradition, c.1820–1977, in Hobsbawn, E. J. and Ranger, T., (eds), *The invention of tradition*, pp.101–04
Cannadine, D., 1990, *The decline and fall of the British aristocracy*, Yale University Press, Conneticut
Cullen, L. M. and Smout, T. C., (eds), 1977, *Comparative aspects of Scottish and Irish economic and social history, 1600–1900*, Edinburgh University Press, Edinburgh
Finn, G., 1991, Racism, religion and social prejudice: Irish catholic clubs, soccer and Scottish society – I The historical roots of prejudice in *International journal of the history of sport*, 8(1):72–95

Finn, G., 1991, Racism, religion and social prejudice: Irish catholic clubs, soccer and Scottish society – II Social identities and conspiracy theories in *International journal of the history of sport*, 8(3):370–97

Grant, R., 1989, *Strathalder: A highland estate*, Triple Cat, Farnham

Gray, M., 1957, *The highland economy 1750–1850*, Oliver and Boyd, Edinburgh

Grigor, I. F., 1979, *Mightier than a lord: The highland crofters struggle for the land*, Acair, Stornoway

Graves, A., 1876, *Catalogue of the works of the late Sir Edwin Landseer*, Smith, Elder & Co, London

Gunn, N., 1931, Highland games, *Scots magazine*, xv(6):412–16

Gunn, D. and Murray, I., 1991, *Neil Gunn's country*, Chambers, Edinburgh

Hunter, J., 1974, The politics of highland land reform, 1873–1895, *Scottish historical review*, 53(156):45–68

Hunter, J., 1976, *The making of the crofting community*, John Donald, Edinburgh

Hunter, J., 1991, *The claim of crofting: The Scottish highlands and islands, 1930–1990*, Mainstream Publishing, Edinburgh

Hutchinson, R., 1989, *Camanachd: The story of shinty*, Mainstream Publishing, Edinburgh

James, C. L. R., 1963, *Beyond a boundary*, Hutchinson, London

Jarvie, G., 1991, *Highland games: The making of the myth*, Edinburgh University Press, Edinburgh

Jarvie, G., 1993, Sport, nationalism and cultural identity in Allison, L., (ed.), *The changing politics of sport*, Manchester University Press, Manchester, pp.200–31

Lennie, C., 1976, *Landseer and the Victorian paragon*, Macmillan, London

Maclean, M. and Carrell, C., 1986, *As an fhearann*, Mainstream Publishing, Edinburgh

MacPhail, I. M., 1989, *The crofters war*, Acair, Stornoway

Mandle, W. F., 1987, *The Gaelic athletic association and Irish nationalist politics, 1884–1924*, Helm, London

McConnochie, A., 1923, *The deer and deer forests of Scotland*, Witherby, London

McCulloch, M., 1987, Neil Gunn: tradition and the essence of nationalism, *Cencrastus*, 26(1):29–34

Nairn, T., 1988, *The enchanted glass*, Radius, London

Orr, W., 1982, *Deer forests landlords and crofters*, John Donald, Edinburgh

Pringle, T., 1988, The privatisation of history: Landseer, Victorian and the highland myth in Cosgrove, S. and Daniels, S., (eds), *The iconography of landscape: essays on symbolic representation, design and use of past environments*, Cambridge University Press, Cambridge, pp.142–61

Robbins, D., 1991, *The work of Pierre Bourdieu*, Open University Press, Milton Keynes

Satterley, G., 1992, *The Highland game: Life on Scottish sporting estates*, Swan Hill Press, Shrewbury

Scott, J., 1991, *Who rules Britain?*, Polity Press, Cambridge

Somers, R., 1985, *Letters from the highlands: after the great potato famine of 1846*, Melven Press, Inverness

Spaven, M., 1991, Defence and the Scottish environment in *The Scottish government yearbook*, Edinburgh, Edinburgh University Press, pp.188–208

Stephens, F., 1874, *Memoirs of Sir Edwin Landseer*, London

Sugden, J. and Bairner, A., 1991, The politics of sport in northern Ireland in *Studies*, 80(318):133–41

Sugden, J. and Bairner, A., 1993, *Games of two halves: Politics and national identity in Northern Ireland*, Leicester University Press, Leicester

Thompson, D., 1990, *Queen Victoria: gender and power*, Virago Press, London
Victoria, Queen, 1868, *Leaves from the journal of our life in the highlands from 1848 to 1861*, Smith, Elder and Company, London
Winstanley, M. J., 1984, *Ireland and the land question 1800–1922*, Methuen and Company Ltd, London

12

FROM ZINES LIKE THESE?
FANZINES, TRADITION AND IDENTITY IN
SCOTTISH FOOTBALL

H. F. Moorhouse

INTRODUCTION

In this chapter I want to use a case study of one form of cultural output –
Scottish football fanzines – to criticize a trend in the scholarly analysis of
football in Britain and to discuss whether the ways that football has been
linked to group and individual identities in Scotland is changing.

Fanzines are widely regarded as one of the most 'positive' features of
contemporary British football. Quarried and promoted by the liberal press,
perused and adulated by academics, they seem to offer some light in the
gloom surrounding the game in the last decade. In the most direct academic
expression:

> football fanzines can be seen as a particularly significant example of cultural and
> political contestation over and within sporting forms, one that has had some success
> in defending cultural ground and winning political arguments. (Jary, Horne and
> Bucke, 1991, p.592)

These authors view fanzines and the Football Supporters' Association – a
movement they regard as closely associated with fanzines – as a form of
popular resistance to 'distorting commodification' and 'cultural manipu-
lation', and one whose implications are far less ambiguous than those of
football hooliganism. Generally:

> fanzines are united in their view that the game is, or rather ought to be, theirs, not
> the private property of businessmen or remote administrators, or the plaything of
> press and television or police and politicians. (Jary, Horne and Bucke, 1991, p.584)

Fanzines are said to resist the incorporation of soccer as a centrally managed
commercial and commodified leisure provision and strive to maintain the
subservience of full-blown commercial values to vernacular football values.
They give the supporters, or rather, the young fan who stands on the terraces,

a 'voice'. and the general role of fanzines and the FSA (Jary, Horne and Bucke, 1991, p.591) is said to be:

— Translating articulate terrace football spectator opinion from an unwritten culture to a lively, engaging, and persuasive, written form;
— raising consciousness about a variety of football issues and defending the values of spectators, and football terrace values in particular;
— promoting and defending football, especially in helping to articulate widespread opposition to the take-over of clubs by business interests with little feel for the culture of the specific club or for football and terrace culture in general.

Because of this counter-hegemonic thrust and their participatory, grass roots, spontaneous mode of organisation, Jary, Horne and Bucke, (1991, p.593), insist:

In final summary, football fanzines and the FSA provide an example of a genuinely popular cultural contestation with dominant economic and cultural tendencies.

There are two immediate criticisms I would make of this kind of analysis, an argument which is close to becoming the rule among many of those who study football (Duke, 1991; Redhead, 1991; Williams, 1991). To begin with many of the pivots of the argument are evoked rather than being specified. We are not told what 'full blown' commercial values applied to sport might be, though we are offered the examples of American franchises skipping from town to town or the vague suggestion that the time structure of the game might be altered to allow more advertising in its televised form. Equally, the values of 'terrace culture' are assumed (and assumed to be 'good') rather than being detailed – a dangerous procedure, as it could well be that the culture of the young standing fan may be quite reactionary and exclusive in some ways, of which an inherent patriarchy is the most obvious example. Secondly, Jary, Horne and Bucke display the usual tendency of English analysts of football to equate 'Britain' and 'England', one consequence of which is to blind them to the possibility of telling cross-cultural comparison. We are, for example, told (Jary, Horne and Bucke, 1991, p.585) that one of the main features of *British* fanzines is that:

they oppose the way in which the game nationally is mainly controlled by business-men, and increasingly dominated by commercial criteria, including the introduction of 'executive boxes', proposals for club mergers and ground sharing, the increasing domination of League football by an agenda set by five big clubs and the interests of television.

Now, some of these features may apply to Scotland (though as I will show not in quite the straightforward ways Jary, Horne and Bucke, suggest) but there is certainly not a big concern in Scottish fanzines about the English Premier League! Analysts should remember that throughout the 1980s Scottish foot-ball remained relatively free of some of the constraints which affected English football, the ban from European competition, for example. Thus some of the springs which propelled the rise of fanzines in England were not present in

Scotland, yet most of Scotland's 38 clubs have or have had, fanzines. This suggests that the Scottish fanzines emerged partly for similar reasons to those which led to the rise of fanzines in the south but partly as an echo of the English fanzines. This is not the point of a pedant, because it indicates that relationships *between* fanzines and *between* their respective clubs might well be an important aspect of 'the fanzines movement' and these might not be harmonious. One feature of fanzines, one which Jary, Horne and Bucke fail to dwell on, is their myopia, a disinterest in, if not downright hostility to, other clubs and their fans. This is certainly a characteristic aspect of the Scottish magazines.

In addition, a stress on experience north of the border is important since football 'tradition' and 'traditional values' there are not the same as those rather vaguely ascribed to the English game. I have discussed elsewhere (Moorhouse, 1984, 1987, 1989, 1990, 1991) five features which have served to structure Scottish football and it's relations with popular culture. Among these are that it has had its professional competitions dominated by two clubs from one city – Rangers and Celtic of Glasgow, and that it has had clubs, including the two just mentioned, linked to ethnic groupings and antagonisms – 'Protestant', 'Catholic', 'Irish' – which have other institutionalised forms in the wider society. Now, if these are among the features that have structured the nature of the Scottish game and attitudes around the game for a century and more, then they are likely to find expression within Scottish fanzines. Moreover, if, as I have also suggested (Moorhouse, 1991), economic imperatives and developments within Europe are beginning to destabilize all these traditional foundations, then we might well expect the nature of the values expressed in Scottish fanzines to be rather different from the (rather idealised) 'norm' outlined for the English quota of *British* fanzines by Jary, Horne and Bucke.

Then, Scottish fans always seem to have been in a tighter relationship with their clubs and boards of directors than was the case for English followers. For example, the 'brake clubs' that attached themselves to both the big Glasgow teams, and others, from Victorian times are an interesting, and quite under-researched, type of fan attachment which seems to prefigure apparently 'modern' forms of support. By the turn of the century, they were developed enough to organise presentations to players, form united associations, issue badges of membership, hold annual socials and suppers and negotiate with clubs about discounts for match tickets.

Members must have communicated but we do not know if these brake clubs had anything like fanzines, and they probably did not, but Scottish football culture in the past certainly produced some publications which prefigure this supposedly 'new' development. A contemporary Scottish publication carried an article about 'The First Celtic Fanzine', which, it declared, was *The Shamrock*, costing sixpence and which flourished between 1961 and 1963. It was published by the Shamrock Supporters Club of Edinburgh and took a virulently anti-board stance with highly personalised criticism, and championed the cause of a baillie who wanted to usurp the existing directors. It was uncompromising in its attitude to Rangers but also denounced the Scottish Football Association and referees for their treatment of the club, while complaining about the state of the terraces and condemning the board for its unwillingness to spend money on new players. Some of its tone is revealed in this editorial,

> The decline of Celtic has reached such a stage that it cannot be tolerated any longer. The supporters must organise and the lead must be given by influential business and professional men . . . after all the supporters are the only part of the club that cannot be done without.

This dates from October 1963 but could be slotted easily into any contemporary Celtic fanzine (*Not the View*, Issue 12).

Rather earlier, but rather less equivalent to modern efforts, were some publications of the late 1940s and 1950s around Rangers, and I am very grateful to Mr Robert McElhone, editor of the *Rangers Historian*, for letting me have access to his collection of this material. These items begin with the *Rangers Review*, the Rangers FC supporters association magazine, price sixpence, first issued in April 1947. Generally, these small magazines were most deferential to those who owned and ran the club, and carried player profiles, cartoons, poems, quizzes, moans at the press, accounts of the old time dances and bowling competitions organised by the thriving supporters association founded in 1946, but also a few articles on more controversial matters. So the first issue, carped about 'the hooligan element' to be found among the Rangers support, though in the third issue an old supporter argued that much of the supposed 'hooliganism' occurring at Rangers-Celtic games was really a media fabrication. This review seems to have been discontinued in favour of a larger *Rangers FC Supporters Club Annual* which first appeared in 1950, by which time the association had nearly 10,000 members, gathered in 117 branches in eleven areas covering much of Scotland. The association was clearly for the 'respectable' fan and took pains to distance itself both from the current 'hooligan' element and the brake clubs of old. The association organised a wide range of social activities, helped in ticket allocations, and some areas produced their own newsletters. Eventually, the editor of the *Annual* and the officers of the association fell out and he began to produce his own little magazine – the *Rangers Supporters Bi-Monthly Review* (later the *Rangers Digest*) which first appeared in November 1955 and which he claimed, a year later, had 2,000 readers and was unique in Britain. Like any modern editor he was quick to note that sales of his product were the subject of some harassment by officialdom.

My reason for drawing attention to these Scottish forerunners of fanzines is two-fold. Firstly, it seems likely that the history of fan-produced publications has been somewhat truncated. Instead of stopping the search for 'origins' in the mid-1970s with punk fanzines and *Foul* magazine (Jary, Horne and Bucke, 1991; Lacey, 1989; Shaw, 1989) analysts of football might do better to search and see whether there were not similar past publications associated with clubs – if only leaflets and petitions – which anticipate the modern form, especially in relation to supporters associations. For in all the talk about fanzines there has been little attempt to elaborate what their theoretical relation is supposed to be to already existing institutions which purport to speak for fans. Fanzines are, apparently, seen as 'more authentic' than supporters clubs (and shareholders associations) though there is at least a possibility that they may only be expressing an *aspect* of 'real' fan culture which is not nearly so unitary as is often assumed. More significantly, I want to underline that the big Scottish clubs, anyway, have always had a more developed relationship with their supporters than English clubs. Both Rangers and Celtic still have an extensive and complex network of supporters' clubs, and meetings between representatives of these and officials of the clubs are relatively frequent. Thus, in Scotland there has appeared to be a reasonable exchange of ideas and at least a continuing *illusion* of 'participatory democracy', which might suggest there is no real call for fanzines at either club. However that might be, the extensive pre-existing associations of supporters in Scotland, is one reason why the FSA, in Jary, Horne and Bucke's view intimately linked with the rise and strength of fanzines, has made very little progress north of the border. Scottish fans tend to shun more inclusive movements in favour of club allegiances. As ever, then, Scotland appears to contradict claims about trends in British football culture which are rooted in English evidence.

To investigate more fully the kind of issues I have sketched above I want to consider the material contained in Scottish fanzines; to look at the detailed content of the fanzines of Rangers and Celtic, and specifically, that contained in the full runs of the most prominent publication associated with each club *Follow, Follow* (first issued in 1988) and *Not the View* (1987).

STANDS RANGERS WHERE IT DID?

Several fanzines are associated with Rangers FC but I will concentrate on *Follow, Follow* which was the first Rangers fanzine to appear and is still the most prominent. While the main Celtic fanzine reveals its oppositional stance to its club's board in its very title, the phrase 'follow follow' suggests the celebratory aspect of support, the fanzine taking its name from one of the most popular of Rangers' anthems. It could (as could any of the other fanzines) easily have adopted other titles clearly coded, to Scottish ears, in a more 'sectarian' way.

Rangers dominate Scottish football at the moment. They have won the League championship five times in the last six seasons, and look set to win it again in 1993. They have the finest football stadium in Britain, a ground in which, it is often suggested, Rangers will soon meet the elite clubs of the Continent as part of some European Super-League. In financial terms too, Rangers are leaving other Scottish teams far behind. The club is controlled by David Murray, one of the richest men in Britain, forms part of his Murray International Group and seems to enjoy considerable benefits out of this arrangement. Certainly the club has few financial problems. Such success, both on and off the field, presents a problem for fanzines – there does not seem much to complain about. As the editor of *Follow, Follow* put it in the first issue, 'Compared with any club, we have a good stadium, a good board and most importantly, a good team. We want to ensure, through helpful criticism, that the fans get a fair deal, that the team continues to improve and that the club maintains its status as the most famous in the world'. *Follow,*

Follow was started because, 'we felt that the views of Rangers fans were not being properly aired either in the press or in the sanitised pages of *The Rangers News*' (the club newspaper). So, an examination of the contents of *Follow, Follow* should reveal not only if and how some of the traditions of Scottish football are being maintained, but also how what appears to be a highly successful amalgamation of big business and football club has been received by some ordinary fans. I want to consider two themes which are prominent in the content of *Follow, Follow*:

the relation of the fans and the club to 'sectarianism';
the relation of the 'traditional' supporter to 'new'.

FOLLOW, FOLLOW **AND 'SECTARIANISM'**

One of the main features of this fanzine is a constant, not to say tedious, sniping at its great Glasgow rival. Issue 13, for example, was a big 52 page edition and, on my count, well over twenty of these contained something derogatory about Celtic and/or its supporters. Few other clubs, English, European or Scottish get a mention, a fact which the fanzines of 'provincial' Scottish clubs find very irritating, but *Follow, Follow* is full of jibes at, or criticism of, the 'tims' or 'beggars' or 'scum' whose stadium is 'the piggery', and who live under the sway of a collective paranoia that they are the victims of a widespread masonic plot involving the media, the football authorities and, especially, referees. *Follow, Follow* provides many examples of such 'paranoia', plus its own 'evidence' of how 'the tims' are treated far too favourably by authority and the media, especially in a tendency to ignore Celtic's and its fans' 'support' for the IRA. For very often the relentless, usually humourless, deprecating references to Celtic supporters take on a sharp political edge. Issue 5 posed the 'quiz question': 'Which famous football club celebrated its centenary in 1988, has won the European Cup once and has been runner up once?' which was answered in the next issue as: 'The nearest you can get to this is Hamburg SV, who formed in 1887. A few people answered 'Celtic', but we must point out that we did ask for a name of a football club and not a pseudo-religious, paramilitary organisation' (also see Issue 24). *Follow Follow* is quick to highlight connections between the other half of the Old Firm and IRA sympathisers, the most spectacular of which, one that made the mainstream Scottish media, was when the fanzine editor taped the editor of the official club newspaper of Celtic, who subsequently resigned from his post, making remarks which condoned IRA bombings (Issues 9 and 10).

This unblinking perspective on Celtic leads the Rangers magazine into deep waters. Like most fanzines, *Follow, Follow* is strongly against 'hooliganism', thus it can sound like the voice of that 'respectable' fan that Jary, Horne and Bucke can hear. However, just like many on the terraces, and one of the reasons any division of supporters into 'rough' and 'respectable' categories is relatively unstable, *Follow Follow* can easily spot occasions when violence around football is quite justified. Issue 18 reported on a game at Celtic Park between the Glasgow giants and claimed that two attempts by the police to remove, 'a massive banner, made up of eight Ulster flags and a Union Jack sewn together' from the Rangers end had been beaten off, the police had been given a good hiding, and the inspector who had provoked the confrontation had been 'coined'. It explained its view:

> Hooliganism is not to be condoned at any time and the police have to be supported. The guys who got the nick rucking with the Bill in order to defend the colours are not hooligans. They were merely showing the same devotion to our country's flag that their forefathers exemplified at the Boyne, the Somme, Passchendale, Tobruk, El Alamein and Monte Cassino . . . Anyone arrested during the flag incident that day should contact FF.

A letter queried why the police tried to remove this flag when the 'fascist tricolour' of the IRA was allowed to fly freely in other parts of the ground.

The fanzine's constant indictment of Celtic and their support means that the magazine has been widely criticized for its 'sectarianism'. Issue 2 reprinted criticism of its opening issue along just these lines by national newspapers, and detailed the fanzine writers' attempts to reply. Now, deploring any expression of racism is another pervasive theme in *Follow Follow*. Issue 1 warned against racist abuse, contrasting the warm reception of the black Englishman Mark Walters at Ibrox with, 'the hostility and sickening racism' he had been subject to elsewhere, 'His reception at Parkhead and Tynecastle put back their efforts to somehow portray themselves as "progressive" or "family" clubs'. Issue 2 said that several men outside Ibrox had been selling the usual Orange and loyalist cassettes but also had, 'a nasty little number called "The Pope's a Darkie" '. The writer had remonstrated with the sellers and most had agreed to stop offering the cassette. One who had demurred had been warned that he would be subject to violence if he continued to do so. When Celtic signed a black English player, Elliot, *Follow, Follow* urged its readers not to barrack him on racist grounds, 'For years middle class Beggars went around claiming we were all potential Nazi Party members. Then came Mark Walters and we saw who the nazis were when they threw their thousands of bananas at him along with the foulest racial abuse imaginable' (Issue 8). Thus there appeared to be a contradiction, noted by many (including some correspondents), between the fanzine's continual campaign against racism and criticism of Celtic fans for their 'racial intolerance', while according to these critics, its producers were busy promoting their own brand of religious bigotry and 'sectarianism'.

However, the writers of *Follow Follow* refuse to recognise any such contradiction, and constantly deny that they are bigoted or 'sectarian'. They are involved in a running argument with the *Chelsea Independent* fanzine which, according to *Follow Follow*, urges Chelsea supporters not to adopt Rangers as their Scottish team because it characterises all Rangers fans as 'rampaging madmen' and 'sectarian', though *Follow Follow* is also firmly against any kind of cross-support because of the behaviour and racism of the Chelsea fans (Issues 4, 5, 11 and 12). They repeatedly insist that no-one is attacked in the fanzine because of their religion or because they are Irish. What they say they attack are those who are racist, bigoted and display support for 'IRA sectarian murder gangs', and many Celtic supporters and the club fall into these categories, though, much to *Follow Follow*'s annoyance, the Scottish media chooses not to publicize this:

> I've absolutely no doubt that if FF was to constantly slag the East Enclosure lads, print articles against the Poll tax and support the IRA we would be the darlings of the media and the fanzine world. Unlike other fanzines we recognise that not all our fans are angels. We are aware that a minority are an embarrassment to Rangers and to Protestantism both of which they occasionally claim to support. Our message to them is short and sweet. Piss off back to Parkhead where you won't feel out of place. We have not, and will not encourage bigotry or violent attacks on other fans (Issue 5).

Moreover, *Follow Follow* sometimes displays a scepticism about all the talk of 'sectarianism' around the Old Firm, a scepticism in which I join (Moorhouse, 1991, p.205). Most academics who write or say anything about Rangers (including this author!) get savaged in its pages but no one has received more criticism than Bill Murray for his various books and interviews about the Old Firm (Murray, 1984, 1988). The fanzine writers are, among many other things, dubious about what they see as his use of fiction and gossip to 'prove' the 'significance' of a 'sectarian divide' in Glasgow, and his general overstatement of the whole issue:

> Glasgow isn't and never was Belfast. The songs and chants in support of the UVF or IRA are all pretty Mickey Mouse. In world, and even Scottish terms, the Old Firm are small beer. There aren't if the truth be told many potential mass murderers amongst the fans most of whom work and live in peace with the opposition six days a week. Punch-ups, stabbings and the occasional death will continue to occur – but you'd get the same in any big city football rivalry. Football though a big thing in many people's lives is not going to change the world. These are the sort of conclusions Dr Murray should have come to. With a little honesty and objectivity in presenting the facts he might have done some good by bringing that realisation to a wider audience. (Issue 2 and see 3).

The fanzine is suspicious of all the TV crews and journalists from glossy magazines who day-trip to deepest Govan in the search for colourful sectarianism, racism and nascent National Front support (e.g., Issues 9 and 18). Its writers see no contradiction in being both strongly anti-racist and proudly protestant (see articles on both subjects in Issue 13), though they accept that the latter is not at all 'fashionable' with 'social worker types'. In fact, the editor argues, Protestantism is historically associated with pluralism and liberalism yet, 'For all of my life Rangers fans have been vilified as scum, drunk, as being violent, unintelligent, bigoted, unsportsmanlike . . . For many Tims "bigot" is the sum total of their vocabulary' (Issue 24).

In 1989 Rangers signed the Scottish international centre forward. What was quite sensational about this was that Maurice Johnston was a catholic and Rangers were famous for operating a 'no catholics' policy. They were regarded as a 'bastion of protestantism' in Scotland and not playing catholics in the team was part, a much criticized part, of the Rangers tradition, How did *Follow Follow* react? For the first (and last) time an ex-Celtic player featured on the front cover. Johnston knelt at prayer, 'Forgive me father for I have signed' (Issue 8). Inside the fanzine argued:

FF has never been embarrassed by the fact that Rangers have been a symbol of unionism and Protestantism, we have never apologised for that and never will. At the same time, because we are confident in our beliefs, we have never felt the need to pour scorn on other peoples' beliefs – nor have we hidden bigotry behind certain codewords. Signing Maurice Johnston changes nothing . . . Rangers as a club have never done anything publicly to encourage Protestantism or unionism. The club has remained a Protestant one because the supporters wanted it. No-one else.

The fanzine received about 50 letters about this great cultural event – half for and half against the signing. Many correspondents regarded it as a neat slap in the face for their rival, as having taken away the moral high-ground Celtic ('Europe's most sectarian football club') had enjoyed, and/or as being a necessary adjunct of Rangers new drive to dominate the Scottish game.

In the subsequent edition, *Follow Follow* jeered at Celtic supporters who were trying to argue that Johnston was not a *real* catholic, 'Most people are nominal Protestants and Catholics . . . Most Scots live in a secular society' (Issue 9). That just about set the tone for further references to Johnston and his wholehearted performances *on* the field (scoring against Celtic) and *off* it (alleged to have sung the 'sectarian'. 'The Sash My Father Wore') won over most supporters. A catholic had played for Rangers and the sky had not fallen in, Ibrox was still crowded, Glasgow had not exploded.

FOLLOW FOLLOW: 'TRADITIONAL' AND 'NEW' SUPPORTERS

Issue 13 contained an interview with Drew – 'a non-bigot' – who had not attended a game since Johnston had joined Rangers. His reasons for not going were quite complex. For him the signing was only part of a much greater change that was taking place. He did not approve of the player, 'not because he's a catholic but because he's Mo Johnston – a guy whose got no respect for himself or his family, a troublemaker'. Rangers were not the team he had been raised on, nor were the supporters. Even before Johnston the atmosphere at Ibrox had been altering, the support had got quieter, they were not 'the Bears' of old but were prepared to take anything thrown at them, they were beginning to lose the club, 'you know the man in the street is not going to be able to afford to watch Rangers eventually. Rangers belong to the man in the street'.

In fact, frequent dissent is expressed in *Follow Follow* about Rangers' attempts to discourage singing, chanting and swearing among the fans (i.e., traditional ways of watching football). The fanzine is clear as to why Rangers wish to see an end to such behaviour. It is to please the 'Johnnie-come-lately-crew of fat cats . . . these people will disappear just as quickly when things go wrong' (Issue 1). Alistair Hood, Rangers' implement for enforcing 'better behaviour', attracts almost as much abuse in the fanzine as Celtic for his efforts to ban traditional (i.e., loyalist and Orange) songs and flags:

If some of our new 'Business friends' object to singing and swearing then they should stay at home and watch the TV because there is no ground in the UK where at least eighty per cent of punters wouldn't be thrown out in the course of a match for swearing. It may not be nice but its a fact of life. There is no such thing as a polite football ground. (Issue 5)

The writer said he had never thought that songs about the Boyne or Derry had much to do with football but no-one could find them offensive unless they were social workers, IRA sympathisers, anti-Protestant bigots or some combination of these. Hood had trained security cameras at the East Enclosure, where the 'traditional' (though young) Rangers' fans tend to congregate, the enclosure being the only, small, area of terracing left at Ibrox, fans who sang 'The Sash' there were ejected but Hood would not, claimed the fanzine, throw out 'camel coats' who intoned just the same songs. The exuberant East Enclosure often vent their feelings vocally at 'those elitist bastards in the stands with their season tickets' (Issue 2). Somehow the fanzine became the 'voice' of this rather small section of Rangers' support, rather to the chagrin of its writers most of whom seem to have seat season tickets (which give a better chance of obtaining scarce tickets for big games – always a preoccupation for followers of the Old Firm). *Follow Follow* engaged in a campaign to 'Save the Enclosure' (Issue 11). It included a postcard for fans to voice their complaint and the next issue claimed that 300–400 cards had been sent to the club. It noted that Rangers had agreed to maintain the terrace as long as possible and said that there would always be a cheap pay-in section at Ibrox, whether standing or seated (Issue 12).

Murray's takeover of Rangers was cautiously welcomed by the fanzine, he seemed to have the business experience necessary to run Britain's biggest football club, but some of his plans raised more doubts. Some land deals looked like 'asset-stripping' and it was suspicious of rebuilding parts of the ground to create more executive boxes.

> If businessmen are daft enough to part with £30,000 a year for a box lets take the money off them, so long as the ordinary punter benefits on and off the pitch from that injection of money. The money will be going to enable us to buy and pay better players, fair enough, but what does that matter if huge sections of the Stadium are populated not by Bears but by the camel coat mob? (Issue 6)

Follow Follow intensely dislikes the 'fat cats', the 'Sleepy Hollow battalion', the 'camel coats', who constantly quit their seats during a game to get food, who leave games early, 'whose only contribution to the atmosphere in the Stadium will be the clanging of their gold chains and half-sovereign rings' (Issue 6), but who seem to get privileged access to scarce tickets over the old arrangements run through supporters clubs. The fanzine accepts the fans who have drifted back to Rangers with success, though the writers are quick to note that they had still been in attendance at Ibrox in the early 1980s when crowds were down to 10,000 or so, but they abjure, 'the new superclass created by Holmes and kept as pets by Murray who get all the joy that is going' (Issue 10). The fanzine demanded publication of figures for the distribution of tickets and suggested that Rangers should become a true 'club' where all members would have the same rights.

Strangely, in the midst of all the success, the future seems gloomy, 'What is the point of winning in Europe if we are just the same as everybody else?

. . . We've said it before that nobody is more ambitious for Rangers than we are, but what is the point of it all if the players and supporters aren't bound together by fervour, love and pride?' (Issue 9). Increasingly articles and letters in the fanzine complained about the 'sterile atmosphere' at matches and the way the club was becoming just a business and was losing touch with the real fans, as in the poem in Issue 16, part of which ran:

> The Enclosure will be seated,
> The bouncy, bouncy will be gone,
> We'll hear the rustle of tenners
> Where we used to hear a song.
> Instead of scarves there'll be bowlers,
> Umbrellas instead of flags,
> Replace hairy arsed Orangemen,
> With public school fags.

Contributors began to argue that as gate money had become less important to the overall finances of the club there had been a move away from acknowledging the protestantism of its working class support in favour of attracting sponsors who wanted a sanitized audience. A Rangers director, quoted in Issue 16, did nothing to ease such fears, '. . . in future, it will only be the well-heeled who will be able to watch football live'.

In short, *Follow Follow* pursues a distinct, if simplistic, strand of 'class' analysis in its outline of what Rangers 'stand for' and foresees a situation where continued domination over 'the tims' seems likely to be achieved at the cost of the alienation of its most faithful supporters. However the fanzine is distinctly fatalistic about whether anything can be done to avert this prospect.

ASSESSMENT

It is hard not to be amused by a fanzine that carries advertisements for a cassette 'There's Something Stirring in King Billy's Bogs' and for a marmalade 'King William's Orange Preserve', but 'irreverent' is exactly what *Follow Follow* is not. It is serious, edgy and embattled, holding on for some 'cause' that tends to be appealed to rather than being specified.

Superficially, this fanzine does seem to promote some of the not so noble traditions of terrace culture in Scottish football but, as I have tried to show, the reality is a little more complex. In fact, *Follow Follow* poses some tricky questions for analysts of football and Scottish society. What are 'sectarianism' and 'religious bigotry' exactly? How significant are they in modern Scotland? Do Scottish authorities condone the songs, flags and slogans of the Celtic support which do, often, seem to express support for organisations committed to breaking up the 'United' Kingdom and which conduct bombing campaigns in English cities? The editor of the Rangers fanzine has certainly urged his readers not to support *any* of the para-military organisations involved in Northern Ireland arguing they will never provide a permanent solution for the problems of that province. It should be added that, as with all media outputs, quite how far the readership shares the obsessions of the very small number of fanzines writers is problematic and, until investigated, academics should be wary of assuming that producers of fanzines 'speak' for anyone but themselves.

For *Follow Follow* reveals other features of fanzines generally which should make academics more wary of hailing the genre. It is against most change, it has an unreconstructed view of who 'real supporters' are, for the most part it is silent on the fine detail of football finance, on tactics and training, on the rights of players, and the problems of football supporters other than those in a small niche of its own stadium. It is intermittently, but resolutely, sexist. Its writers seem uninterested in anything else going on in Glasgow or Scotland, which is not surprising since they go to almost every game and watch many others on TV. They dislike business people who 'don't invest a penny of their own money in football', on the other hand they are very suspicious of anyone who seems to, since they are probably working a financial fiddle and/or passing too many tickets to their pals. They have the lowest opinion of virtually all referees, journalists and academics. They tend to regard practical experience as the only form of valid knowledge. What *Follow Follow* really promotes is total commitment and loyalty to watching one football team, which, this fanzine is self-aware enough to appreciate (if some academics are not), is not of great social moment. In short, the ideological form of this fanzine, like most others, is just that working class 'us' versus 'them' delineated by Hoggart (1957) many years ago, though shot through with even more exclusiveness than in its classic social forms. The question is whether it is really likely that such an ideology can create an effective pressure against all the economic, political and social forces driving football in Scotland, Britain and Europe to a new cultural location?

IT WAS A GRAND OLD TEAM . . .?

Celtic FC have spawned a handful of magazines. These have somewhat different perspectives and one *Tiocfaidh Ár Lá*, overtly aligned with the IRA, has been the subject of some ire in *Follow Follow* (Issues 23 and 25). I will concentrate on *Not the View*, one of the first in Scotland and claimed to be the biggest selling club fanzines in Britain. The club's official newspaper is *The Celtic View*, so the fanzine's title makes plain an oppositional stance.

Celtic have been having a very lean time of it in the last few years. In addition, the club has huge financial problems centred on, but not confined to, the need to totally upgrade their dilapidated ground or create a new stadium. There seems no obvious way to finance either of these options. In a period when Rangers have forged ahead the Celtic board have more and more appealed to the club's 'unique tradition' as a way of legitimating their continued control. Such difficulties, on and off the field, are fertile ground and *Not the View* emerged because, 'A group of like minded supporters who go to the Jungle every Saturday decided that it was time for the views of the ordinary fans to be heard' (Issue 1). An examination of this fanzine should reveal not only if and how some of the traditions of Scottish football are being maintained, but also how some ordinary fans, the 'Jungle' being the area of terracing which attracts Celtic's most vociferous supporters, regard the relation of big business and the control of a great club in a context of incipient decline. I want to consider two themes which are prominent in the content of *Not the View*:

the relation of the fans and club to 'sectarianism';
criticisms of the board of directors.

NOT THE VIEW AND 'SECTARIANISM'

Antagonism to the other half of the Old Firm is certainly displayed in *Not the View*, although to a lesser degree and with more humour than in *Follow Follow*. Issue 1, for example, carried an article about Rangers long standing reluctance to sign 'handsome players', guying the 'no catholic' policy. In Issue 23, Pat Nevin then of Chelsea, but formerly with Celtic Boys Club, was asked, 'Everybody knows about the sordid connections that exist between Chelsea fans and the Huns; what are the reasons for this and has it ever affected you on or off the pitch?' Rangers, club and fans, are almost always referred to as 'the Huns' (a Glasgow colloquialism) and many mentions of Rangers are swiftly followed by 'masonic lodge' or similar. There is a lot of repetition of Glasgow gossip about 'sectarian' behaviour, for example, that one of Ranger's English players dressed up as the Pope and scrawled anti-catholic graffiti on a tablecloth (Issue 4). However, the main expressions of antipathy are the regular articles about, 'the power wielded by Glasgow Rangers within the Scottish game' (Issue 11), on how Rangers get easier 'draws' in cup competitions (for example, Issue 15) and a litany detailing all the biased referees that favour Rangers. So, Issue 9 (and others) carried a mock 'advertisement' 'Referees Wanted' in which necessary qualifications included 'must give penalties to Rangers' and equipment needed included 'a sash and apron'. An article in Issue 23 'analysed' the penalties awarded for and against the two teams in the past thirteen seasons. It found that Celtic had been given four more penalties in those years but argued that Celtic were so 'attack minded' that, obviously, they should have had a lot more. When it looked at penalties against, 'The figure ignores penalty claims turned down which most fans would acknowledge Rangers benefit from more than any other team'.

Sometimes, however, *Not the View* finds it difficult to maintain a stance as the mouthpiece for the victims of 'sectarianism'. Following the abuse of a black player of Rangers by Celtic fans *Not the View* printed an apology on behalf of 'those Celtic supporters who feel as we do on this issue' (Issue 4). The fanzine hoped this racial intolerance among Celtic fans would cease immediately. However, it regarded the normal behaviour of Rangers and their fans as equally abhorrent and argued that it was a pity that Rangers could not, 'rid themselves of a much more deep-rooted and widespread intolerance among their supporters . . . could it be that if they were to throw out everybody who practised or condoned sectarianism they would be playing in front of an empty stadium, and that includes the directors box?' (Issue 5 and see 7).

Rangers signing of a catholic was a great blow to Celtic fans not just because Johnston had, apparently, been on the point of re-signing for their club. The fanzine could only greet the apparent ending of discrimination grudgingly. 'Souness himself must be given some credit for ending a 116 year "tradition" of blatant sectarianism and signing a "Catholic", albeit the worst Catholic since Heinrich Himmler and pulling off a superb publicity stunt in the process, but in my view his reasons are cynical and his methods despicable. Indeed, everything you would expect from the present Hun regime' (Issue 14). Johnston himself was guilty of 'betrayal', he was a 'Judas', he was the subject of continuing debate in the fanzine, should he be referred to as 'le *petite* merde' of 'le *petit* merde', for example.

I have noted that *Follow Follow* supports the right of the fans to sing traditional songs against the efforts of the club to stop them, but in Issue 19 of *Not the View* an appeal was made to all Celtic fans about the next Old Firm clash, 'Put all religious and political songs to one side . . . leave that to our friends from Ibrox', though the sentiment here was a little spoiled since the justification was the fact that the match was being televised and that 'sectarian' songs would not project the best image of the club. Issue 24 praised the efforts the club was making to try to eradicate some of the songs emanating from the Jungle and suggested other methods: 'It is to the Club's credit that they bring this subject into the open, unlike Rangers who perpetually ignore their responsibilities in this issue' . . . Moreover 'it seems that the board are indirectly, but correctly, expressing concern at songs and chants connected with the highly emotive subject of Ireland; a subject which we will continue to studiously avoid in the pages of NVT since we agree that Celtic Football Club is not the context within which to address such issues.'

It should be said that relative eagerness to discuss Scottish football's links with Ireland, the IRA, or associated issues is not the only thing which differentiates the two fanzines. *Not the View* tends to carry much more material about the team, matches, nostalgia, football quizzes, etc. than *Follow Follow*. Then whereas *Follow Follow* sometimes alludes to 'the cause' it feels is associated with its club, *Not the View* appeals to something much looser: the 'mystical aura', that 'something different' or 'special' about Celtic, its 'unique tradition' which, in so far as it is ever specified, tends to be located with Brother Walfrid, and this supposed club founder's concern to help the Catholic poor of the East End of Glasgow, contrasting his mission with the contemporary club's donations, or rather lack of them, to charity.

CRITICISM OF THE BOARD

The fanzine was founded to enable its writers to criticise what they saw as the root of the club's problems: the Celtic board. From the first issue to the latest, *Not the View* has highlighted the fact that Celtic FC are a *private*, limited company and as such cannot hope to generate the cash required to compete with the elite of Europe. The fanzine has consistently advocated that the club should 'go public'. They see twin advantages in such a move: Celtic could raise much-needed capital and individuals who purchased shares could have their say at the Annual General Meeting. Here the fans of Rangers are certainly seen to have an advantage:

We can all have a good laugh at the Huns as they go through the annual ritual of the shareholders meeting, which at times resembles the Nuremberg rallies with fat loonies in Rangers strips demanding that no "Tims" ever be allowed to darken the doorstep of Ibrox. But at least they can make their views, however bigoted or stupid they may be, known to the directors face-to-face . . . Who are the Celtic directors accountable to? (Issue 1)

Or as put in Issue 24, under the title 'Happy Families':

Yes the image of Celtic as a 'family' club will be under threat if outside financers are allowed to invest in the Club (and there are people out there willing to do so) but whose 'family' does the Club belong to. Although we supporters feel that Celtic is 'our' Club, legally and in every other way it belongs to the Whites, Kellys, Grants and Farrells, and this is a situation that the first two mentioned will do their utmost to preserve.

The constant critique of the board has led to some interesting articles about the economics of the game. They outlined the present ownership of Celtic, 'a kind of family dynasty under the control of a few people' (Issue 2), while Issue 32 showed that only about 76 people have some right to a vote about club affairs, with two families being quite dominant, 'What Celtic means to us as ordinary supporters bears no relation to how the aforementioned families view the Club. To them it is like the family silver; a precious heirloom to be handed down from generation to generation'. In the face of arguments that going public would open the club up to being taken-over by people who were not in tune with the traditions of the club, (even a 'Hun'!), *Not the View* carried pieces detailing legal mechanisms that could easily be put in place to make the club take-over proof (Issues 4, 20 and 22). Other articles have painstakingly dissected the club's various proposals for new stadia.

Gradually *Not the View* has explored the dead end of a tradition of 'stewardship' of a great football club by professional men drawn from a few families. These are the miserly 'custodians of the biscuit tin', the receptacle in which, as Scottish football culture knows, they are supposed to hoard Celtic's takings, especially those that come from a systematic under-reporting of the gates at Parkhead. Such a traditional arrangement, such a lack of economic expertise cannot, the fanzine argues, by its very nature provide sufficient resources to keep Celtic competitive and avoid the club being driven by Murray at Rangers, 'it is he, together with the help of a few others, who will dictate in what form the game in Scotland will enter the twenty first century' (Issue 36). The appeal is for the club to be opened up to tycoons, 'We need real businessmen in charge, preferably wealthy enough not to need employ-ment at Celtic Park in order to make a living' (Issue 18). The fanzine has embraced the various self-made men, mainly property developers, who have come forward offering to solve Celtic's problems only to be repulsed by the board, even though some of the money-making schemes these men propose seem to be what the fanzine otherwise abhors.

Not the View can advocate the introduction of entrepreneurship and invest-ment of personal fortune while sniping at, 'vulgar commercialism being made into an art form at Ibrox' (Issue 28), though recently a correspondent wondered why it was possible to buy a season ticket for a seat at Ibrox for less than a season ticket to stand at Parkhead (Issue 38). *Not the View* certainly deplores most of the Celtic board's own ham-fisted attempts to increase revenue, for example, opening an expensive restaurant and naming it after Brother Walfrid. It cannot believe that decades of under-investment can be offset through increased sales of scarves and pies. It was dismayed by a recent 'Celtic Family' scheme (cruelly parodied by other Scottish fanzines) where purchase of a £35 card gave the holder discounts from various businesses. *Not the View* sees this as an attempt to yuppify the Celtic image and as revealing the board to be quite out of touch with the lives of the majority of the fans, who are working class people struggling to make it through a hard recession. The scheme has not been a success.

Crucially, however, *Not the View* has appreciated its own limitations as an agent of change. It has tried to develop other tactics which might influence those in power, though this is difficult because supporters' clubs are unlikely to complain too much for fear of reprisals in ticket allocations and critical letters to the club newspaper tend to go unpublished. Issue 10 urged readers to write to the board with their complaints. In Issue 12 an article mused on how to put more pressure on the directors. The fanzine did not want to cause any conflict between fans and, judging by letters to *Not the View*, no form of action was likely to get 100 per cent backing. Somewhat hopelessly, they urged the manager to tell fans the truth about what was happening inside Parkhead and added:

> We as supporters, can and will do all we can, but that can only be so much. We appeal to those inside the Club who have some influence over the Board to listen to the voices of the fans and act now, before we go down the tubes completely.

Not the View printed a questionnaire in Issue 11 and reported on the response in Issue 13. About 400 people had replied and, for example, in answer to the question, 'Would you buy shares in Celtic if they were offered' 369 had said yes, fifteen were not sure, with the noes registering 28. In Issue 18 the writers were pondering other options: a boycott was a non-starter if only because it would never get mass support, a petition would leave those who signed it open to retaliation from the club's 'Securitate', a walk-out would upset the players and fans would be reluctant to take part, a sit-in outside the ground would mean a confrontation with the police, while one inside would mean getting dirty and being harassed by the stewards. In short, there seemed no easy way to exert pressure.

Issue 19 appeared after a spontaneous display of anger against the board during a match and a demonstration outside the stadium after the game. *Not the View* understood the frustration but saw such action as counter-productive. Chanting slogans was pointless, 'nobody can sack them, they have absolute power within the Club to do what they want'. The fanzine hoped to organise a public meeting which might be the beginnings of a totally independent supporters body, and proposed that at a forthcoming game fans should leave the part of the Jungle directly opposite the directors box empty as a silent protest. This plan fell flat (Issue 20). The public meeting idea was postponed (Issue 22) and taken over by a 'Save our Celts' group (Issue 26) which held its inaugural meeting in February 1991. It set up an Independent Celtic Supporters Association, which was publicised in the fanzine, but had little purchase on recent events.

ASSESSMENT

Not the View promotes the ideology that there is widespread discrimination, systematic discrimination, in Scottish society against catholics and Celtic football club though its writers sometimes wonder whether this is just their own 'paranoia'. The 'evidence' it offers for this discrimination tends to be jokey stories recycled from the mass media and, in Scotland anyway, there is a much more complex relation between fanzines and the mainstream press than most analysts allow. In Glasgow there is something of a circularity in the borrowings between fanzines and mainstream newspapers concerning 'stories' about 'sectarianism' in football, while in 1992 a member of the Celtic board offered the editor of another fanzine, *Once a Tim*, space in the club newspaper to attack the mainstream media's coverage of the club (*Evening Times*, 20 November 1992, *Once a Tim*, Issue 13). By reflex, however, *Not the View* tends to regard the Scottish media as part of 'the protestant ascendancy' and almost totally biased against Celtic. *Not the View* is virtually silent about what *Follow Follow* charges Celtic and its supporters with – support for the IRA and its tactics. In short, the Celtic fanzine adopts a routine, unreflective, easy, portrayal of the 'significance' of 'sectarianism' in Scotland though there is no explicit discussion of competing religious ideas and institutions. In this sense this fanzine is very true to the traditions of Scottish football and much of its academic analysis.

Not the View is most untraditional in its desperate advocacy of an extension of corporate capitalism in the legal form of the club. In early 1992 *Not the View* reprinted some of the points it had made in issues 1 and 2 adding:

> Nothing has happened in the last five years to make these early editorials any less valid today. In fact, if anything, the situation is now worse than ever. Two families have quite openly stated their intentions to run the football club the way they want it run and no-one will be allowed to interfere . . . the men on the board are merely interested in holding on to control of the club at any price. (Issue 34)

Which, if nothing else, shows how little purchase a fanzine is likely to have over the affairs of a football club (and see the similar disclaimer in *Follow Follow*, No. 12). Both the fanzines I have considered here seemed to be able to get a maximum of 400 people to respond to some of their simpler initiatives and so they cannot even deploy paper armies to shape events (as the FSA in England has done to some extent, though not to the extent analysts often claim). Outlining a few 'victories' is all very well, but the regressive kernel of many of these needs at least some discussion as do all the 'defeats'. It is easy to celebrate fans having a 'voice' (though studies of the specific contents of fanzines would show that this articulates some debased themes) but, and increasingly in the late twentieth century, fans are having to struggle with financial and legal complexities, some of which arise well outside Britain.

Fans (and most academics) are not well trained to comprehend such compli-cations and they cannot really affect them *except* by choosing, as consumers, not to attend matches, and, of course, fanzines tend to be produced by just the people who will not advocate, let alone exercise, that particular option. Caught in the trap of their own commitment there tends to be a search for, or acceptance of, the 'good' businessman. *Follow Follow* does not particularly warm to Murray, it regards him with suspicion and constantly compares him and the present regime quite unfavourably with Bill Struth and the Rangers of earlier times, but it knows the old days have gone with the wind. *Not the View* also appreciates that the old ways will not do, but pins its hopes on the arrival of some figure similar to Murray, though one, of course, 'sympathetic to Celtic's traditions'. Big business and compromise with 'commercial criteria' is preferable to a slide into irrelevance.

The task for those who analyse British soccer is not to romanticise the content nor exaggerate the significance of fanzines but to trace the limitations of their ideology and organisation, and to consider just how they fit with other ways fans can affect the owners and controllers of football. Here *Not the View*'s belief in the rights conferred by wider share-ownership needs at least a thought, and there are, for example, the many radio phone-ins where, in Scotland anyway, directors are often put on the spot before mass audiences. Demonstrations, non-attendance, etc., all need consideration. Such an over-view of the efficacy of various ways of influencing owners and controllers of football might well suggest that fanzines are really not, 'the "rational " end of a continuum of "oppositional" forms of popular football culture' (Jary, Horne and Bucke, 1991, p.592). Indeed, through their reiteration of the need to attend whatever the quality of the product, whatever the treatment of fans, they may be regarded as rather *irrational*.

CONCLUSIONS

English analysts have eyed fanzines far too uncritically. From my case study of the content of two prominent fanzines in Scotland I would say that they represent clear expressions of the 'subordinate value system' which Parkin (1971, pp.88–96) saw as characteristic of the British working class, a value system which is essentially accommodative, defensive and parochial rather than being oppositional, radical and inclusive. It's main conceptual categories tend to be an 'us' versus 'them', though in fanzines the 'us' category is often even more exclusive than in working class ideology more generally – not only supporters of other teams but many of those who attend games of the same team are put in the 'them' camp. In Scottish fanzines all the 'tims', 'huns', 'wee huns' (Hearts), 'part-time beggars' or 'wee tims' (Hibs), 'sheep shaggers' (Aberdeen), etc., etc., derogate and are derogated with great gusto. They can all spot 'bias' against their team, on any number of bases, at a hundred yards distance and, compared with this common complaint, common problems, and there are plenty of these, do not get much of an airing. The subordinate value system endorses only knowledge derived from experience and as fanzines, in the main, despise writers, 'sociological claptrap', and most forms of talking about football which do not simply laud their team (or disparage all others), they are likely to remain the prisoners of a rather restricted view of 'what the game is about' and how its problems might be solved. What stands out from my study of Scottish fanzines is their narrowness of vision and general negativity. However, this does not matter much since for a whole number of reasons, as I tried to suggest, fanzines have a very limited power to influence events. Praising them for their 'counter hegemonic' thrust and the like is simply to hymn the position of the powerless and to avoid confronting the exact forces which are changing the nature of soccer as a cultural product.

As regards what the fanzines suggest about the relation of Scottish football to individual and group identity, more attention has to be paid to the whole conceptualisation of 'identity'. We can, for example, conceive of 'identity' as a series of levels. People:

1. may know an identity exists;
2. may understand what that identity involves;
3. may believe in what that identity involves;
4. may allow that identity to affect behaviour;
5. may make that identity one of their main identities.

Much media and academic discussion about Scottish football proceeds as if most Scots adopt 'protestant' and 'catholic' identities at my levels four and five, and this version of the situation is eagerly swallowed by English audiences. However, I judge the vast majority of the population now take them at levels one and two, if at all, and my case study of two major fanzines reveals that they can hardly be judged as agencies for promoting any profound 'sectarian' *activity* in Scotland. Both explicitly preach against 'sectarianism' and have little to say to their readers about religion in any form. Of course, 'identities' are situationally relevant and people can move through my levels speedily in certain eventualities *but* such eventualities are highly unlikely to occur in modern Scotland.

'Ethnic' allegiances have recently been floated around some English football teams, but lack strong social moorings and, by the same token, in modern Scotland *talk* about ethnic antagonism is rather more prevalent than evidence of meaningful ethnic division. Analysts slide too easily between what was and what is, there is a sleight of hand from rhetoric to reality, the clash of the Old Firm is taken as the symbol of something more profound but it is more properly understood as a burlesque of what now exists. Such faults are characteristic of Finn (1991), whose arguments and evidence about the existence of some widespread anti-Irish 'prejudice' in Scotland are the less compelling the nearer he gets to the present day. A recent text on 'understanding Scotland' scarcely feels the need to mention 'sectarianism' (McCrone, 1992) and those who want to go on asserting its continuing relevance need to consider why such a dogged student of Scotland does not feel it necessary to wield this term. I certainly doubt that many people in Scotland now 'need' a 'religious label', or that these really are 'significant', or that 'the fusion of religion and football is a remarkable social force in modern Scotland' (Walker, 1990, p.156). Nor will it do to claim that, 'anti-Irish and anti-Catholic sentiments are dredged up from the murky depths of those as yet inadequately analysed but commonly shared collective myths' or that,

'Ireland and things Irish still induce a strong, almost visceral anti-Irish senti-ment in many Scots and a desire that Irish associations be "eliminated"' (Finn, 1991, p.394) when what, for example, *Follow Follow* argues, with more evidence than diviners of contemporary 'sectarianism' usually provide, is that Celtic and their fans seem to show support for groups who advocate the use of, and use, weapons against civilian targets in many parts of the United Kingdom. Talking about 'dual identities', the validity of 'honouring' Irish roots, 'conspiracy theories', and asserting that, 'the failure of Scottish society to recognise the validity of different Scottish social identities has been well captured in the treatment of the Irish-Scots soccer clubs' (Finn, 1991, p.383) scarcely gets to the root of this criticism of a continuing 'Irish connection', and adopts a view of 'Scottish society' that does not seem to include the local and national state, political parties, the football authorities, the legal system or an education system which is divided at the wish of the Catholic Church.

In my view, study of Scottish football and Scottish society, would benefit if academics and journalists would put a moratorium on the use of a whole bundle of terms like 'sectarianism', 'sectarian hatred', 'bigotry', 'tribalism', (a lovely example of racism being used to condemn 'prejudice'), protestant/catholic/Irish 'community', 'religious tensions', and the like, until they are ready to specify exactly what they want to refer to by such concepts and provide some evidence, other than the chants at Old Firm games, to show that some 'religious divide' really is a strong motivating force of individual and group action in Scotland today. Such abstinence might, I believe, pro-voke a move into much more fruitful areas for investigating identities in modern Scotland. In all truth, the fanzines I have considered scarcely say much about what it is to be 'Scottish'. Their tight concentration on their clubs does, perhaps, promote the idea of Scotland as a unit separate from all others, but, of course, *Follow Follow* sturdily promotes the Union. Other fanzines may be more emphatic about some connection between football and a Scottish national identity but that is for other research to show. What is apparent to me is that the fanzines I have studied can hardly avoid responding to the new forces acting on Scottish football and Scottish society, whose sources lie well outside the country. Multi-nationalism, in all its economic, political and cultural forms, seems to be steadily dissolving traditional ties, 'communities' and old allegiances. It is this, in part, which probably accounts for the strong elegiac strain which is a major part of the content of many Scottish fanzines, but the search for ways to spring to new glories seems unlikely to involve any national solution.

ACKNOWLEDGEMENTS

I am very grateful to my friend Alastair Hollywood whose undergraduate dissertation – 'Not the Hampden roar: Scottish football fanzines and how they differ from English fanzines', April 1992 – first suggested some of the themes pursued in this chapter.

BIBLIOGRAPHY

Duke, V., 1991, The Sociology of Football: A Research Agenda, in *Sociological review*, August, 39 (3), pp.627–45

Finn, G. P. T., 1991, Racism, religion and social prejudice: Irish catholic clubs, soccer and Scottish society, parts I and II, *International journal of the history of sport* 8, (1) and (3), pp.72–95 and 370–97

Hoggart, R., 1957, *The uses of literacy*, Chatto and Windus, London

Jary, D., Horne, J. and Bucke, T., 1991, Football "Fanzines" and Football Culture: A Case of Successful 'Cultural Contestation', in *Sociological review*, August, 39 (3), pp.581–97

Lacey, M. (ed.), 1989, *El Tel was a space alien – the best of the alternative football press*, vol. 1, Juma

McCrone, D., (1992), *Understanding Scotland*, Routledge, London

Moorhouse, H. F., 1984, Professional Football and Working Class Culture: English Theories and Scottish Evidence, *Sociological Review*, May, 32, pp.285–315

Moorhouse, H. F., 1987, Scotland Against England: Football and Popular Culture, in *International journal of sports history*, September, 4, pp.189–202

Moorhouse, H. F., 1989, 'We're off to Wembley!' The History of a Scottish Event and the Sociology of Football Hooliganism, in McCrone, D., McKendrick, S. and Straw, P., (eds), *The making of Scotland: nation, culture and social change*, Edinburgh University Press, Edinburgh, pp.207–27

Moorhouse, H. F., 1990, 'Shooting stars: footballers and working class culture in twentieth century Scotland' in Holt, D., (ed.), *Sport and the working class in modern Britain*, Manchester University Press, Manchester, pp.179–97

Moorhouse, H. F., 1991, 'On the Periphery: Scotland, Scottish Football and the New Europe', in Williams, J. and Wagg, S., (eds), *British football and social change: getting into Europe*, Leicester University Press, Leicester, pp.201–19

Murray, R., 1984, *The Old Firm: sectarianism, sport and society in Scotland*, John Donald, Edinburgh

Murray, R., 1988, *Glasgow's Giants: 100 Years of the Old Firm*, John Donald, Edinburgh

Parkin, F., 1971, *Class inequality and political order*, Paladin Books, London

Redhead, S., 1991, 'An Era of the End, or the End of an Era: Football and Youth Culture in Britain' in Williams, J. and Wagg, S. (eds), *British football and social change – getting into Europe*, Leicester University Press, Leicester, pp.145–159

Shaw, P., (1989), *Whose game is it anyway? The book of football fanzines*, Hemel Hempstead, Argus

Walker, G., 1990, 'There's not a team like the Glasgow Rangers': Football and Religious Identity in Scotland' in Walker, G. and Gallagher, T., (eds), *Sermons and battle hymns: Protestant popular culture in modern Scotland*, Edinburgh University Press, Edinburgh, pp.137–59

Williams, J., 1991, 'Having an Away Day: English Football Supporters and the Hooligan Debate' in Williams, J. and Wagg, S., (eds), *British football and social change – getting into Europe*, Leicester University Press, Leicester, pp.160–86

Williams, J. and Wagg, S., (eds), 1991, *British football and social change – getting into Europe*, Leicester University Press, Leicester

Fanzines consulted:

Aye Ready
Blues Brothers
Dens Scene

Follow Follow
Heartbeat
Hibs Monthly
No Idle Talk
Not the View
Once a Tim
The Celt
The Final Hurdle
The Gorgie Wave

INDEX